P9-BJH-310

Tales of a Street Bull

by

Enzo

Copyright

Copyright © 2021, Stenson All Rights Reserved.

The moral right of the author has been asserted.

Apart from any fair dealing for the sole purpose of private study, research, criticism, or review, as permitted under the *Copyright Act 1968*, no part of this publication shall be reproduced by any means without prior permission of the publisher. Every effort has been made to make this book as complete and accurate as possible. Although the author and publisher have prepared this book with the greatest care and have made every effort to ensure accuracy, we assume no responsibility or liability for errors, inaccuracies, or omissions. Before you begin, check with the appropriate authorities to ensure compliance with all laws and regulations.

The purpose of this book is to educate. The author and publisher do not warrant that the information contained in this book is fully complete and shall not be responsible for any errors or omissions. The author and publisher shall have neither liability nor responsibility to any person or entity concerning any loss or damage caused or alleged to be caused directly or indirectly by this book.

Acknowledgment

My dear friends, David and Karen Gillespie, your friendship means a great deal to me, as well as Athena.

It is friends like you both who, with your encouragement and nudging, kept me on track. You two are the greatest, and we love you both, as well as our Friday night get-togethers.

To the rest of my family and extended family, who also have tolerated me and encouraged me, this book was first intended to be a journal of some of the strange calls I went on. I wanted to write them down so you could look at them and see what law enforcement was in the 'old days.' All of you, Kyle, Jenean, Milan, Holly, Tim, Maggie, Austin, Kori, Rachel, Trenton, and Trinity are my pride and joy. Every day you make me a proud father and grandfather. I hope you enjoy this 'memoir.'

Dedication

This book is dedicated to my wife. She has stood by me in every venture I have attempted, no matter how they have turned out. She has been by my side for over 30 years, helping me, guiding me, and, especially, loving me. So many things have happened in our lives together most couples would have never survived – not us. She has been my best friend from the day we met on Saturday, May 13, 1989. We fell in love on that day, and there is nothing that can stop us. You are the greatest!

My older brother, Dennis. He was my inspiration to get into law enforcement and my guide as I worked my way through the academy and career. His advice to me was truly brilliant and set me on a path to being a good police officer. I owe much to him for his guidance and leadership.

He did not survive the COVID outbreak to see the end product of this book, but if you are looking down now, I hope you are proud of this accomplishment.

God rest your soul, 10–7 – we've got the watch and your 6.

Contents

Why Did I Become a Cop?

If you had asked me when I was in high school or even in college if I wanted to be a cop, I would have told you: "Not on your life." It was not on my radar anywhere.

I have always had respect for what they did or maybe a fear which kind of parlayed into respect. I always knew it was in my best interest to say "yes, officer" and "no, officer" when pulled over for something I did wrong, plus I knew I would not be pulled over unless I deserved it.

I grew up in a military family. My dad's career was in the Air Force, so my brother and I learned to respect a uniformed person, including law enforcement and firefighters. Both of us were expected to go into the military, which we did. It was never said, but the inferences were always there, plus we grew up with the famous quote by President Kennedy: "Don't ask what your country can do for you, ask what you can do for your country." Military service was a foregone conclusion.

After graduating from high school, my older brother went into the Marine Corp, and I went into the Navy one year later; that means I was smarter (LOL). This gave us both more of a regimented background, which would come in handy when we became cops. Just as a side note, I had more fun in the Navy than my brother did in the Corps—again, smarter.

Once out of the Marines, my brother began his mission to become a police officer. It was something he decided early in life, and he was focused on pursuing his goal. Me, on the other hand, had not quite hit that stride. Law enforcement was just not something I had any desire to do.

After spending four years in the Navy, I got out and started college. At first, I wanted to do radio broadcasting, but I lost interest in that quite rapidly; I do not really remember why it just didn't hold much of an interest. I studied it for a short time, but it wasn't until a good friend of mine — with whom I was in the Navy — introduced me to forestry, and I finally settled on a career.

I was not interested in becoming a forest ranger, which was way too foo-foo for me. My apologies to my forest ranger friends, but that is a touchy-feely career, and I wanted to do the labor part. I studied exactly what I wanted to do: setting up timber sales, reforestation, fighting forest fires, building logging roads, and so on.

My favorite thing to do in Forestry was fight forest fires, just an adrenalin rush beyond belief. When I was putting out a fire, I was at my best being around the wildfires with the flames all around me; I know you will think I'm weird, but it was just an immense amount of fun. Ask anyone who fights forest fires, they don't do it for the money because it's not a tremendous amount of income considering the risk, but you do it for the excitement.

I moved up the ladder of the forest fire leadership in short order. I started as a crew member on an attack crew, but after only a few years, I became 'Air Attack Boss' on large fires (sometimes called 'project fires') and 'Fire Boss' (the big guy) on medium size fires. I was running the show, and that was awesome! I loved being in that position. So you're probably asking, "If you loved it so much, why did you leave forestry?"

There were two things I did not realize about myself: 1) All this forestry training and firefighting were actually prepping me to be able to deal with extreme stress, and 2) I was a cop, and I didn't realize it. I had this inner desire which never exposed itself until my wife and me at the time went to visit my brother in California. He had moved to California, where he was working his dream as a Long Beach police officer. While we were there, he invited me to go on a ride-a-long. *OK*, I thought, *that sounds interesting and maybe some fun.*

When he made the invitation, I didn't realize how much I'd enjoy myself. Keep in mind that I had a great job and was moving up the forestry ranks, so there was no monetary incentive for me to jump to a new career. I really had no major desire to leave the forest, or at least that is what I thought.

The ride-a-long was a graveyard shift, and I stayed the entire time. I watched as my brother made traffic stops along with some other mundane stops and contacts. One of the calls was the most interesting when we caught a burglar as he was exiting out a window on the ally side of a building. I thought, *how cool was that?*

As the night progressed, I thought a boy should not have this much fun. I know some of you think, *really, this is fun?* For me, it was as if I was like a kid in a candy store. Why hadn't I thought of doing this before?

When the shift was done, Dennis changed out of uniform into street clothes, and we went back to his house. My wife asked me if I had a good time, to which I began a dissertation of the night's events. She could see I was excited, and at the end of my verbal novel, she reminded me that I had a great job, and she was not interested in being married to a police officer. It was not because she had any disrespect for cops, but she was visibly afraid. She stated her reasons were because she did not want to wait up nights worrying if I was coming home or not. That was not only a wet blanket on my excitement but an icy, wet blanket to boot. So, it was fun, but I just put it in the back of my mind, and we never discussed it again.

When we got home to Olympia, Washington, I went back to work, and even though I knew I was working at a great job, I began to find fault with it, and the luster of forest management had dimmed a great deal for me. Nevertheless, I persevered. I looked forward to fire season to get the excitement back. I did, and I drifted away from law enforcement and put myself back into the woods.

About two years after that ride-a-long, my wife and I split up and began divorce proceedings. Police work was still out of the picture as I saw it at the time, so I didn't even give it a thought, even though my biggest obstacle was no longer in my way.

At least that was the case until one night when I got home and picked up the newspaper to skim through it like I normally did. I don't know if God sent me to this page or it was just dumb luck, but when I turned the front-page over, there was a full-page ad for Tacoma Police Department. It screamed out at me: "HIRING NOW for police officers." Right then and there, the thought of becoming a cop and that night with my brother rushed back into my brain. I was stoked up to get back on track and begin the process of getting hired by the City of Tacoma. There was nothing to stop me from beginning the process; the female persuasion was no longer a factor. I immediately called my brother and began picking his brain about what to do and what not to do. Armed with his advice, I began planning my attack to become a cop.

The next day I called in sick to work at the Washington State Department of Natural Resources (DNR), grabbed my birth certificate, my forestry degree, and everything else I could think of and what Dennis advised me to take with me. Off to Tacoma I went. I first went to the police department, and they sent me to the personnel department. OK, so I was a bit excited about this and unsure where to go or get the other details. I spent about an hour at the City of Tacoma personnel office filling out paperwork: application, fingerprint cards, background check form, and some other stuff I cannot remember what it was. I was given a test date and decided I needed another sick day.

Once I was done there, I decided to head to Seattle to apply with them, too. I mean, why not? I was on a roll. Finding the City of Seattle personnel office was a hunt and peck system. I never spent much time in Seattle so getting around was a bit difficult. Keep in mind, folks, there was no GPS or Google to get a location in those days. Once I got to Seattle, I had to find a phone booth to get an address, and then it was locating the streets by pure guessing. Once I found the address and figured how the streets were laid out, it became easier to locate the Municipal Building where the office was located. I contacted the personnel office, and they told me they were always hiring, so I spent another hour there as well.

When I applied for Seattle, I actually wanted to get hired by them just because it was a larger department. Bigger city, so more opportunities, right? But as things would turn out, I bombed their test for some reason — not sure what happened there. That actually turned out to be a Godsend. After getting hired by Tacoma, I learned how screwed up Seattle's system was, so thank goodness I did not get hired there — Tacoma was a much better place to work.

After taking the written test for Tacoma and completing a joke of an agility test, I received a letter in the mail two weeks later telling me I was number 36 on the list of candidates. At first, I was quite disappointed because I didn't think I'd get called, but Dennis let me know that was very high, and there was no doubt I would be getting a call to further my process of becoming a police officer. He assured me the background check would eliminate several candidates before me, and he was right. Two weeks later, I got a call from the training sergeant asking me to come in for an oral board. I was told at the end of the oral board that I received 94, and with that, I knew the process was well on its way. One thing led to another; physical, another joke of an agility test, and psychological profile, which was weird. One thing after another, and then suddenly, within about 30 days later, I was done with everything.

One week later, on Monday, March 28th, 1983, I received a call at my work from the training sergeant of Tacoma PD. When I answered, he asked, "Do you still want to be a cop?"

My answer: "Absolutely."

His next question: "Can you start the academy on Monday, April 4th?"

Oh no, I thought, *now I have to say no.* I had not told anyone at work or my estranged wife but felt a duty to my current employer to give at least a two-week notice. Though I choked on those words, I told the sergeant exactly that. He did not miss a beat and told me the next academy class starts on Monday, May 2nd, and asked if that worked for me. Phew, I felt I just dodged my first bullet and let him know I was looking forward to showing up on that day.

To help expedite, he asked if I could come in for one day between now and the academy date to get fitted for uniforms. We set up a date in just a couple of days, and I had the uniforms in a week. Once I hung up, I submitted my notice giving myself a week's vacation before the academy.

Though I was extremely excited about this new adventure, there was still this little feeling nagging me in the back of my mind: what if I decided this was not for me, or what if I failed the academy, or what if or what if or what if. I was not having any second thoughts, just a bunch of 'what ifs.' So, I went to the big boss of the department—I was working at the DNR—and requested a six-month leave of absence, just in case. I thought that I might as well ask; all they could say was no. I was surprised it was granted. *Cool!* I thanked him and left with an ace in my back pocket. At the same time, I didn't think I really needed that ace, but why not? Let's cover all avenues, just in case.

The Academy

At the academy in Burien, WA, I was having a good time. My class started with 40 members, and we were building friends with a common goal: getting through the academy and fighting crime. We enjoyed each other's friendship, and there was some great competition between each other but all in good spirit. Getting the highest score on the test was a badge of honor and having a little bit of fun with the instructors, with respect, of course, was also a status symbol. One of those times during the knock and announce rule discussion we had a slight bit of humor. The instructor told us that after knocking on the door and before kicking in the door, the police had to knock very loud and announce their presence, such as "Tacoma Police, Search Warrant." So, when he attempted to review and make a point, he knocked on the podium very loudly and asked the class, "Now, what do you say?"

From the back of the class, one of the recruits said, "Ah, candy gram." The entire class roared with laughter. The problem was that the instructor did not get the joke. If you are like him, please research 'Saturday Night Live Land Shark skits,' and I'm sure you will see the humor.

While there, ironically, the first movie of the Police Academy Series had hit the theaters. As a group effort, we all went to see it, and I scored the movie marquee poster. Little did I know I would end up collecting all six movie posters. Our academy was nothing like the academy in the movie, and we were all glad it was not. There was no regimented marching; we did not live on the campus, no 'stand talls,' etc. The movie was quite corny, but we just had to make our pilgrimage to it, if for no other reason, the name of the movie lured us there.

After only the first two months at the academy, I just knew I was not going back. Given how nice my old boss was to me in giving me a six-month leave of absence, I felt I needed to do the right thing, so I called and let my former boss know that I was not coming back. He was gracious and thanked me for giving him the heads-up. He wished me well and let me know he felt I would be a good cop.

That's it in a nutshell of how I became a cop. I give credit to my brother as he was truly an inspiration for the best career path I have ever sought. I tell people all the time; I became a cop, I lived as a cop, and I will die as a cop—no matter what else I do in my life, it defines me. Thank you, Dennis!

Those who work in emergency service have a ton of stories. It doesn't matter if you're a firefighter, ER nurse or doctor, ambulance worker, cop, or any other member of this community service-oriented folks; the stories are varied and are retold. Like any story that is retold over and over, some facts may be a bit embellished. At the same time, we, who work in these fields, think the stories are mundane, but others will ask you over and over to repeat these tales of woe for amusement and amazement—thus the editorial license we allow ourselves.

One does not have to work in emergency service (law enforcement for me) for over thirty years—as I have—to compile a library of events. Even those who are rookies begin the accumulation of sagas that will make them the center of attention at parties and family gatherings. Be careful, though; there may be little ears or those who may be just a bit sensitive to the graphic parts of your rendition.

In the next pages are some of the stories of what happened to me as a police officer. With 22 years with Tacoma Police, four years with US Marshals, working as District Court Manager for King County, and with my work in Homeland Security, I have some funny stories as well as some tragic ones. For the most part, people are just funny but beware, some of these stories are a bit rough, and the language may be a bit dicey at times because that is just the way it is. They are from real life, and sometimes real life is just ugly, no matter what you do.

I hope you enjoy these tales and realize this is the way police work is. Just so you know, I had fun as a cop. Nothing about my career do I regret—even when I screwed up. Screwing up is a part of the deal. As my brother once told me when I was a rookie, "If you don't get a complaint from time to time, you aren't doing your job." So true!

Beach Ball

When I first became a police officer in Tacoma, I did not know exactly what was in store for me. It was not as if I was a 'wet behind the ears' sort of guy. I had been in the Navy and did a tour in Nam, so I thought I was a bit savvier than the next rookie — I was mistaken. On my first night on the street, I showed up on the graveyard and met my training officer. I was crisp and sharp with spit-shined shoes. He was patient and understanding. Though most of the other veteran officers were nice, some of the old 'dogs' just gave me a courtesy smile and moved on.

My training officer and I got into the prowl car and headed for the East Side. He drove because he said he was not ready to relinquish the driving to me yet, and that the passenger officer does all the writing. OK, I half expected that. The East Side of Tacoma, known to the cops as the Four Sector, is a blue-collar neighborhood. They are friendly to law enforcement but prefer to handle 'problem people' their own way — usually, that means the suspect calling us for help, like the time a burglar was treed by a block load of very angry residents. These people were so incensed that they became angry at me for not letting them dispense their own brand of 'justice.' I was able to talk them down, but I thought at one point that I would have to call for backup to protect myself from the victims. I was happy I did not have to.

My first night on patrol was relatively slow, just some minor fights and car break-ins, but that was about to change. About 2:00 a.m. (0200 hours for all you cop and military types), we received a call for an armed robbery in progress. At the intersection of East 56th Street and McKinley Ave are a market and a Shell Gas Station. The gas station is a 24-hr place directly across the street from the market, allowing the attendant to see directly into the market. A young male, who was on duty at the gas station, could see through the long bank of windows of the market. What he observed and reported was three men in the store, and he could see that at least one had a gun. As luck would have it, we were only two blocks away when the call came in. We turned off our lights and slowly drove a block to a good vantage point. There the 'bad boys' were running from register to register. From what we could see, it looked a bit chaotic. I could not believe that it was my first night out of the academy and I had got a robbery in progress call. Most cops go their entire career and only respond after the fact. My trainer and I were eyewitnesses, saaaaweet!

Our view was a bit obstructed as there were advertising posters all over the windows, so we could only see the heads of the suspects — you know those butcher paper ads that have "ground beef $2.00 a pound" and that sort of thing. It was a bit surreal because the robbers' heads looked like they were floating from register to register, kind of like one of those bobblehead dolls. As we sat there waiting for these guys to come out of the store, other units were coming into the area and setting up. My training officer let them all know that I would be the primary officer and calling the shots. Oh great! Not only was this my first day in the field, but I was also being tossed into the fire. I found it interesting that he trusted me to take down three-armed robbery suspects, but he did not trust me to drive; I still haven't figured out that logic. Nevertheless, all I could think about was, "Academy, don't fail me now!"

As we watched, what seemed to be an eternity, I was scanning the area. I could see some of the other patrol units in the distance waiting. I also saw a white, two-door, 1962 Buick Skylark (I made it a hobby as a kid to recognize cars on sight) parked in front of the store on the sidewalk. Given there were three suspects in the store, and this was a two-door car, and there was no way three men could fit in the front seat of this car, somebody had to sit in the back. I knew we would have the advantage when they came out of the store as they tried to enter the getaway car. This all comes into play very shortly. As I was analyzing all this, the robbers' exodus began.

I was not expecting what I saw as these Three Stooges came running out of the store. Two of the three exited quickly and jumped in the front seat of the Buick I mentioned earlier. That took me by surprise at first, given there was another guy, and it would have been much easier if the guy who jumped in the front passenger would have gone it the back seat first. *Oh well*, I thought. Then I heard the two in the car yell at their friend still inside to hurry up. Suddenly a massive human began coming out the market doors. Was it human (I asked myself) because I had never seen anyone fill a doorway with zero room to spare? It was not that he was tall or a big man of large stature — this guy was fat beyond anything I had ever seen before. I have heard of people this big but had never actually seen anybody like that. This guy, who I would call 'Huey,' was at least 500 pounds. If you don't know why I named this guy 'Huey,' take some time and research 1950s cartoon characters by the name 'Baby Huey.' Then you will understand my motivation behind the name.

When Huey got to the car, the front passenger could have easily moved to the rear seat, but no. This rocket scientist decided to lean forward so Huey could 'slip' into the backseat. Needless to say, but I will anyway: the idiot in the front nearly was crushed as Huey tried to wiggle that gargantuan body into that small car's tiny backseat. With all this going on, it was a bit difficult to maintain a serious vein, but nevertheless, we moved in on the slapstick trio's scene unfolding before us.

As soon as we radioed that we were moving, we saw the lights of the other police vehicles come on, and before you know it, the suspect's vehicle had nowhere to go. My training officer pulled our patrol car to the rear of the Buick, with Huey about a third of the way in the car. The front seat passenger was trying to breathe while yelling at the oversized robber: "Get off me!" Once we were in place, I had the helm and ready to take control. Out of the car, we came with guns drawn. As stupid as these Three Stooges were, they recognized being outgunned.

I reflected on my training and began ordering the trio out on the ground, spread eagle, face down. It went smoothly until I noticed Huey not flat on the ground. As a matter of fact, he was so large he had one hand on the pavement, but the other was in the air, and he was lying on his left side. Knowing what my textbook training told me to do and how to position the suspects on the ground, I yelled at Huey to lay flat. He began to move to his stomach, but the momentum of moving rolled him to his right side, having the same effect, this time with his left arm in the air. When Huey landed on his right side, I heard a couple of chuckles coming from the other officers, or maybe it was my training officer—I really did not know at that point. I was in concentration mode and doing what I was taught. My textbook said for all the suspects to lay flat on the ground, and by God, this guy was going to comply. I barked the order: "Lay flat on your stomach, or I shoot you where you lie!" In my peripheral vision, I saw my trainer take a quick look at me and then shrug his shoulders. Huey did his best, and as he desperately tried to lay flat, but he teetered back and forth as his stomach was like a huge beach ball he was trying to steady. After only a few seconds, Huey cried out in desperation, "I...can't...breathe!" I had to admit I honestly believed he was having some serious difficulty, but with that statement, laughter permeated the night air.

It did not take long to get the hombre off the pavement, but we ran into a problem with Huey. Another textbook procedure is that all suspects must be handcuffed behind the back, which was a bit too much to complete as this guy's girth was way more than one set of handcuffs behind the back could handle. Not even two sets hooked together accommodated Huey's girth. Eventually, we had to hook together three sets to do the mandatory behind-the-back cuffing, and even that was a bit of a stretch.

The next problem was getting him into the back seat of the patrol car—that was just not happening. A call went out to the paddy wagon from downtown for assistance. It didn't take long for the wagon to show up. As soon as it did, the wagon master (driver) asked, "Are you sure he's going to fit?" Though he was joking, he did not know how close to reality he was.

The back of the paddy wagon had a double door, so the entry was quite wide—not quite wide enough to make it easy to get Huey in the back. When he stood up on the back step, I swear I heard the wagon groan. Also, it began to sink rapidly in the rear. As the wagon sank, Huey lost his balance, and his massive form started falling toward us. The streetlights became darkened as they were eclipsed, and I began seeing my life flash before me—I just knew I was going to be crushed, and no one would ever find me again. But as quickly as they could other officers rushed to help me from imminent death, four of us pushed back this lumbering block of humans, and with all the strength we could muster, we were able to shove Huey through the doors. He popped into the wagon like a champagne cork bursting out of its bottle. Huffing and puffing, we all felt relieved to survive the ordeal.

While gathering information for my report, it was unbeknownst to me that some of the senior officers, which included my training officer, concocted a little joke at my expense. When I got back to the car, my mentor (the guy I thought I could trust) told me I had to ride in the paddy wagon with Huey. The reason I was given was if Huey made some sort of statement, we needed an officer to write it down. I did not know better, so — OK, I got in the back. I found out later there was no such policy or procedure. Nevertheless, off to the jail we went.

As Huey and I rode together, I tried to engage him in conversation. He was breathing awfully hard and sweating like someone who had run ten miles in the heat. I wrote it off on his weight and all that had happened. After a few moments, his face lost all its color, and he began gasping for air. I asked the stupid question we all ask when someone is obviously sick or quite ill, "Are you OK?"

"Of course not!" would be the correct answer, but Huey said, "I'm having a heart at...!" At that, he fell between the two metal benches, out cold, not finishing his statement, but being the bright rookie I was, I surmised he meant to finish that sentence with "attack." His size filled the narrow aisle with his fat spilling over the edges of the benches and onto the seat portion. His body pressed against my legs, pinning them against the side of the metal bench. There was so much weight pressed against my legs as I desperately tried to pull my legs free. I pulled and pulled and could feel my shoes being left behind. You know that feeling when you get stuck in the mud and lift your foot right out of your boot? That was the way this was but now add crushing pain! Once I got my legs free, I pounded on the partition separating the wagon master from us and told him to head to the hospital.

Huey lay there, motionless. I hoped he would not suffocate, given what happened on the sidewalk when he was arrested. I just knew this guy was going to choke to death right there in the back of the paddy wagon. I looked for a rise and fall on his body but could not discern any movement through the fat. Getting to his head to check for breathing meant climbing over Mt Huey, but I was afraid that would restrict his breathing. *Don't you dare die on me*, I thought. Just as I was about to take on that task of checking his breathing, we arrived at the hospital — thank God I was spared that nasty task!

The doors flung open, and standing on the outside of the van were hospital staff, fellow police officers, and a gurney. The looks of the hospital staff were priceless. It was bewilderment of just how we were going to get this guy out of the wagon. Two of the cops crawled in over Huey and squatted over the benches to get a better grip on his limp mass. The three of us lifted as best we could by using his shirt and arms, hoping it would not rip. Reaching down between sweaty rolls of fat was, at best, revolting, and he smelled of perspiration that filled the small cavern of the van. As we lifted, the hospital staff pulled on Huey's legs. Inch by inch, we were able to get Huey out and on the gurney. It was a lift-move, lift-move, lift-move method. I do not think we ever actually got Huey lifted. It was more of releasing the pressure on the wagon floor so we could move Huey an inch or two as the ER staff pulled. Once he was out, I immediately retrieved my shoes and was surprised to see they survived—mostly intact.

What a relief I felt as we began to move the gurney away from the wagon to the Emergency Room. My relief was short-lived when suddenly the gurney collapsed on one end—at Huey's head. Unable to stop him, he slid slowly, headfirst, down the gurney onto the pavement. There he was with legs still on the gurney, pointed upward and head, face down on the pavement. All I could think was, *you've got to be kidding!*

One of the hospital staff members (who I assumed was the doctor) yelled at me to "Grab his foot!" I grabbed Huey's left foot, and the doc grabbed his right one—away we went. Using the broken gurney as leverage, we headed for the ER—with a nurse trying her best to protect Huey's face from bouncing on the pavement. It was a valiant effort by her but mostly unsuccessful. Once inside, the rest of the staff could see what was going on and rushed to help—most with a gasp of "Oh my God!" With about 9-10 people in the room, we were able to right the gurney and roll Huey to a larger and more stout hospital bed.

After moving him, I looked at the gurney, and I could tell it was trash and had given its life to get Huey into the hospital. It was now just deformed and twisted metal.

When I left the hospital, I was teased by my fellow officers who let me in on their joke, and I was labeled as the 'Fat Robber Killer,' but Huey did not die like many thought he would.

I saw Huey about two months later in court. He told me that he did, in fact, have a heart attack, and it was fairly massive, but the doctors told him his age is what probably saved him, for now. Huey was only 20 years old at the time of the robbery.

He's Looking At You

Many times, police officers are asked to do things that just boggle one's mind. Case in point – an eyeball, yep, you read that correctly. Here is what happened.

Downtown Tacoma in the 80s and before was just a terrible place with a lot of work for cops. Fights in bars were quite common, but this one was a step above most.

This occurred at about 10:00 a.m., wherein two drunks got into an argument over whether there was sugar in peanut butter or not. Most drunk arguments seem to take on a life of unbelievable stupidity; obviously, this was no different.

The argument became quite out of control when fists started flying. From what I was told by witnesses, almost every fist missed its mark. No one seemed to care one way or the other, including the bartender; they just seemed to be enjoying the little may lay. These two guys, hell-bent on sugar or no sugar, stumbled about as they beat the tar out of air molecules with haymakers after haymakers. That was okay until one decided he had had quite enough and picked up an empty beer bottle, smashed it on the bar (just like you see in old west movies), and now armed himself with the broken bottle.

The bartender decided, as much as he did not want to, he needed to call the police. When we got the call, we were told that one subject was armed with a piece of glass. Sharp glass is one of those things you never want to encounter for the obvious reason – it will cut the crap out of you. We pulled the patrol car within a block of the bar – unlike the movies, you do not go lights & siren to the front door, which can cause a hostage situation. From the car, we drew our weapons and ran up to the door. As we looked in to see where our armed person was, we could see one man on the floor bleeding profusely from his face and the armed suspect standing over him. Unbeknownst to us, at this point, the armed drunk had actually stabbed the other guy in the left eye. As we moved into the bar, we pointed our guns at the suspect and ordered him to drop the bottle. I suppose looking down the barrel of two cops' service revolvers was just too much for him, so he complied. Immediately, my partner Scott called for medical aid as I took custody of the suspect, placing him in handcuffs. The bartender came around with a bar towel—God knows what germs were on it given how filthy this place was—and he put it on the eye of the victim.

Medical aid (Tacoma Fire Department) got there quickly, had the victim bandaged and in the back of the medic unit vehicle in record time. They were off to the hospital in truly short order. I suppose someone getting stabbed in the eye is not an everyday incident, even for paramedics.

After collecting the broken beer bottle and interviewing the witnesses, except for the bartender—he was not a cop-friendly sort of guy—we transported our suspect to jail. As correction officers were booking the suspect, our dispatcher asked us to call her on the phone. I made the call, and she was a bit hesitant to tell me what it was she needed us to do. After a moment or two, she finally blurted it out. It seemed when our victim got to the hospital, the doctors determined that his eyeball was missing. They were not sure if they could put it back in but were asking if we could go back to the bar and see if we could find it.

Most of you reading this might say, "No way! Are you kidding me?" That was my first reaction, but I just decided, oh well—it's just a part of the job. We told the jailers we would be back for the booking number later.

We headed back to the bar, walked in, and began looking around. As soon as we turned on the flashlights and began looking, the bartender said, "You guys got a search warrant?" I looked at him and informed him we did not need one for the public area and then told him what we were looking for. I was going to add 'smart ass' at the end, but as soon as I said 'eyeball,' he and the two patrons fled the bar to the street. The bartender just wanted to know when we were done, and he didn't want to see it. We commenced a search and were in it for about 30 seconds when the dispatcher asked us to call them again. I made the call, and the dispatcher told me it seems the doctors found the eye. Due to the amount of blood, the eye was shoved way back in the socket, so they assumed it was gone. Once they located it, they were able to put the victim under and pop the eye back into place. No guarantee he would be able to see out of it, but nevertheless, it was now back in place. I must admit I was glad the search was over.

When we were about to leave, Scott said, "We have to get back at that bartender." Okay, I was good with that. My partner was a bit of a prankster, and he was not about to let this go just yet. I saw him rummage around the bar, and with a big grin, he held up a white cocktail onion. Oh man, I knew where this was going, and I was totally good with this plan. He put the onion between his left thumb and forefinger. Then he picked up a bottle of Tabasco sauce and sprinkled it all over the onion and his hand. As we walked out of the bar, he placed his right hand over his left so one could only see part of the onion (AKA: eyeball) and see the dripping red Tabasco sauce (AKA: blood) from his hand. The bartender, with a serious, concerned look, asked, "Did you find it?"

Scottie said, "Yes, it's right here."

A patron asked in a drunken slur, "Well, what are you going to do with it?"

Scottie paused for a moment and looked at me. I looked back at him and said, "Yeah, what are you going to do with it?"

Scottie looked down at his hand and said, "Eat it, of course," and then immediately popped the onion in his mouth. As soon as Scottie did that, one of the patrons vomited a stream of beer. Me, on the other hand, began hysterically laughing. I had no clue he was going to do that. As I walked to the patrol car, unable to stop laughing at both what Scottie did and the patron vomiting all over himself, the bartender and the other drunk were screaming at us, saying we were sick bastards. "How could you do something like that," and so on. Finally, the bartender screamed; he could not believe I thought it was so funny.

My answer was, "Because it's hilarious!"

They were dropping F-bombs over and over as we drove away, saying they were going to call the mayor, our chief, and anyone else they could think of. We just ignored them. I must admit I thought they would have caught on this was a prank. Nope, and that made it even better.

About ten minutes later, our sergeant called on the radio to come to the station. On our way, we thought, *oh man, are we in trouble now?* When we got there and walked into the sergeant's office, Scottie said, "What's up, Sarge?"

"You know damn well what's up," he replied. "I know there has to be more to this story, but I got a phone call from that bar you were at saying one of you ate some guy's eyeball," he continued. The sergeant had a big grin on his face, so I knew he was ready for a good story. After we told him what happened and what we did, he began to laugh and wished he had been there to see the entire thing. "Of course," he said, "make sure you don't do that again." We assured him we would not, but as we headed to the door, the sergeant stopped us and said, "But if you do, invite me next time. I've got to see this shit." We assured him we would and headed back out on the street.

You Won't Be a Problem
for Anyone

The 'strip,' as it was called in my early days as a Tacoma cop, comprised of 11th Street to 15th Street on Pacific and Commerce Avenues. There was some overflow, but that area was the main area of sinful decay if you will. On that six square block area were those seedy bars to house the drunks, porn peek-a-boo movie theaters to house the perverts, and seedy hotels to house the prostitutes and their customers. The area, at the time, was abandoned by the city. The city council seemed to look the other way and really didn't want to know what was happening there. Drugs, sexually transmitted diseases, and alcohol flowed without check. The police department's responsibility was just to keep it all corralled and contained.

In Downtown Tacoma, the seedy bars seemed to generate seedy people, and that clientele was an accepted bunch by the seedy bars. I am sure you can make the connection. That said, it took a great deal, and I mean a huge amount, to get kicked out of the bars. These were bars that, as long as you had money, you were guaranteed to buy the next bottle of beer. The people who patronized these places are not the kind of people you'd want to call a friend.

Like anything in life, there is always an exception to the rule. I had the pleasure of meeting him. My partner and I were working a swing shift and started our shift in the area as any normal evening when we got a dispatch for an unruly drunk in one of the bars. I mean, to have a call for an 'unruly' person in one of those places was strange. Everybody in these places was unruly, and it was a way of life. To be called to get someone out of the bar was truly the exception to the rule. You had to be a total asshole to be kicked out, especially when you still had money in your pocket. The bar owners usually would tolerate a great deal, but once you were broke, they showed the broke guy the door.

When we got to the bar and met the bartender, he pointed out a guy he wanted to remove. It was a simple contact, and the guy left without much issue. *Okay*, I thought, *easy enough*. We told him not to go back to the bar, and he was agreeable to that. He did ask if he could go into any other bar, and we told him he only got 86th out of the one we removed him from. "Okay," he said, and off he went.

One would think that if you got kicked out of one bar, you might want to adjust your behavior to make sure you didn't get booted out of another one. But as it was, brilliance was not a part of this guy's gene pool. Through the course of the night, this guy got thrown out of five different bars, all because he couldn't help himself other than to be nothing but a pain in the butt. On the fifth bar, I told him we were sick of responding to calls just because he couldn't control himself. I let him know that if we had to come back again, we were going to make sure he wasn't a problem to anyone, ever again. His response was not the same as the agreeable guy from the first call, but it instead was, "Fuck you, pig." I told him if we got another call, this would all come back to haunt him. What do you think happened? Yep, another call came in.

When we arrived at the call, I didn't say a word but grabbed our obnoxious drunk and dragged him to the car. My partner knew what I was up to, and he had the back door ready. This guy wasn't very big so getting him where I wanted wasn't a big ordeal for me. I patted him down and commenced stuffing him in the back seat. I have to admit I was none too kind. That wasn't a major issue in those days—no cell phone videos, and it was an acceptable practice not to be friendly.

He went in headfirst, and as I was about to close the door, I saw he was wearing slip-on shoes. I had an immediate idea and grabbed his shoes from him before he could react. When I closed the door, he yelled, "What the fuck are you doing with my shoes?"

"You'll see," I responded. My partner gave me a quizzical look, and I told him I have plans and we needed to head out to the Tide Flats.

The Tacoma Tide Flats in the early 80s was a desolate area and had a whole lot of nothing. There was little to no business and large empty tracts of land. Today it's a bustling international seaport, but back then, it was a no man's land for the most part.

As we drove out to the Tide Flats, I held up the guy's shoes so he could see them. I asked, "Do you want these back?"

He said, "Yeah, ya mother fucker!"

I rolled down the window and tossed them out the window. "You can have them back when you find them," I said. I then received a flurry of 'fuck yous.' My partner told me he had no clue I was going to do that and wished he would have thought of it.

As we drove out into the Tide Flats, I began telling our little drunkard we would make sure he was not going to be a problem to anyone, and we always took care of guys like him. The drive continued on into a remote area. There was nothing anywhere near us, and it seemed we were miles from any building. We began going off-road along the levee for the Puyallup River as I continued to speak softly that we know how to make sure guys like him never come back to Downtown Tacoma. I was trying to get this smuck to believe we were going out to kill him, and it seemed to be working. Our drunk asked me several times what my partner and I were doing, plus I could hear this genuine fear in his voice. My only answer was, "You'll see. Maybe you should pray now."

When we got underneath the Eels Bridge, it was the perfect spot. The levee was muddy, and there were several mud puddles where we stopped. I got out and opened the back door. I told our then very afraid drunk to get out of the car. He refused, screaming, "You're screwed, man! Whatever you do, the evidence is in the car! You're screwed, man; you're screwed!" I was laughing inside but annoyed as well. I reached in and grabbed him as he screamed, "Oh my God! Somebody help!" We were under a bridge that carried heavy traffic. No one could hear him. There was a nearby huge puddle where I made sure he landed in. He immediately peed on himself and then went into a fetal position, crying and repeatedly saying, "Oh God, Oh God!" as we drove away.

Today if a cop did this, they would get days off, fired, and/or sent to jail. In the early 80s, this was considered good police work and still should be. Guess what? It worked out exactly the way it was intended – he was never seen in Tacoma again.

Another happy ending.

A Little Pepper (Spray) With That

When I first came to the Tacoma Police Department, Downtown Tacoma was a seedbed of sin. There were a tremendous number of vice crimes going on that would keep any cop busy for hours. But, from a cop's point of view, it was fun to work there. Cops, or at least real cops, did not seek to get employed by a law enforcement agency to sit on their butts all shift. Keeping busy with arrests, contacts, traffic stops, and taking calls was what it was all about, as well as it helped the shift go by.

With all that said, as one can imagine, cops got the strangest and sometimes quite nasty calls. This was the one that happened in my first couple of years.

As stated, Downtown Tacoma was well known for its seedy activity. One of the major contributors to that stigma was the number of alcoholics roaming the street. It was not uncommon to see drunkards sprawled in doorways passed out, usually vomiting or pissing on themselves, or maybe even taking a dump in a doorway.

On one occasion, a drunkard had apparently exited one of the many seedy bars; he leaned against a light pole, commenced to pull out his Johnson, and urinated on the sidewalk. I was with two other officers when dispatched to check on him. When we got there, he was leaning against the pole, and he appeared to be done with his business as his somewhat unmanly manhood was still hanging free without a waterfall coming out the end. What was so amazing was that though he was passed out, the manhood was standing upright. Of course, he was leaning against the power pole but asleep. We tried our best to wake him up by yelling, shaking him, and even throwing a cold glass of water in his face that we got from the bar to wake him. Nothing worked. The other two officers came up with the bright idea to see if pepper spray may stir our little 'Sleeping Not So Beauty.' So they started with a little zap in the face—nothing, not even a twitch. *So let's try some more*, they thought. After three hits with pepper spray, he did stir a bit, wiping his face with his hand a couple of times, but that was it. To say we were a bit astonished would be an understatement. I can't remember anyone in my entire career who was that drunk. Oh well, those officers and I decided that he wasn't a threat to anyone, so there was no reason to arrest him, even for the exposure of his little Johnny. I was about ready to walk to the car when my friends said, "Wait a minute." I looked at those guys as they walked back to the drunk. One of the officers stood there, rubbing his chin in deep thought.

I asked him, "What are you up to?"

That officer turned to me and said, "We have to make sure when he wakes up he knows we were here." I did not like the sound of that at all. To my amazement, that officer pulled out his pepper spray again. *So are you going to spray him in the face some more? I thought. It didn't work before; why does he think it'll work now?* The difference this time was it wasn't in the drunkard's face but on his penis. That officer sprayed him so much that the pepper spray was dripping off this guy.

Both officers got in the car, and one said, "Wait until he goes to take a piss after he sobers up." I have to admit—I did get a chuckle out of that.

Maybe he'd try harder to find the men's room next time.

Two Finger Kate

There seems to be a growing number of groups in the United States that want to have most drugs legalized or have places where addicts can do their drug of choice in a safe place. I totally get the concept behind the idea, and I suppose there is some merit to it. My thoughts would be, instead of spending so much money on the war on drugs, we should spend it building and funding drug rehab facilities. I never, in my entire career, met a drug user who did not want to get clean. Never!

While working Downtown, I worked with street-level drug enforcement. I did surveillance of drug deals and following up on the bust. The 'junkies' I busted always complained there was never enough 'bed space' for them to get into treatment. Why? Because of all the money spent on putting these sorry souls in jail. If these people could get the treatment they needed, then guess what? They could have become a productive citizen. They would pay taxes, and they would add to the economy by adding to the GDP. It is a simple concept. Even if they relapse, at least for that period of time, they would be 'clean,' making a positive impact. When they fall, we should pick them up and clean them again, so they become a productive citizen once again. How many times do we do that? As many times as it takes, period.

But our system is not geared like that right now; I do not know if it will ever be. So, where does that put the addicted drug user? Drug users will do whatever it takes to get the drugs they need so they can be 'right.' That all said, I do not want anyone to get the idea the drug user is all innocent. They are the ones who decided to put the needle in their arm, the powder up their nose or put their lips on the glass tube. Saying this is a disease is pure hogwash. The drug user has to take responsibility for their actions; without it, no treatment in the world will be effective. This is a story about one of them who has issues with responsibility.

Kate, as she was known before this incident, had and still does have a major problem with drugs, or maybe she is dead by now; I do not really know. She did not care what drug she got, just something to take the edge off. She was well known to my partner and me as a user who would do anything to get her drugs. We had arrested her for stealing from her mother while her mother was in the hospital seeking treatment for a heart attack. She broke into her mother's house, took almost everything of value, and sold it for drug money. Needless to say, we didn't have much concern or respect for Kate. Kate was quite the self-centered – 'the world owes me' attitude person.

On one of Kate's many escapades to acquire drugs, this one truly was the top of the heap of sheer stupidity. Around the 4th of July, Kate got her hands on an M100 and decided it was a good idea to try and blow up a phone in a phone booth (for those who do not know what a phone booth is — because they do not exist anymore — watch an old Superman movie). Her attempt was to put the M100 in the change flapper, blow up the phone, and steal all the change in the bottom of the phone. So, I get the idea behind the reason for the pyrotechnics, but she needed to think this out a bit more.

For some of you reading this story, you might have never seen a phone booth let alone how well the phones were constructed. The coins were kept in a mini–Fort Knox. An M100 stood a snowball's chance in hell of doing any damage to the coin compartment. I suppose when you are a junkie, you are not really thinking very clearly. Due to the construction of these phones, the blast would not penetrate the phone at all; the blast would come directly out toward Kate.

Kate searched and found a victim, isolated phone booth in the south end of the city. Where the flapper for the return change was a bit small, so she shoved the firecracker into the little compartment. As she pounded on the M100, she broke the fuse in several places. On and on, until it was 'stuck' in the flapper.

Every time she tried to light the firecracker, it went out fairly quickly. Finally, once the fuse was down to the smallest of nubs, Kate was able to light it for the last time. Once again, let us remind everyone that druggies do not think very clearly. She had got the smallest of all the small nubs; just what do you think was going to happen here? It blew up in a split second. So, what did she do, light it, of course? Brilliant! Boom went the explosive.

Remember I stated that the coin container was built to withstand a nuclear blast. With that, where did you think the vast majority of the blast go? It couldn't penetrate the heavy-duty steel wall it was against, so out it came right at her hand, the path of least resistance. The blast was also very concentrated given the size of the flapper, which took Kate's thumb, first & middle finger all off.

Someone from a nearby residence heard Kate's screams and called for medical aid. The paramedics got there and, in panic, along with Kate's demands to "get me to the fucking hospital, you assholes!" the paramedics failed to retrieve her partial hand. So, who got that call? You guessed it.

Once we got the call, both my partner and I argued about who had to pick the thing up, but we got a bit of a surprise as we went there. As we approached the booth, we could see the back end of a dog sticking out. When we got within about 50 feet of the phone, the dog exited the booth, looking right at our approaching car. I looked at my partner and said, "No, no, no way." As soon as we stopped the car, the dog went back into the booth, and as we exited the vehicle, the dog ran off with 'something' in its mouth. I walked up to the booth and looked in. There was a lot of blood inside but no hand. The simple deduction will tell you the dog was not running away with a mouthful of Snauusages®. Nor were we going to chase the dog as he was too fast. Neither were we going to shoot the dog to get her hand back. All I could say to the dog was Bon Appetite. So off to the hospital we went to let the doctor know what happened.

While filling in the doctor, Kate got wind of what happened. She started cussing us out with, "You fucking assholes go find that fucking dog," and so on. The doctor told us he was quite done with her, given exactly what she was yelling at us as he got the same.

Due to the resulting injuries Kate sustained, we dubbed her 'two-finger.' Every time we saw her after that day, we called her by her new name. Usually, she just retorted back with a "fuck you." She hated us even more after that. By the way, the phone booth? It fared well. Some powder burns but nothing else. It was operational despite the minor comedic blemish.

$25 And an Elevator Ride

Some of you might want to skip this story. Why? Because of my response to an extremely unruly 'customer.' That said, I do regret anything I did or how I took care of a problem. Most of you would probably agree with the outcome and how I ensured the outcome. So, with that quasi warning, read at your own risk.

Handicapped people always get my respect, and I try to help them every chance I have. If the handicapped person is homeless as well, that multiplies how difficult life can be for them. Not something I would ever want to experience, nor do I completely understand what a person in those situations goes through on a daily basis. Drugs are not the only reason people are homeless – I have met several of them who are just in hard times. That all said, when others help, no matter who we are, we should accept that help with grace and gratitude and not be a jerk like this guy.

I was working the day shift in Downtown was dispatched to the Wells Fargo Bank for trouble with a customer. It was in the summer of 1992, but don't ask me the actual date. For the life of me, I can't remember.

The Wells Fargo Bank building is the tallest building in Tacoma and is fairly centrally located in Downtown. The actual bank is located on the second floor, and the access is via an elevator or the escalator. At the main level of the building, you are greeted by a large desk where, most of the time, two security officers are located. To this day, I still don't know their function or what they are being paid for as they never do 'security' functions. It's mostly a meet-and-greet counter. Every time I had been to this building, that is all I have ever seen them do. Basically, letting you know what elevator to take to any given office.

As my partner and I entered, we could hear the yelling of a male voice coming from the bank area at the top of the escalator. He was saying, "I want my fucking money." We ran up the escalator and found the following scene: To the left was a long counter with four teller stations, but only two were occupied. One of the tellers was crying and obviously very upset, and the other teller was trying to console her. At the front of the teller counter and just below the actual countertop was a marble front. A large crack ran diagonally from the high point on the right, all the way down the length of the marble to the low point on the left. On the floor, directly in front of the counter, was a 15-pound dumbbell-style weight. To the right of the teller area, near the exterior wall, was a large potted tree that appeared to have been pulled over; dirt from the tree was in a large area directly in front of the pot with wheel tracks running through it. Just right in front of the tipped-over tree was a man in a wheelchair who had a hold of another man by his tie, choking him. The man in the wheelchair was the one screaming about his money.

We separated the two men, and given that the wheelchair man appeared to be the aggressor, we started by interviewing the man wearing the tie. Well, at least, we were trying to start there. The man wearing the tie identified himself as the bank manager, but as we spoke to him, 'Wheeling Willie' (my nickname for the guy in the wheelchair) would scream even louder and made every attempt to make it miserable to interview the bank manager. After several minutes of trying to calm down Wheeling Willie (WW) with no success, I told my partner I would get him out of the bank so we could get to the bottom of this incident. So I wheeled WW into the elevator even though he was still in this non-stop verbal tirade. He was so vialed that as the doors closed, he looked at the upset teller, flipped her off, and said: "Fuck you, bitch!" For now, I will keep you in suspense as to what happened after the doors closed because we have to find out why we were there in the first place. No cheating; you can't look ahead.

My partner was now with the bank manager and tellers getting the entire story. He was able to find out WW came in demanding his $25, which he assumed was still in his account. What he failed to do was tell the bank teller the account was ten plus years old with zero activity. This was the late 80s when computers still had not been anywhere near as refired or accurate as they are today (2021). Information such as the last time WW had accessed his account would be crucial because it would have made things just a bit simpler to try and locate. But given WW was not a very cooperative sort, the teller was having extreme difficulty finding his account. Why was she having so much of a problem, might you ask, yes you may. Because this location was not always Wells Fargo, it used to be First Interstate Bank, which was consumed by Wells Fargo. WW had actually opened the account with First Interstate Bank, and in the exchange, some small accounts were lost in the shuffle. The procedure to locate the account was taking a long time because WW was stubborn and demanding. The poor teller was at odds with why she could not find what she needed to address this jerk of a customer. And WW was getting angrier every second that went by, and that built on the anger he already had when he came in, making this a stressful encounter.

Once the teller figured out what had happened, she asked him to fill out a withdrawal slip, routine at any bank. This would have been a simple solution, but this was WW, and he was not going to make it easy for anyone. Instead of filling out a simple form so he could get his $25, all WW would do was scream that he wanted his 'fucking money.' When she stated she could not give him anything without the slip, WW grabbed his 15-pound weight and threw it toward the teller. Thankfully his aim was poor, and the dumbbell (no, not WW) struck the marble front, cracking the stone. That was when the teller became distraught and began to cry. WW had zero compassion and screamed a slurry of vulgarities, calling the teller a 'cunt.'

Hearing this commotion, the bank manager got up to intercede. As the manager came, WW quickly wheeled over to the large tree and pulled it over, spewing dirt onto the carpet. The manager caught up with WW and stood in front of him, ordering out of the bank. WW was not deterred and continued his rant of wanting his money, pointing at the teller, screaming the 'C' word and how incompetent she was. Finally, the manager ascertained it was over $25, so he offered WW what he had in his wallet, $20. That was not acceptable to WW. That was when he grabbed the bank manager by his tie, choking him. Now you have the scene when we arrived.

Back to the elevator. When the doors were closing, and WW had made that rude gesture to the terribly upset teller, it just pissed me off. No matter what happened, when you combine his outrageous behavior, I would not let him get away with it. As the door closed and I heard the doors come together, I doubled my fist and gave both to him across his head from right to left. WW had no idea that was coming, and given I was standing behind him made it all the better. I hit him so hard he tipped off from his chair over to the left. Before it could reach the floor, I grabbed his hair with my left hand and the chair with my right. I brought him and his chair back to an upright position and slammed both of them down. After setting the chair correctly, I pulled WW's head back, got down to his ear, and said, "Now you shut the fuck up. You got that asshole?"

Ever so meekly, he said, "Yep." So, when the elevator stopped on the bottom floor, I wheeled WW out with a smile and made happy greetings to all as we headed out of the building to the courtyard area. There, we waited for my partner.

Once my partner showed up, he told me the entire story and said while he and the bank manager were talking, they heard the sounds of thumping coming from the elevator immediately after the doors closed. The bank manager had asked my partner, "Do you think your partner needs help?"

His response was, "No, it's not my partner that needs help right now." Thanks for that vote of confidence, partner; you were right.

As we drove in silence to the jail, my partner told me, "I don't know what you did in the elevator, nor do I want to know but whatever it was, seems to be working."

"It was just a heart-to-heart talk," I told him.

One last thing. At the jail, when the booking officer asked for WW's name, he didn't answer. The booking officer asked again, and still, WW said nothing. Seeing the anger welling up on the booking officer's face, I realized I had to let WW know it was okay to answer the booking officer's question. *Man*, I thought, *this guy is a quick learner.*

Cary V

Though this tale isn't truly one of the seedy Downtown locations, it is about one of our regulars from that area, and Cary V was one who 'escaped' (if you will) for a moment. Cary V was an interesting sort of guy. On one occasion, my partner and I caught him masturbating on the corner of Union and South 19th Street during rush hour traffic. If you don't know Tacoma, these are two very busy streets all day long, so during rush hour, it's even crazier. Cary would just do stuff like this without a second thought. Obviously, he was not all there mentally and became one of our regular 'customers.' Cary was also a bit of a big guy, so when he wanted to fight, he was quite the handful.

This tale is maybe more about my partner than Cary. It's just that Cary was the original focus of how this tale got started. My partner and I got the dispatch about a guy masturbating in public. Once we got the call, my partner and I both knew it was Cary; I mean, it was got to be Cary since he was the only one who would ever do this kind of crap. The description of the suspect and what he was doing just meant it had to be Cary. As we approached, we could see it was our best customer, as we thought. He had his head back and eyes closed, and he was going to town on his manhood. It was one of those things where you're saying to yourself, really? And at the same time, just shaking your head because you are expecting exactly that from this guy. We rolled up to him, making sure our car is not in any direct line of fire of any ejaculated substance, plus we were trying to block the motorists' view of Cary's activities.

As we got out of the car, we turned on our light bar, and that got him to open his eyes. Once he saw us, he tried to run away while trying to stuff his 'package' in his pants. The combination of those two things, along with his weight, made him a bit slow. I tackled him, and as he fell to the pavement, his fist full of penis hit his nuts, causing him a fair amount of pain. That took the fight out of him right away, and we were able to get him handcuffed. When I had to pull his right hand back to be placed in handcuffs, I noticed that he was right-handed—we all knew what he was doing with it. Need I say more? Yuck! That was so nasty! I was happy that when he fell, he was still holding on to his little trouser snake, and with the fall, he ended up shoving the package into his pants rather forcefully. Oh, thank God, we just had to zip him up. That was much better than the alternative. We put him in the back of our car and took him away from the motoring public on a public obscenity charge—no more roadside show from him. Something told me that, just maybe, many of the motorists might have got quite the chuckle of the sideshow they were experiencing when we chased Cary down and tackled him.

We went straight to the sector one substation for the processing before we headed to the jail. When we got to the substation, we placed Cary at the head of the report writing table as we would with any subject under arrest. My partner sat at the right of the table, and I was standing at the head with my back to Velez; whereas, Velez was facing my partner. As my partner was gathering information for the report, I began talking to my lieutenant about the arrest. Suddenly I heard Cary cough up some phlegm in his throat, and before I could turn around, he spat it at my partner, hitting him in the face.

As I am sure anyone reading this right now would agree that being spat on has got to be on the top five list of things that are just plain disgusting to happen to a person. Cops feel the same way and compound with what this jerk was previously doing— it just added to the disgust.

Without even a second thought, when I spun around and saw what had happened, I laid my right fist on the right side of Cary's face as hard as I could, not only knocking him out of his chair but literally knocking him out. It was an automatic reaction, but seconds later, I felt I did the wrong thing. Not because Cary didn't deserve it, but because he actually deserved more, but my partner had jumped up to get his lick in. But there was Cary out cold on the floor, and Al was standing over him looking at me, then looking at Cary and back at me saying, "Shit!" My partner wanted to punch him so bad, but I had taken the shot and deprived him of that opportunity.

I looked at my partner and apologized for taking his shot. Cary woke up moments later, and off to the jail he went. We didn't have a concussion protocol in those days, so he went from knock-out to lock up.

Cary was one of those guys who was not right in the head in a sexually deviant way, and many times, he would get quite violent. Last I heard, this caught up to him when he was killed by an angry dad when Cary tried to molest the gentleman's teenage daughter on a bus. It would seem, only from what I heard, the dad beat the living tar out of Cary, causing him even more brain damage, and he subsequently died from his injuries. The dad was arrested and got community service hours. Fair? You be the judge. As for me, it worked.

The Bicycle DUI

Law enforcement has many aspects that just end up being ridiculous for both the officer and the suspect. This tale, I feel, falls into that category. This was a normal summer's early evening while I was cruising in the Downtown area of Tacoma. Nothing exciting nor happening of any importance. I was feeling good about my day and enjoying a relatively peaceful patrol. I had a couple of traffic stops, which went well, mostly because I just issued warnings. I even had a shoplifter at a grocery store whom I had the option to release on a citation, and they went away swearing on their mother's grave they would show up in court. Honestly, I can't remember if he did or not.

So as I cruised Downtown, I was expecting the rest of my day to go as well. That kind of thought pattern usually meant what? That's right; the day was about to change and not in a positive manner.

As I got to 17th & Pacific Ave, traveling south on Pacific, I observed a fellow on a bicycle ahead of me. Being an avid cyclist, I am very aware of cyclists and understand their dilemmas, needs, and screw-ups, probably much more than an average officer. This one, though, was one for the books. Even for the most critical cyclist, one would scratch their head and say, "What the...!"

What I saw was a guy riding a mountain-style bike, okay nothing abnormal there. It looked, even from a distance, to be a bit beat up, and I could hear squeaking coming from it as the rider pedaled downed the street. So it sounded like he had done little to no maintenance on his ride. As I got closer, I could see it was a semi-trashed Huffy, basically junk. Yes, I am a bicycle snob.

What marveled me the most was this guy's ability to stay atop the bike. I had no idea about his cycling skills, but he was having a great deal of difficulty remaining upright. He was weaving back and forth across the lane, which had nothing to do with the poor condition of the bicycle but, instead, he was apparently dozing off. I could see the rider begin to slump to the right, and when his body got to about a 45-degree angle, causing the bicycle to go in that direction as well. He would then jerk back upright only to jerk the bike to the left, and then the process would repeat itself. As I watched, he also leaned straight back toward the rear tire while still holding onto the handlebars – I have to admit I was impressed by how limber he was when he got in that position. Then he'd do the same thing as he leaned to the right as well. It was crazy and awe-inspiring at the same time.

Though all that was happening, my attention was also drawn to something else going on with this 'cyclist.' All of us have seen those plastic shipping crates that milk cartons come in. One was tethered to the back of the bike with about a 15-foot rope. I also noticed that on the back of the bike was a rack – so the reasonable assumption was maybe this poor, misguided person had tied the crate to the rack, but it had just fallen off.

As I watched this scene, it became clear this guy was not just a bit intoxicated but actually quite drunk. So I moved in directly behind him to initiate a traffic stop; I had to get this guy off the road before he got killed or caused an accident. Once I was about 20 feet away, I turned on my emergency lights. I did not want to spook him and have him crash into a parked car, so I decided not to turn on my siren yet. As I waited for him to stop, he fell back toward the rear tire twice. Each time I thought, *okay, he sees me now*. I mean, this guy was near upside down, and I swear we made eye contact. Nevertheless, he continued on his drunken way, swerving back and forth with the crate tossed back and forth in a near half circle. One swing struck the tire of a parked vehicle. It became apparent to me I had to hit the siren to get his attention. With that, I 'burped' the siren. The reaction was not what I expected.

Most people, riding a bicycle with me chasing in a patrol car, would just pull to the curb. Not this guy. As soon as I gave the siren a short blast, the rider popped straight up and turned around with a sharp snap. We made eye contact once again, so I figured he would now just stop. Nope! He began pedaling faster and went into a tuck position (upper body lowered to the handlebars), which I figured was an attempt to make himself more aerodynamic to get all the speed he could from that rickety bicycle. Let me emphasize the word 'attempt' because he failed miserably. To exasperate his escape (please inject as much sarcasm tone you would like with the word escape), he was only trying to go in a straight line – so basically to outrun me. This was about the stupidest thing I had to deal with all week.

What compounded this 'pursuit' was he was not stopping for anything. So for his safety, I had to turn on my siren all the way, plus I had the duty to let dispatch know I was, technically, 'in pursuit.' Not only was that embarrassing for me, but use your imagination for a second and wrap your head around the sight of a patrol car with lights and a siren blasting behind some drunk on a bicycle; it was a bit insane. Let's say it's just a sight you don't see every day. Also, keep in mind when I told dispatch what I was doing, their response was, "You are pursuing a what?" I could just hear the laughter coming from all the other officers who heard me repeat myself.

I was also using my external speaker as much as I could. Just saying things such as "Stop, pullover, you're going to hurt yourself on that thing," but to no avail. It wasn't until he swerved so violently to the right that his bike hit the curb, he bounced up out of the seat, going headlong over the handlebars. As I watched, I thought, *oh my God, he's going to hit his head on the pavement!* Thankfully he kept from doing that. He flipped in a complete 180, landing on his back, unhurt for the most part. I was grateful he did not land on his head, not because I was concerned for his injury, but to be very honest, I dodged a great deal of paperwork along with having to take him to the hospital. Those trips take all day.

I stopped my patrol car right behind the now sprawled out cyclist and his upside-down as well as the rusty bike. As I walked up to him, I could see my drunken friend lying on his back, trying to get up but unable to do so. Not because he was hurt but due to his drunken state. I asked if he was okay, and he said in slurred Spanish, "*Yo estoy bien, señor.*" My Spanish is limited, but I got that he was okay. I helped him to his feet, and with my broken Spanish and his broken English, we were able to communicate. As I spoke with him, he was slurring his words, could hardly stand up, and smelled like a brewery.

"*Demasiada cerveza* (Too much beer)?" I asked him.

"Oh, no *señor. Muy poco* (very little)," he replied.

Sorry, but I didn't believe him. I had little trust in that answer, but I really did not want to arrest this guy. Man, arresting a drunk on a bicycle was more paperwork than I needed. So my solution was to take his milk crate and use the rope he had to tie it to his rack. At least that would keep it from swinging back and forth. Using makeshift sign language, along with broken Spanish, I told him he could no longer ride his bicycle because of how drunk he was. "Okay," he said, so I hoped I got through to him, and when he began walking his bicycle on the sidewalk, I thought, he's got it. I got back into my patrol car and drove off, satisfied and feeling comfortable with my decision to let him go on his way.

That feeling did not last very long. As I drove down the street, I began to question my decision. Traffic was a bit thick, but I was able to get back to where I stopped the guy within about 5–10 minutes. He was gone, so I thought I'd better take a peek around just to make sure he was actually doing what I asked him to do. I drove about six blocks when I spotted him. There he was, back on the seat of the bicycle, weaving back and forth as he pedaled down the street, just like he was before. What I found to be very irritating was he actually had untied the crate, and it was swinging back and forth behind him again. It was like he was using the crate as some sort of stabilizer – it was not working at all.

I got my patrol car right in behind him, and it was very clear to me he had no clue I was there because I could hear him signing as he rode. So when I got about six inches from his rear wheel, I blasted the air horn on my car. He came about three feet straight up off the seat and landed half off the bike to the right. He turned quickly, and he had a look on his face of an 'aw shit, I've been caught again.'

Thankfully this time, he decided to pull over and stop. So no hitting the curb, no crashing, nothing. As I got out of my car, I let dispatch know I was out with a DUI and my location. Routinely you tell them the license number of the car as well, so when I didn't say anything, dispatch asked for a 'plate number.' "There is none," I told them.

"Car make?" they asked.

"It's not a car," was my response.

"Is this that bicycle again?" was the question, and I could hear the laughter again in the background.

Reluctantly, I said, "Yes."

After a short talk with my Hispanic drunk, I reported to dispatch. "One in custody for DUI." I can't say for sure, but I just knew the dispatchers were falling out of their chairs about now.

Despite all that, the process for this DUI went smooth, and if he were driving a car, we'd impound the car. With riding a bicycle, I placed the bike in the property room. I didn't book him into jail either. Once I put his bicycle in the property room, he would not be able to get back on that thing for the next 48 hours. Let's hope he was sober by then. The last I saw him was him walking down the street. One would think that would be the end of this story. Nope.

For the next week, I was contacted by several officers, and I mean several, asking me when I might be in their neighborhood so they could make sure their kids weren't riding their bicycles. My response: "Keep them away from the liquor cabinet, and all will be fine." I never made another bicycle-related arrest for the rest of my career.

Dracula

What a strange name for this next story, isn't it? No, I don't believe in Dracula, Frankenstein, Sasquatch, UFOs, or any other sort of ghoulish monster or myth. On the other hand, I have to admit I did, very deliberately, decide to write this one tale on a Halloween Day (October 31st, 2016, to be exact), but in no way will it be a blood and guts sort tale. No one is biting anyone on the neck or bats flying about or someone rising out of a coffin after the sunsets. As a matter of fact, you will not even see any horror film villain, but there is a reference to Bram Stoker's undead human. It will include a strong belief the nightwalker actually exists. The subject of this tale, whom I will call 'Screamer,' had a strong belief the dark soul was real and alive – he just made a serious miscalculation. I just hope you find the humor in it all.

I'm sure anyone can imagine that police officers encounter many walks of life. We see horrible things, of course, but many more funny things pass our way – or at least they are funny after the fact. As one might imagine, we also encounter those that are mentally deficient. I know some of you may feel those folks are tragic, and you are right. They do need our assistance and help. At the same time, they also can be quite funny. They say and do things that are off "in a galaxy far, far away" (Star Wars).

While working the beat in downtown Tacoma, I had my fair share of every imaginable person a cop could have encountered. Most of the people who were having mental concerns brought it on due to drug addictions of one sort or another. Not all, of course, but in my experience, drugs had a great deal of influence on what demons they were dealing with. Screamer was not outwardly crazy, but he just did very odd things from time to time.

He was a "normal" looking guy, whatever normal is. Screamer didn't dress weird or seem strange when I talked with him the first time. If you saw him walking down the street, you'd never know he had some issues. It wasn't until he made this very odd claim that it truly hit me he was a few bricks short of a full load. I had many conversations with Screamer on several occasions prior to this encounter. We had conversations about many things, and he confided in me about his addiction to heroin and how he was trying to get off it through treatments but had relapsed the past three times. These conversations were over about a three to four-month period. He also told me he had respect for law enforcement, and I never had any reason not to believe him. Even though in the back of my mind I always felt he was a bit strange, I just chalked it up to the heroin talking. The day Screamer went off the deep end, it was nothing less than a stellar, crazy, off-the-wall leap. I mean, if the Earth was flat, he was falling off the edge of the planet. I suspected this was one of those relapses with his addiction.

One day Screamer showed up on the street wearing a headband with five bicycle mirrors attached to it. Those bicycle mirrors that cyclist wear on their helmets—you know, the small square ones on a short boom, so they stick away from the helmet on the left side, allowing the cyclist to see what's behind them. There was Screamer walking around town with those mirrors. He had the mirrors mounted with one pointing forward and the other four spaced equally, so they covered the front half of his head – none to the rear.

At first, I just thought this was a temporary addition to his wardrobe, but after a month of seeing this every day, my curiosity got the best of me. I just had to ask. So I approached Screamer and asked, "Okay, you've got to tell me, what's with the mirrors?"

As soon as I asked the question, he furtively looked in every direction as if he was looking for something or maybe someone. After seemingly completing a thorough search, he looked directly into my eyes and asked, with earnest, "You won't tell anyone, will you?"

"Of course not; your secret is good with me," I said with a hint of light sarcasm, which went unnoticed by Screamer. As he looked about, he went on to tell me he was having an affair with Dracula's wife. There it was, he stepped over the super crazy line, and I just had to see where this was headed. I told him that was a bit dangerous and I wasn't sure if I should congratulate him, but it still didn't explain the mirrors.

He looked at me like I was the one who was crazy and said, "Yes, it does!" I told him I must be a bit stupid because I still didn't get it (keep in mind many crazy people think that you are thinking just like them). He rolled his eyes in a manner of 'come on, don't you get it,' but went on to tell me that when he is walking down the street and if Dracula was looking for him; he could see the vampire coming at him from the front but not from the rear. I told him again that I still didn't get it. He was now getting quite frustrated and annoyed with me and screamed, "The mirrors are so I can see him coming from behind me, you idiot!" Well, there went his secret for the world to know. That outburst didn't seem to register at all about his desire to keep this affair secret, so much for the twisted mind.

I began to laugh out loud. He looked at me with this anger on his face and said, "What's so fucking funny?"

Through the laughing, I told him, "Everyone knows Dracula has no reflection, dude. So you will still never see him creeping up behind you."

His face lost total color, as white as can be. He began saying, "no," over and over. Fear had racked every cell of his body with this revelation. I could see him visibly shake, and I thought he was about to pass out. I asked him if his bed partner had alerted him of this little fact. He bent his head down and said, in a very soft voice, "No." His head then popped up, and he said, "Oh, I see you're just fucking with me, aren't you?" I suppose I was, just not in the way he thought. I repeated to my adulteress friend that everyone knew this about Dracula except for him, obviously.

About this time, across the street, a businessman was walking on the sidewalk. I told him to go ask that guy, pointing at the gentleman walking. Without the slightest hesitation, my now quite confused and scared dope addict ran directly across the street. In doing so, he was nearly hit by two cars, which of course, made me cringe a bit. Not because he was going to get hit by a car but the paperwork that would have been created by the incident.

Thankfully, he got across safely with only two irate drivers. He ran up to the businessman, sort of jumped in front of the man, and yelled. "Does Dracula have a reflection?"

The man looked at me as if to say, "What the hell!" I told the pedestrian to answer his question. The confused man, having no idea what was going on, told

Screamer the harsh truth and said, "Of course not, and everybody knows that. Now if we are done..." and the gentleman walked away. Screamer, this very poor demented soul, looked at me with sheer terror, then looked toward the now businessman who was going about his day shaking his head, and Screamer looked back at me again.

I have to admit; I would have never expected the next thing to happen. I kind of expected him to fall to the pavement in a weeping heap or roll up in a doorway, sucking his thumb, but not at all what he did. Instead of cowering, he ran down the street, with his hands over his head, waving back and forth, screaming at the highest pitch one would imagine, passing the gentleman and continuing down the street. For blocks, I could hear him screaming. That was the last I ever saw my misguided, deranged friend. I don't know where Screamer ended up. I kind of miss our little discussions...naw, not really.

Home Rotten Home

This is one of those stories that you just shake your head in wonder and amazement at the same time. The call was trouble with a transient. My partner and I were called to a loading dock for a food packaging plant and were told a transient was hiding under the loading dock. *Okay*, we thought, *we will just drag him out; no big deal*. This should be easy enough. It seemed when I think it would be an easy call, it turned out quite different.

Here is the scene: The loading dock was a large concrete platform where trucks would back up to and a large roll-up door where employees came out to unload the trucks. Around the loading dock were several dumpsters to throw away spoiled food before bringing it into the plant or at least shortly after employees went through the food.

When my partner and I got to the loading dock, it was dark, so I started looking under the dock and saw no one. A couple of employees stepped out, and I asked if the guy had left. They said no and told me he was right there and pointed to the end of the dock. I looked in the direction where they were pointing and still saw nothing. Again they said, "He's right there." I went back to the place they were pointing, moved some dumpsters out of the way to see better—still nothing. I thought that they saw a ghost or something because I was searching and there was not a thing. That was until one of the dumpsters I moved out of the way opened from the inside. Suddenly I saw a face. What the hell was going on? It would appear we have a real-life Oscar the Grouch here!

You have no idea how close this guy came to being shot. When that lid opened, it scared me half to death, and as a normal reaction and via hours of training, I upholstered my weapon, stuffed it in the guy's face saying, "What the fuck!" Of course, the crew on the loading dock saw a great deal of humor in my reaction and heard the chorus of laughter as I engaged my smelly, vegetable-covered 'friend.'

This guy, who I will affectionately name 'Oscar' the dumpster diver, stood up in the dumpster dripping with lettuce and an assortment a vegan would appreciate. The smell of rotting food permeated the air, not only from inside the dumpster but from Oscar himself. I ordered Oscar out of the dumpster, more of a 'get the fuck out of there,' but he refused. He claimed residency in the dumpster, telling me it was his home. I've heard of 'tiny homes,' but this was ridiculous. He further told me he wasn't going to give up his home to anyone. I assured him I had no interest in occupying the dumpster and also let him know the dumpster was not his — so "get out!" Once again, he refused.

Oh my God, I did not want to put my hands on him, given he was covered with rotting veggies of all kind (basically a walking bag of expired salad), and I didn't have rubber gloves – that was not a common tool that cops carried around in the 80s, unlike today. Nevertheless, he wasn't coming out unless we physically grabbed him, so that's what we did. I holstered the gun and began the nasty task of yarding this guy out of the dumpster. Cops have to do nasty stuff all the time but pulling a guy out of a dumpster, which he claimed residency, was one for the books.

As my partner and I yanked his nasty body out of this rotten veg container, he yelled, "Don't throw me in the puddle!" At this point in the story, I want to thank Oscar for such a good idea. I would not have thought of it on my own as it really didn't enter into my thoughts until he mentioned it. Time for a bath, Oscar!

Next to the dumpster was a very large and deep puddle, and that's where he went. The puddle contained mostly muddy water, but at least he could get a bath before going to jail.

After getting Oscar cuffed and out of the puddle, off to jail he went. After booking Oscar, all I could think about was getting a shower and burning my uniform. Oh, by the way, and as a side note, the jail officers donned hazmat suits while dealing with Oscar; that's how nasty he was even though he received a 'bath' before getting to the booking desk. And you know what? That's how nasty we were, as well.

A simple call and simple arrest, right? Something gnawed at me that we would be seeing this guy again. I was hoping he learned his lesson about setting up housekeeping in a dumpster, but that was not to be. Return 'customers' are quite common in law enforcement.

About two months after dealing with Oscar, I got a radio call from one of our detectives asking me if I'd recognize the guy my partner and I pulled out of the dumpster. Sure, no problem. The detective said he would meet me at the sector one sub-station. As I waited, I thought about what dumpster Oscar was found in again. When the detective showed up, he showed me a photo of Oscar, not a booking photo nor a photo of him in a dumpster. It was a picture of Oscar at the morgue.

It seemed Oscar was up to his tricks, but he didn't keep track of the garbage can pickup dates or set his alarm. What happened was a dumpster Oscar was in was loaded into a garbage truck, then compacted and later put on a refuse train. It is a reasonable assumption Oscar would have been waking up by the lifting of the dumpster. Probably he was, but if you've ever been around a garbage truck, you know how much noise they make. Plus, the driver is in the cab, so external noises are muffled by all those conditions combined.

Once the garbage was compacted in the garbage truck, either Oscar was crushed or suffocated – either one will do the job.

Thus the train shipped Oscar, along with the garbage, to a landfill about 160 miles away to Yakima, WA. The train unloaded the cargo, but it wasn't until the operator of the machine that aerates the garbage found Oscar.

The aerating machine lifted the garbage into the air as it moved through the huge pile of trash and had huge steel wheels with large steel spikes to help punch holes in the garbage, which would, of course, include Oscar.

From what I understand, Oscar was thrown over the machine during the aerating operation, not to mention the several holes in him or the number of broken bones from the compactor. I was also told the machine operator was having a great deal of difficulty with the entire incident. He thought he was the cause of Oscar's demise. I hope he got some professional counseling.

So what did the detective need from me: Oscar's real name or at least the one he gave me.

Well, I am sure Oscar has a better place to live now.

Take Me NOW!

If you have never read the book *Sybil*, I suggest you do so. Briefly, it's about a woman who had multiple personalities and how each one of the personalities affected their host, Sybil. Her personalities could come and go as needed for any situation she encountered. The woman I dealt with on this call was not as affected as Sybil, but she was equally disturbed.

I was dispatched to Tacoma General Hospital (TG) while working a swing shift (2 p.m. to 10 p.m.). I was told there was a potential patient who was at the triage desk at TG, creating a disturbance. I was also told she was upset she was unable to visit a male friend who was in the ER but who had stated he wanted nothing to do with her. Basically, she was not taking no for an answer.

When I arrived at TG, there was an emergency vehicle parking at the ER in front of where the triage desk is located, blocking my view into the area. Another unit was also dispatched, but I got there first. After parking my patrol car, the ambulance moved, which allowed me to clearly see the desk, and it was staffed with two nurses whom I knew (Becky and Janine). I made eye contact with them both. I couldn't really see what was going on, but they both waved at me to come in. Once I got out of the car, I could hear a woman's voice screaming, "I want it, I need it, take me now! Somebody fuck me, damn it!"

It wasn't until I got through the ER doors did I see the source of the screaming. Directly in front of the triage desk and on the floor was a 40ish female. She was fully clothed and lying on her back. She was rubbing her breast while jutting her hips up and down in what looked like she was actually involved with a sexual procedure – I am sure you get it. This was confirmed with the types of things she was saying, as mentioned before. She upped her comments when she saw me come through the door. She reached out toward me and said, "Fuck me, man. I really need to be fucked." I looked at Becky and Janine and asked what was going on. They told me her so-called boyfriend didn't want her around, and when she was refused, she started doing what I was observing.

I was a little reluctant to approach her and wanted to wait for the other officer to show up. Then I looked around the ER waiting room and saw horrified families, and they were looking at me to end this silliness. So I began to talk to her and tried to get her to stand up. I asked her several times to hold down her comments as I slowly approached her. I begged her to stand up so we could go outside. Nothing doing, she laid there with offers of sex. "Get on top of me; what are you waiting for?" she said.

This went on for what seemed like an eternity, and I was wondering where the other officer was. Nevertheless, I continued to approach and try to get this woman calmed down. My mistake was I got just a bit too close. Suddenly she grabbed me by my Sam Brown belt and pulled me to the floor on top of her. She wrapped her legs around my waist and started humping me like a rabbit on speed. All the while, yelling, "Fuck me, damn it, fuck me!"

At this point, I could hear female laughter, which I knew was coming from my now two former friends. I knew I had to do something to get out of this if I had any chance of regaining any dignity. I figured if I just stood up with this woman, I could pry her off of me and end this call once and for all. I brought my knees up to get leverage and had my hands on the floor to push myself to a standing position. I was about to stand up when my backup finally showed.

I just want you to take a moment to try to envision the scene he saw when the officer walked in and keep in mind this woman, who had not stopped the bionic hip action; she was going to town as well as screaming how she wanted to be taken. Okay, I am sure you have now figured it out, and you can stop laughing at me. I looked at the other officer and said, "Get your ass over here and give me a hand!" I was not a happy camper at this point.

He just looked and said, "Man, it doesn't look like you need any help."

"Not funny at all, now get over here," was my answer. I was able to get up, and between that, we were able to pry her off me; we placed her in handcuffs and in the back of my car.

After getting all the information I needed for my report, I drove this crazy woman to the station. As I drove, she was in the back and not happy with me any longer. I suppose an evening of canoodling was out of the question at this point.

She was nonstop cussing me out. I became used to that, but her voice was something out of a demonic horror movie; it sounded as if it was demon-possessed and had a need of an exorcism. It was never-ending; she spewed vulgarity and when I say, never stopped, I am not exaggerating. We got to the station, and I brought her into the report writing room, which was the normal procedure at the time. Because she was so disruptive, I had to strap her into a specially equipped chair that had a harness. I began writing down the face sheet information (name, address, phone, etc.) when suddenly she went completely quiet. At first, I thought something happened to her, but when I looked at her, she was alert and just being quiet. I figured she had just decided to accept what was going on and accept she was headed to jail. But I was wrong.

Her entire demeanor had now changed like she was being possessed by an entirely different person. Now she was becoming a sticky sweet lady begging for forgiveness. She apologized for her behavior, saying it was just not like her to do what she had done.

She didn't know what came over her and so on. She went on and on, asking to be allowed to go home, and was sure we could come to an agreement and arrange something so she could go home. Each time she made a request, I told her no, and that just sparked her to be even sweeter than before. This behavior became equally as annoying as her evil side. After some time, I just looked at her and told her, "You can try all day to be this so sweet person, but given what has happened tonight, no matter what you say, you are going to jail."

She paused, looked directly at me, and in her most demonic voice, she screamed, "Well then, fuck you," elongating the "fuck you" part. And then the tirade of vulgarity began all the way to the booking desk again. That was music to my ears because when I got her up to the jail, she failed the booking, and the 'brown wave' came out and drugged her to the nearest holding cell.

I think I preferred her evil side because that seemed to be her natural state.

The Olympus Hotel

At 815 Pacific Ave in Downtown Tacoma there sits the Olympus Hotel. One would think the name came from the mountain in Greece, where Zeus lived, but nope. There is nothing about the Olympus Hotel that would have anything to do with a god or even a demigod, quite the opposite. What it is named after is Mt Olympus in Washington State: the highest peak in the Olympic Mountains, located in the Olympic Range, which are on the Olympic Peninsula, just northwest of the capital, by the name of Olympia. That's a bit of a boring pattern, don't you think? It appears the founders of Washington State didn't have much of an imagination.

The first day I walked into the hotel, I was conducting a security check. I felt an immediate need to take some time and research this building. The entire place had the appearance of what was a very nice place on some bygone day. But in 1983, one would never know that unless you were willing to look past the deterioration the many years had taken on this once grand hotel. This place had become a dumping ground by Western State Hospital, our largest state mental institution located in an adjacent city. The people who resided there had no desire to be there, could barely care for themselves, and that transposed into lack of care for this jewel in the rough.

Downtown Tacoma had, over the years, become a seedbed of vice and sin. Drugs and prostitution were prolific, and the Olympus was smack dab in the middle of the worse place possible, given many some residents who had mental condition due to abusing drugs. The atmosphere for recovery was not the slightest bit conducive to their needs. It was exactly the opposite.

Brief History of the Olympus Hotel

You are probably asking, "Why are you giving me a history lesson when I bought this book for cop stories?" Because a lot of times, cops deal with what things were like in the past and how it all changed. It's just good to know what the potential is of anything or anyone. Bear with me, and you'll see what I am talking about.

The Olympus was built in 1909 and was a central part of many community activities. It had the state-of-the-art elevator service to each floor that included the retractable gates one sees in movies of older East Coast apartments or hotel buildings. The front desk of the Olympus still has the original key slot bank behind the hotel clerk's counter. If you are not familiar with this, in those days of the early 20th Century, when one rented a room, you checked in your room key when you left the hotel and then got it back when you returned. Kind of an unnecessary step at today's standards, of course, but it assured you would not lose your key. Obviously, there were no electronic card swipes in those days.

One of the other things that intrigued me was when you walked into the foyer area, and there was one of those large round sofas with the high round, peaked backrest. Something one would see in a fancy hotel of the late 1800s to early 1900s. The entire floor of the entry had black and white penny tiles, which appeared to have been there since day 1. Think about that for a second. This floor was put in way back in 1909 when each tile had to be placed individually. That took a great deal of painstaking labor, as well as skill.

If you do a bit of research on the internet, you'll find this building had a great history with Tacoma. It was the center of many charitable events or community activism. In the basement of this once grand hotel, it was the place to go for entertainment with a fine restaurant, which could make for a romantic evening. Going to the Olympus for dinner and dancing meant you had some more money than the average Joe. During the prohibition days, it was also a place to get a drink or two, so maybe it started its wayward journey way back then.

But like so many things that were good, it seemed it eventually had to come to an end. The Olympus decline began in the late 50s to the 60s. In 1974, the hotel lost its battle with nicer hotels and newer accommodations for the traveler. Downtown Tacoma was becoming entrenched in the seedy part of life, which no one wanted to be a part of, let alone come Downtown to spend the night or even have dinner. Why would someone want to feel afraid they may get mugged, offered sex from a walking disease factory, or get hit up for 'spare change' at every street corner? It wasn't on my radar of things to look forward to doing, so I am sure that it wasn't on the vast majority of good citizens' list as well. To sum this all up in a short sentence, Downtown Tacoma had fallen off the edge of the earth and was dragging the Olympus with it.

So let's fast forward to 1983. I was walking into the Olympus to do what? Not to rent a room, obviously. I was there to see how many druggies I could round up or at least do my best to cut into the drug trade. The once-great bar was the perfect place to find something illegal.

As I walked in, I could see a number of patrons who were seated in booths. When they saw me come in, a row of obvious junkies began fidgeting as I approached. I knew what they were doing, but in no way could I get to them fast enough, so I just ordered them out of the booth. Without any complaint, they got up. In those days, you could do that—order them to get up and move, and they complied. You know why? Because I would have grabbed them by the neck and threw them out of the booth. Today, you'd have to get a warrant signed by three judges (exaggerating), a blood test, and a willingness to sacrifice your firstborn child (heavy exaggeration here).

The seat cushion was removable, so out it came. *Oh, look at what I just found!* Five balloons of heroin and six bindles of cocaine (inject sarcasm here if you wish). Oh my! The shock and horror on their faces to even think they were near drugs! Yeah, right. I couldn't pin this on anyone, but at least I could cut into someone's profits. I collected the narcotics and felt satisfied that at least these drugs were off the market. This was how it went with the Olympus Hotel, day in a day out. Occasionally, you'd catch someone red-handed, but it was not the norm.

The hotel closed in 1974 and then reopened in 1978 as a small apartment building, but it continued to head into the sewer. What made it even worse was it seemed nobody cared until around 2010, when the building went through an extensive renovation in an attempt to bring it back to the original state of 1909. It didn't quite make it there, but it did make a great deal better. Compared to what it was like, it's a thousand times better today. It is drug-free and no longer a place for criminal activity. The apartments were all redone and are for low-income folks.

See, that wasn't so bad, was it? With that little bit of background, the rest of this section will just be a few of the stories that I dealt with in Olympus. I hope you enjoy these tales.

I Blame KISS

As I've stated in previous tales, crazy people can be fun. At the same time, as one could imagine, they can be quite dangerous as well, not just to police officers or the general public but to each other. They sometimes see things or hear things that are not there, or at least the rest of us don't hear or see. Why don't we? Because it's not there.

Once again, we are back at the Olympus Hotel in Tacoma. This is the early 90s, and bands, such as KISS, are very popular. I am sure you are wondering why I mentioned them, but that will come into play soon.

As many calls go, this one began long before dispatch got the call. As a matter of fact, by the time dispatch got the 911 call, it was way too late, and the damage was done. At that time, we were reactionary and not preventive.

It started on the fifth floor with one of the residents running back and forth in the hallway, pounding on doors, yelling, "They are coming, they are coming!" in an ever so frantic manner. I don't know if this guy was a reincarnation of Paul Revere, but in this case, I am sure he didn't just see two lanterns in a church steeple, and I can assure you he did not have a horse. I honestly never knew this guy's name, so I'll just refer to him as 'Paul.' I think that's appropriate, don't you?

As Paul was running rampantly up and down the hall, screaming the alarm of something or someone coming, it began to take a toll on all of the occupants on the fifth floor but even more so with the occupant of room 504, who I will refer to as Gene because I can't call a guy Joan. You'll understand that joke in a bit, so don't jump forward to find out what I meant by that because it's more fun to wait, okay? Good. Also, don't get this Gene mixed up with my partner Gene. Many times I felt my partner was equally as insane as this guy, but that may be another story in a different book.

Just so you understand, Paul didn't just make one pass through the hall as his namesake patriot did in his famous ride. Oh no, this was a constant running up and down the hall with an occasional run to the adjacent floors, stopping at each door. He would pound on the doors with both fists, scream his warning and move to the next room and do the same. Witnesses said when they opened the door, he had panic in his eyes, and they were quite frightened of him and his message. Remember, these were people having some mild to serious mental problems, so telling them "they are coming" could mean many different things to these people. I mean, this could mean space aliens, people with straight jackets…just about anything. Who knows what goes through the mind of the insane until they verbalize it. Just look at Paul. What was he envisioning which sparked him to make his dire warnings?

Also, so you have a better picture of what the residents were experiencing, the walls and floors at the Olympus were never insulated for sound deadening, so sound traveled without restriction through this building. The building was built in 1909, and due to the construction of those days, which was never updated to this point, the building acted as a giant megaphone, and the sound reverberated throughout the building.

Hopefully, that gives you the picture of what these folks were dealing with, along with their own private demons. Paul was adding to their living hell as he screamed his dire message. Most of them huddled into one corner or another of their rooms in some sort of fetal position, hands over their ears hoping this devil would just go away.

Sometime after the fourth or fifth time, Paul beat on Gene's door. Gene answered and told him to shut up and stop. I know Gene was probably a bit forceful in his tone, but as it went, it didn't stop Paul. Paul just continued his 'midnight ride,' even though this was happening around three in the afternoon.

As Paul continued, Gene was now experiencing some serious anxiety and tried to cover his ears in hopes of, at least, dulling the warnings Paul felt he needed to alert his neighbors about. Gene cried because he felt helpless in getting Paul to cease his verbal onslaught. "Will he never stop?" he asked himself. "Why is he doing this?"

Suddenly Gene heard a rustle outside his fifth-floor window, which opened on its own, and as Gene watched the portal slide upward, he wondered, *what is happening?* And then there they were: Gene Simmons from KISS and Joan Baez (if you are too young to know who she is, she was a folk singer from the 60s and 70s). Both of them were crawling through the window into his room. After getting inside, the two entertainers began to chant, "Kill him, kill him, kill him," and so on. This confused our misguided soul Gene.

Gene looked at his window guests and said, "But I can't. I don't have a gun."

The chanting stopped, and the lead singer from KISS pointed to a corner in Gene's room and said, "You have a baseball bat."

Joan then said, "Beat him on the head, like Maxwell's Hammer (Beatles; Abby Road 1969) until he can't torment you any longer."

They are right, Gene thought. He could smash Paul's head in until Paul stopped — that would work. Gene got up, walked over to the aluminum baseball bat, picked it up, and examined it closely. He turned around to speak to his guests, but they must have slipped back out the window. He wondered if he should really do this, but then he still heard them chanting again, "Kill him, kill him, kill him!" Gene had to do this; I mean, the lead singer of KISS and peace activist Joan Baez told him to kill Paul. This was a done deal, and he had to obey.

He walked over to the window, looked down to the street and up to the roof, but Simmons and Baez were gone. "I didn't know they could fly," he said later when I interviewed him.

My answer to him was, "Neither did I." Gene continued to examine the bat; he swung it around like he was warming up in an on-deck circle.

Then it happened again. The one thing that pushed him over the edge, the nail in the coffin, one might say. Paul was once again pounding on the door, screaming. Paul's screams were even louder now. "My God, will you shut up; will you fucking shut up!" Gene screamed through the door at Paul but to no avail. Paul seemed to stay at Gene's door for a very long time, pounding and screaming, pounding and screaming. Gene looked at the bat once more as the entertainer's commands repeated in his head. Gene ran to the door, swung it open, and hit Paul in the chest with the blunt end of the bat. Paul stumbled backward, losing his balance. There in the hall, Gene had the ability to take the first swing in a chopping motion, landing dead center on the top of Paul's head. Paul immediately fell to the floor while blood spurted out in several directions. Though Paul was now unconscious, he began to convulse on the floor, so Gene continued to take strike after strike at Paul's head, never missing and landing squarely on target. Eventually, Paul stopped convulsing; he was dead.

Once Gene knew Paul was dead, he took the bat, walked down the several flights of stairs to the reception area while covered in blood, and politely asked the clerk to call the police.

When I got the call, I was told it was a possible homicide and was told it was via baseball bat. Further, I was told the suspect was in the foyer area waiting to be arrested. Other units were also en route, but luck would have it, I was the first to arrive on the scene.

The front doors of the Olympus have large glass inserts, so it is easy to see the entire foyer and reception area before walking in. I parked my car about two blocks away and ran up to the building on the sidewalk, staying close to the building's edge so as not to be detected. I immediately drew my weapon as soon as I exited my car. I used the side of the building for concealment and cover if needed as I walked up to the front doors. I looked quickly through the glass portion of the doors to see what I could see. What I saw was Gene seated on a bench that was facing the front door. The baseball bat was erect with barrel side down, and Gene had both hands at the top crossed over the end of the grip. I could also see the bat was covered with blood.

I alerted other units, who were headed my way, of my observations and waited for another officer to arrive before entering the hotel. Once another unit got there, we entered, pointing our guns at Gene and told him to drop the bat and then had him lay on the floor. He cooperated, and the handcuffing procedure went easy. One of the things that truly bothered me was there was blood all over Gene, and it was now being transferred on to me. I advised Gene of his rights, and he said he understood and began telling me the entire story. He took us to where the body was. Other officers secured the crime scene as I waited for homicide detectives to arrive.

Ident (forensics) showed up to process the scene and collected evidence, which included the bat. With the help of the homicide detectives, we determined Gene had struck Paul somewhere around 20 times. To say he was a bit angry would be an understatement. Gene's hits made Paul's head look strange. I am sure one could imagine the disfigurement, so I don't need to go into the gory details.

Gene was tried but not for the crime. Instead, he was tried due to his mental instability history. He seemed aware of his disability and was tired of getting his freedom and then have to go right back to Western State Hospital. He went back, from the last I heard. We kind of all figured that was a foregone conclusion. Have no idea whatever happened to him, given he was never criminally tried for the homicide.

Here's Your Wake Up Call

One of my most rewarding calls was the one at the Olympus Hotel. It probably had the potential to be one of the most dangerous but truly some fun.

At one of our turnouts (roll call) on a graveyard shift, we got the routine briefings such as this guy wanted and so on. This one included a BOLO (Be On the Look Out) on some guy from central Oregon. He was involuntarily committed to an institution down there and had escaped. In the process of the escape, he stabbed a nurse in the eye. That got my attention because of the horrific way he escaped. It was also reported he was headed north.

I was thinking, *okay, he'll go to Seattle; all these assholes* do. So I put it in the back of my mind and headed out to my district and didn't give it much thought, except I was hoping he might stop in Tacoma. I might just get lucky, I suppose.

My wish came true. At around midnight, I was called to the station to meet with the sergeant. Just so you know, when you get that kind of call, it's either you are in trouble, or you may be getting an atta-boy. I knew it was not the latter, so what did I do to piss someone off this time?

When I got to the station and met with the sergeant, I noticed there were two other officers there as well. *Oh good*, I thought, *I'm not the only one in trouble.*

The sergeant started out by asking us all if we remembered the info at a turnout about the escapee from Oregon. Of course, we all did. He went on to tell us there was intel that this asshole was at the Olympus Hotel in a room on the second floor (sorry, but this was so many years ago I can't remember the actual room number). The sergeant went on to say we were going to head there and scoop this guy up. Man, this was awesome, and I was ready to take this guy down. I had only been on the department and a cop for less than a year. I was pumped!

We got into our cars and headed downtown and parked in a nearby parking garage so as not to be detected, and walked to the hotel. The sergeant told me to grab the shotgun out of my car and wanted me to take the lead into the room. This was getting better by the moment.

Once we got inside the hotel, the clerk gave the sergeant the key to the room. Because we didn't have to talk the clerk into giving us the key, it was obvious the clerk was the one who was the source of the intel.

We walked up to the second floor, and as we approached the room our suspect was in, we could all hear a sound of a chainsaw buzzing. It was so loud we could find the room without even knowing the number — this was the loudest snorer I had ever heard. This turned out to be a good thing. His snoring masked any noise we might have been making in the hall.

The sergeant slipped the key into the door and slowly turned the lock open. He eased the door open, and the snoring continued but got louder as he pushed the door to the fully open position. We could see the entire room and our suspect facing the door asleep on the bed across the room. Our weapons were trained on him at every moment while the door was open and he was in sight. His hands were visible, and we didn't see weapons in the room. Though it was dark outside, we had a fair amount of city light coming through the window. I pointed the shotgun directly at the sleeping monster and walked up to him at a slow pace, never taking my eyes off him. This guy was sound asleep; he had no clue we were there. The sergeant was about to turn on the lights in the room, but I put my hand up to tell him to wait. As I continued to point my shotgun at him, I stepped onto the bed and straddled Mr. Sleepy Head. I got the shotgun within an inch of his head and then motioned the sergeant to turn on the lights. As soon as he did that, I shoved the barrel on the shotgun into the suspect's left ear and yelled, "Here's your wake-up call, asshole!" His eyes opened up to see three guns pointed at him, and a side glance, he was looking down the barrel of a 12 gauge shotgun. He didn't say anything, but I just had to add, "Welcome to Tacoma, butthead!" He slowly put his hands out toward the side of the bed. I backed off so one of the other officers could come in and place him into handcuffs. He knew he had been cornered, so he gave no resistance.

After cuffing, we did get the routine lip service about he didn't do anything and how he could kick our butts and so on.

We called the paddy wagon for transport, and I have to admit I was quite surprised there was a The News Tribune reporter and a photographer waiting for us to exit. I suspect the hotel clerk gave them a call.

So off our suspect went to Oregon, but I never found out what happened to him or the nurse he stabbed, but that's kind of routine in law enforcement. I was just happy to be a part of taking this guy down and getting him back into custody.

There's Going to be a Fight

The calls that can get a bit edgy are domestic violence calls. In my career, three Tacoma police officers were killed going at domestics: Jim, Bill, and Craig; I personally knew each one. Craig and I actually worked a few times together, gone but not forgotten. Those three officers were always in the back of my mind when I responded to DVs. Many times these calls don't result in violence to that degree but rarely does the aggressor in these calls surrender without much of a problem. This call was a bit more of a verbal tough guy attitude but did not have the means to back up his 'aggression.' You'll see what I mean as you read the story.

My partner and I got to the Olympus, and we contacted the clerk, who was the one who called. The clerk told us the incident was in room 207, and the female had come down to the front desk to call us to respond. He also told us the female was visibly upset and appeared to have a black eye. When I asked where she was, he stated she went back to the room.

Her going back to the room was no surprise, stupid maybe but not a shock at all. So many times, I saw women do exactly that or something similar, and I even had a wife fight with me because I was arresting her husband, who had beat her up, leaving her with a busted lip and a black eye. The problem on that particular call was the husband went to jail for the simple misdemeanor assault, but she ended up going on the felony of assaulting a police officer. More stupidity than one should have to handle.

So up the stairs to 207, we went. After knocking on the door, a female answered. The first thing out of her mouth was that she didn't need our help. However, her left eye was swollen, and it was obvious she was crying. We told her we could not leave until we knew this was being resolved. She stated it was resolved, and we could go away. I explained to her it didn't work that way. She didn't like what I said, but she came to the realization she was not going to win this discussion with me.

After entering, there was nothing about the apartment that showed signs of struggle, but there was still her swollen eye. We suspected she might have cleaned up the apartment prior to our arrival. I asked how she got the black eye, and she admitted: "My boyfriend hit me." As soon as she said that, she realized that statement alone was going to get him in trouble; thus, she begged not to arrest her boyfriend. I knew we were going to take him into custody, but I told her we just needed to talk to him. She directed us to the bedroom and pointed toward a door. When we walked into the bedroom, it was quite small, barely able to fit the bed and dresser that were in it. On the bed was a very skinny male was lying on his stomach on what appeared to be a full-size bed. The dresser that was crammed in the corner near the head of the bed had a mirror on it.

He appeared to be asleep, so I tapped him on foot to wake him. He jumped up in a start. It appeared he was quite frightened by our presence, and he had good reason to be. This guy could not have stood more than 5'4" and weighed in at no more than 110 pounds, soaking wet. His body was not toned in the slightest, and he was so skinny he looked just like he had stepped out of Auschwitz. His fists were doubled up, and he was shaking.

This might sound a little bit rude, but I was surprised his girlfriend didn't kick his ass given she was taller, and she easily outweighed him by more than double. She was a large woman.

I told him to calm down. I was afraid he was going to pass out or experience a stroke right there. He was shaking so badly, and his face was turning a very pale color. I told him up front that he was going to jail today and that he was under arrest. That seemed to make him shake even more, but his answer was not to surrender as I thought he might do, but what came out of his mouth was not something I expected. "Come near me, and there's going to be a fight." I thought he might be right, but it wasn't going to last very long.

I also was thinking, *aw, come on, really, dude!* I think I have mentioned this before, but in those days, I was doing a great deal of upper body strength workouts, so, not to sound self-centered, but I was a bit of an imposing figure. Plus, there was no way I wanted to hit this guy because I was sure it would have only taken one hit, and he'd be dead or get a massive concussion.

I started to talk to him softly, telling him this was stupid and just relax. I told him the law mandated we make an arrest, and he was the one elected today. As I talked to him, I walked up to him very slowly. Each time I took a step, he would say something to the effect, "if you get any closer, I'm going to kick your ass," with his voice cracking and body shaking; no, maybe it was quivering as he spoke.

When I was within a foot of him, I said to him, "Do me a favor, dude. Turn around and look in the mirror on the dresser. Once you do that, turn back and look at me and be honest with yourself when I ask you if you still want to fight."

I was surprised because he actually looked in the mirror. I had an easy shot at him right then, but, honestly, I thought he was going to give up. But no, he remained verbally defiant, and as he was about to say, again, "There is going to be a fight," I interrupted him. I reached out with my right hand, cupped the left side of his face, and shoved him to the bed he had been sleeping on. As he saw my hand come up toward his face, he screamed, "oh, my God!" like the most frightened little girl I had ever heard. I honestly think he thought I was going to kill him. Nevertheless, he fell softly to the mattress. As I cuffed him, which was little to zero resistance, my partner was laughing hysterically. Hearing laugh our suspect began to cry and said, through his tears, "Quit fucking laughing at me, you prick!" Sorry, but that was funny, Mr. Tough Guy.

Though this turned out a little bit on the funny side, there was one thing that I was a bit bugged about on this call. This little twerp had successfully intimidated a girl who could have easily beaten the pulp out of him. My guess was he preyed on someone who was a bit weak-minded and then took as much advantage of her as he could. That was evident to me, given he didn't put up anything other than his feeble verbal resistance; basically, he was actually a coward to anyone who stood up to him. There was a part of me where I felt I should have punched him in the face. I suppose it's best I did not.

Oh, by the way, what happened after I put him in handcuffs? This is so typical. However, this guy was all mouth and went into handcuffs without a fight to speak of, despite his threat over and over. Once he was in cuffs, though, he started up again with, "Take these cuffs off, and I'll kick your ass."

I told him, "You had your shot, and you didn't take it," but after, he continued, again and again, demanding I remove the cuffs so he could kick my ass. I decided to accept his challenge, so I took my cuff key out of my pocket and walked behind him to unlock the cuffs.

Once again, his voice began to crack as he asked me what I was doing. When I told him I was going to give him another shot at me, he said, "You not suppose to do that. Isn't that against the law?"

"I'm confused," I told him. "Do you want to kick my ass or not?" He declined and kept his hands behind him. "That's what I thought," I told him.

At the jail, he must have learned his lesson because he was not challenging me or anyone else at the booking desk. Good boy.

You Really Don't Want to Do This

This incident and the saving of the life go solely to my partner. We were sent to the Olympus Hotel for a guy sitting on the ledge over the sidewalk. We came in the back door of the hotel so the jumper would not see us come into the building.

The Olympus Hotel is seven stories high, so it's not the typical building a jumper would pick. I suppose all the taller buildings have better security, so this guy couldn't get to the roof of one of those. It's not like one can't die from a jump this high, but if they don't, I assure you they will wish they did. The chance of multiple compound fractures is a guarantee — not to mention the internal injuries, head trauma, and so on. It would be a very ugly consequence and thus not achieving the end result one desires.

My partner and I ran up the stairs to the door leading to the roof. As we opened the door, we could see the man on the other side of the building. He was facing away from us. He didn't turn around at first, and that was most likely due to the traffic noise below. My first impression, as I looked at the guy, was him trying to build up his nerve to jump. I know I'm no psychiatrist, but I had found through my experience with suicidal people if he was actually ready to end it all, he would have done it way before we got there. Most of these people try to reach out and hope someone will have a viable alternative for them. That is not to say they aren't capable of just doing it, but many are open to listening and circumventing this horrible idea. We know this is not a decision one makes without a fair amount of consideration. Taking your own life, for most of us, is something that takes a great deal of contemplation.

Given he was still mulling this over, wherein he had not yet committed the act, that was a good sign for talking him down. So now we needed to begin the dialog without saying the wrong thing that gave him that little spark of courage to take the leap. Those who just want to end their lives won't sit on the edge of a building in broad daylight, waiting for cops to come and talk them down. No, they would just go out there and do it. They won't make calls, and they won't tell others. They would just do it and tell no one.

My partner did not want to just run-up to the guy where he might have heard us running and, out of fear, went ahead and jumped. Cautious movements were the best tactics. My partner had a golden tongue, so he began walking toward the man, and when he got within about 30 feet or so, he called to him, loud enough for the guy to hear him but not so loud to frighten him or give him the idea that we might be angry at him.

The man turned quickly and was surprised to see us standing there. He responded exactly the way we expected, yelling in a panicky voice that if we got closer, he would jump. That statement alone told me this guy had no intention of jumping; he just needed some encouragement to talk him out of it.

My partner was calm, and even though this guy kept saying he was going to jump, my partner kept the conversation low-key, letting him know we were there to help as well as letting the guy feel he was under the control of the dialog.

The guy was shaking as he talked, and he said he was confused and didn't know why he was in Tacoma. My partner asked, calmly and softly, to get away from the wall so we could talk more about what sent him to this point. The guy went through a list of reasons why he could not come off the wall; he knew he was going to jail now, and he would look stupid if he didn't go through with his suicide and so on.

My partner found two large plastic buckets that he moved to within 15 or so feet of the man and turned them upside down. My partner sat on one and invited the man to join him so they could just talk, anything he wanted to talk about. In about ten minutes and after very subtle encouragement, the man swung his legs away from the side of the building and onto the roof. This was an amazing move, and we were very sure this guy was coming off the wall soon. He sat there for about 2–3 minutes, and then very cautiously, as he still did not fully trust my partner or me, he stepped onto the roof and slowly walked toward my partner. This was a major wow moment.

My partner never moved; he just sat there smiling at the man. When the man got to the empty bucket seat, he picked it up and moved it about six inches away from my partner. He sat down and began to cry. My partner reached out and touched the man's shoulder, and surprisingly the man did not flinch. He just kept crying as he spoke. I watched as they spoke to each other. I wasn't going to interrupt or interfere with what was a successful day so far, and it looked like my partner was about to save a life. My partner spoke softly with this disturbed man for about 20 minutes before he agreed to go with us.

The man was most concerned that he would be going to jail. My partner assured him that was not what we had planned for him but instead to get him the help he wanted, desired, and quite frankly, needed.

At that point, the man decided we were trustworthy and told us he willing to go with us voluntarily. Even though we told him he wasn't going to jail, he stood up and actually turned around to be put in handcuffs. I let him know we keep our promises, and only those going to jail get put in handcuffs. No jail for him, so no handcuffs. He began to cry once again.

When we got in the elevator, and as we headed to the ground floor, he thanked us for how nice we were. We told him he deserved it, and my partner thanked him for being cooperative with us.

We transported him to Puget Sound Hospital for evaluation so he could get the help he needed. My partner let him know we wanted him to get better and wanted him to be as nice to the folks at Puget Sound as he was with us. He seemed happier now and assured my partner he would follow the hospital's instructions.

It felt really good about what we did, especially what my partner had done. My partner did nothing less than a phenomenal job with this guy and truly saved our potential jumper's life. I wrote a long report, outlining everything, in detail, what my partner had done and going so far as to say in the report my partner was the only one who saved this guy's life. I didn't, the hotel manager surely did not, and of course, the jumper, himself, did not. My partner was the sole person who got this guy off the wall and out of danger. He was the one who convinced the jumper to surrender and come with us.

The intent of the report was to recommend my partner for a Lifesaving Medal due to his actions. He deserved it. I gave it to my sergeant, and when I didn't hear anything after a week, I contacted the sergeant and asked the status of my partner's medal. My sergeant said he didn't follow up with the request because if he recommended my partner, he'd have to write up everyone when they do something good. I looked at him and said exactly what I was thinking, "You lazy fuck," and walked away.

I figured if this sergeant was too lazy to forward my report to the powers that control this sort of thing, he was probably too lazy to write me up for insubordination as well. It turns out I was right.

Despite the fact that my partner did not get the recognition he deserved, he told me he was okay, given he did something very good that day. He was right… but it still pissed me off!

This was the type of crap that used to get me so angry. Supervisors who just want to sit in the office and drink coffee all day and BS with the other sergeants until it's time to go home. I'm not saying all sergeants are that way, but I have met many who were.

Christmas

Christmas Eve 1987

Christmas is supposed to be the time of year when all of us are supposed to be nicer and kinder to each other. Sadly law enforcement will give you another perspective on holiday—it kind of falls into the same group as full moons, Friday the 13th and the worse. I have found, like many other cops, Christmas seems to be a time when we turn greedy and have very little respect for each other. To get a great overall view, one only has to watch one of the many videos of people crawling over each other or punching each other out over a TV or video game at some store holding a sale. It seems so stupid, but yet each year, it repeats itself over and over.

An example of that is when I used to work off duty for a major retail department store in Tacoma. On December 24th in 1987, I was standing in front of the store. As you can imagine, on a day like December 24th, parking was at a premium as people were rushing everywhere to get that last-minute gift. Despite the parking conditions and the limited numbers, there were usually plenty of parking spots out farther from the store, and many people took advantage of those and just walked the extra distance. Those folks just felt like I did; it was easier to just get a parking spot and walk than trying to do the *Tour de Parking Lot* forty times to get that spot which maybe 10 feet closer.

This tale revolved around two ladies who did the 'tour,' and I lost count of how many times they drove past me, but it was at least ten times. That was truly a bare minimum. Their efforts finally paid off, but not the way they had hoped or expected.

A spot about four stalls away from the front door began to come open. As both of the women were on the quest for the perfect parking spot, within seconds of the backing lights coming on, the car left the two women homed in like they had a radar affixed to their cars, pulling them toward the potential open spot. As soon as the car cleared the stall, both women began heading to the opening. I don't know for sure, but their moves seemed to be choreographed as it appeared they both realized at the same moment the stall was coming open. Without delay and what appeared to be, they were not to be aced out of that spot. Each headed straight for the open slot, increasing speed as they went without delay. Each saw the other going for that small but very valuable piece of real estate, so they decided to use the horsepower their respective engines could muster and make a bee-line for the parking stall.

Neither had the advantage over the other, and that was evident when they crashed directly in front of the open space. Immediately the women exited their vehicles not to assess damage or to see how each other were, not on your life. They began screaming at each other and pointed fingers at each other, directly guilt to the other. As they exchanged insults, they went to a new level of low that is usually reserved for men as they dug into the deepest part of the vulgarity bag, calling each other not only the 'B' word but also the next letter of the alphabet as well. That word is a huge taboo, so I was quite surprised to hear these 'ladies' utter it.

I walked over to these women to try to calm things down. Both were demanding I arrest the other for recklessness! Negligence! Attempted murder! Pick something, anything because "it was her fault," damn it! I told them they were both equally at fault, and I was just going to make sure they exchange information for the collision. After filling out an exchange of information form, I told the two they had to leave, and their shopping at this store today ended before it even began. My decision was based on the hostilities they were displaying. I wasn't going to allow them to go into the store and then have to break up some knockdown, drag-out fight. Their reaction to my decision was as if I just shot the Pope. It was the sin of all sins.

The claws came out, and neither were happy with me at all. How dare I even make a slight suggestion on this Christmas Eve of last-minute shopping? "Who do you think you are, officer?" Seeing how they were a bit reluctant to comply and refusing to leave, I let them know they could leave, go to a different store or have their families spend Christmas with them at the Pierce County Jail; the choice was theirs. Both decided they'd rather be home for Christmas instead of the gray bar hotel. I knew there had to be a brain in there somewhere. So they left without any further argument.

Where they went, I had no idea and didn't care. I was just glad to get rid of them.

Christmas 1988

Christmas is normally quiet despite some attitudes that take over a family gathering. With that in mind, my partner and I were working a swing shift (2:00 p.m. to 10:00 p.m.) on December 25, 1988. We decided that every traffic stop was going to be a warning, small crimes that we could just cite and release. Only a few crimes our hands would be tied, and we had to book that person. It was going to be the ultimate Christmas present to those we contacted. That would make it a good Christmas for us as well as any contacts we might make.

The entire shift went smoothly. We had a few contacts, and everyone we contacted was very grateful for getting a warning. My partner and I felt good about what we were doing, and at about 9:30 p.m., we were making that 'slow roll' to the station. About 20 blocks from the station, we got behind a car that an entire family was in: a male driver, a female front passenger, and two kids in the back seat. Additionally, the car was weaving down the street, leading us both to reasonably feel the driver was drunk.

I'm not much on giving any drunk a break, but there was no accident, and it was Christmas, so we'd just gave these folks a ride home. Easy enough.

I turned on the overhead emergency lights, and the driver pulled left in a sharp motion causing him to strike the curb. I was a passenger officer, so I walked up on the passenger side as my partner went up on the driver's side. When we used that tactic, 99% of the time, the driver would focus on the officer walking up to him and not even know there's an officer on the passenger side. It would allow me, in this case, to view his right hand, and given most people are right-handed, I would be able to see if the driver had ill intent and any gun they might have ready to shoot the driver's side approaching officer. In this case, this driver had nothing. What I did see were two very frightened children in the back seat, one boy and one girl who looked like they were anywhere from 8–10 years old. In the front seat was a woman who had her face in her right hand, which I assume was because she was embarrassed over being pulled over.

I could hear my partner telling the driver that it was his lucky day. I could also tell that maybe the driver was arguing a bit as I heard my partner say, "No man, it's Christmas."

When my partner motioned to come over to the driver's side, I knew this might be going downhill a bit but also thought, *of course, this guy will take our offer to end this without an arrest.* When I got over to the driver's window, I couldn't believe this guy was 1) refusing to exit the car and 2) refusing to accept a ride home. My inner thoughts were, *are you that drunk or that stupid?* I also noticed that the female, who turned out to be his wife, wasn't saying anything. She was just sitting in the front passenger seat, face in hand, and nothing more. I can tell you if that were me, my wife would have said something to the effect of "Shut the f*** up and listen to the officer!" That would have been followed by a punch in the arm as well.

Even after several pleas to just accept our ride, it became obvious this brain surgeon had done surgery on himself sometime in the past, and I was sure it included alcohol. Not only was he refusing to get through this without being arrested, he decided to try and restart his car. That was a big mistake, and there was no way I was going to allow this drunk to get back on the street, especially with the two kids in the back seat.

Assuming he was going to try and drive off, I reached in through the window, grabbed him by the head, and pulled him out of the car. He wasn't seat belted, so he came out quite easily. Of course, this action, seeing their daddy being ejected through the window, caused the kids to begin to cry in fear. His wife, on the other hand, just sat there calmly. Something told me she had been through this scenario too many times before.

After extricating our uncooperative drunken idiot, we placed him on the ground, cuffed him, read him his rights, and put him in the patrol car. I walked back to the car as our own Christmas Grinch was screaming obscenities from the back seat of the patrol car. I looked through the driver's door at the female passenger and said, "I need to talk to you." For the first time, she lifted her head out of her hand and turned her face toward me. She wasn't crying but did have a concerned look. "I have to make sure you are okay to drive. Have you been drinking tonight?"

"No," she said.

"Do you have a driver's license?"

To that, she stated, "Yes." She picked up her purse off the floor and retrieved her license from her wallet. I looked at it, and it was current. After having her do a couple of sobriety field tests, I told her she could drive the car home but wondered if she was okay to drive as she might be too upset. She said she was just fine. As I walked back to the patrol car, the female drove off.

When I got in the car, our arrestee was screaming, and all I could think of was how we tried so hard not to arrest anyone, but now we were headed into overtime on Christmas. Man, that just sucked. With that in mind, I nearly came unglued when our drunkard said, "I can't believe you two are arresting me on fucking Christmas, man!" That comment made me want to climb into the back seat and punch this asshat in the face. I didn't; I just wanted to.

This arrest took us into four hours of overtime, so I didn't get home until around 2:30 a.m. Right, Merry Christmas, everyone.

Thanksgiving

Holidays can be quite stressful. So much to do, so little time to do it. The cost of everything seems to always be going up in an uncontrolled manner. Stress needs relief, whether it be sleep, alcohol, drugs, sometimes violence, or in a few cases, sex. This case is the latter on the list. Yep, sex.

Thanksgiving morning, about 1:00 a.m., 1984, I and another officer were dispatched to a possible domestic in a south end home. Before we get to the turkey and gravy of this story, so to speak — pun intended — I have to outline the home itself we had responded to. This house had a barbershop attached to it at the kitchen/dining room, so basically, the barbershop access for the barber was via the kitchen, but the customers' access was from the street side. Just so you get the layout, as it has a great deal to do with this story. Now, back to this Thanksgiving tale.

I and the other officer arrived at about the same time. The front door of the house was located down a short walkway to a three-step pedestal concrete porch with handrails on both sides. You know the kind, narrow 3'x3' square, in the East they call these porches, stoops, or something like that.

As we walked up to the front door, we were met by a woman who was wearing a very flimsy robe which she was holding together with her right hand, and she wasn't doing such a good job. She was clasping it together in front of her breast, and that seemed to be the only area that was staying covered. Additionally, she appeared to be quite intoxicated given her slurring speech. Her blood alcohol content, which I could only estimate was probably over .2, may have explained her lack of modesty to some extent.

She had an angry tone when she said, "Come in here and look." She spun around in a very deliberate manner and immediately lost her balance. Her spin was fairly good, and at first, I was quite impressed, but her stop (landing) was where it went awry. She began to fall over the railing to the right. Her body went completely upside down on the outer edge of the rail, but she was able to avoid hitting the ground by grabbing onto one of the railing pickets. Nevertheless, as she inverted herself, her flimsy robe flew up, exposing much more than either Officer or I wanted to see. My partner was the trooper, though, as he grabbed her before her head hit the ground or the side of the stoop. She righted herself and never missed a beat as she walked into the house. I do think I saw a little twinkle in her eye as she mustered up a smile for my partner. Awe ain't that sweet, ya little devil.

Once inside, she stood in the hall/foyer and pointed to the kitchen, saying, in her very angry tone, "Look what he did." We walked into the kitchen, and I saw an open oven, a large baking pan filled with what appeared to be turkey drippings. On the floor was a grease stripe from the oven to a door, which turned out to be the entrance to the barbershop. Against the door was somewhere around a 25-pound turkey thrown with stuffing splattered all over the bottom of the door.

Through an interview with our immodest female reporter and wading through this lady's drunken haze, we found out about the poor turkey's demise, whose now resting place actually started about two hours prior to the call. In this tale, I will refer to the couple as Romeo and Juliet just because...I don't know just seemed appropriate for me.

Juliet had gone to bed but set the alarm so she could get up to baste the turkey she had placed in the oven. Not knowing much about baking a turkey overnight, I do remember my mother doing that when I was a kid; of course, she never had to deal with what Juliet dealt with, or at least I don't think so. I just knew that my mom's turkeys at Thanksgiving and Christmas were the best, just plain yummy.

Juliet got up around midnight, put on her flimsy nightgown, and headed to the kitchen. Romeo was still up and in the kitchen as well. He had made a sandwich and was drinking a beer. Juliet grabbed a large kitchen fork and her basting tube and walked over to the oven, which was directly in front of the kitchen table, where Romeo was seated.

When Juliet bent over to open the oven, it was just a bit too much for old Romeo to handle. She was thinking, baste the turkey and back to bed, Romeo had other thoughts, but he was not thinking too clearly given this woman was now armed with a large kitchen fork and hot basting tube.

Note: Both had been drinking earlier, and the alcohol may have worn off a bit in Juliet, but Romeo was still keeping his buzz on. Seeing his bride bent over at the waist, the inner caveman began to stir, somewhat uncontrollably. He put his beer down, got up, and got behind Juliet as she was tending to the turkey. Romeo pulled down his pants and began his attempt at an amorous entry.

At first, Juliet was unsure of what he was trying to do until she looked between her legs and saw his pants on the floor; she was none too happy at Romeo's timing. "Knock it off," she said. But 'no' was not part of Romeo's vocabulary right now; he was determined. Juliet moved to one side and then to the other in an attempt to avoid Romeo's personal probing vessel. Continually saying "no" or "stop it." I am sure it's a bit difficult to baste and have sex at the same time, not to mention, for God's sake, she was in front of a hot oven. Juliet was getting very frustrated with her horny husband, and after about five minutes of his romantic onslaught, she was ready to do what was necessary to stop the missile from landing. She removed the kitchen fork from the turkey, reached around her, and tried to stab Romeo in the buttocks while making a gallant effort to continue to baste. Every attempt was sidestepped by Romeo, so she was not at all successful. Even though Juliet was not quite as intoxicated as Romeo, there was still some residual effect, making her target acquisition a bit poor, thus having a detrimental effect on the 'fork-you' attack. Why she just didn't stand up and poke the little weenie is beyond me.

Given nothing was working on getting this guy to stop, Juliet's frustration reached an all-time high. Instead of trying to stab Romeo any longer, Juliet stabbed the turkey. She placed both hands on the fork handle thrusting the fork deep into the breast of the bird, and with every bit of strength, lifted the turkey out of the pan. Romeo came to his senses and realized what was coming. Horny or not, he didn't want anything to do with getting hit in the face by a large hot bird, supported by a very angry woman. Retreat at this point was the better part of valor. Romeo decided to escape and began his pants down, hobbled 'run' to the barbershop. With a determined and intense look of pure rage and insanity on Juliet's face, she came around, aiming for Romeo, but the bird was too heavy. At mid-spin, the bird and slipped off the fork. What she had going for her was tenacity, and even though the Thanksgiving entrée fell to the floor, the greasy dinner had enough momentum to follow Romeo's path to the barbershop door, and it appeared it was actually going to hit him before he could make a clean getaway. Alas, Romeo was able to get into the barbershop, and the door closed just as the turkey hit the portal, spreading stuffing and turkey parts all over the bottom of the barbershop entry.

I contacted Romeo in the barbershop, and he was seated in one of his chairs. He stated he was going to spend the night in the shop and had every intention of keeping the door locked. I let him know that was probably in his best interest. I think he was having visions of *The Shinning* with his wife peering through the door saying something similar to "Here's Juliet!"

After speaking with Romeo, I contacted Juliet again, and she was sitting at the kitchen table eating the sandwich Romeo made. She assured me she was just going to bed. She looked at the now splattered dressing and turkey and said, "I suppose it'll have to be McDonald's for Thanksgiving this year."

As we walked out of the house, I swear Juliet gave my partner a wink and a wave. "You know you've got a shot at that," I told him. My partner didn't say anything, just scolded me. I don't know if he ever followed up on that or not.

While I was driving away from the call, I was reminded of the scene in the movie *A Christmas Story* where the family has to go to a Chinese restaurant on Christmas day because the neighbor's dog eats their turkey. If you've never seen it, find a copy and watch it.

Family Christmas

This is one of those stories I would have never dreamed could, or would have happened. I have to go back a few years to set this up, and it all comes into play as we progress.

When I was working on bicycle patrol, I worked, for the most part, street-level drug enforcement. In the days I worked the bicycle, it was a new and innovative way of breaking up drug deals. In the early days, the dealers and users saw bicycles coming toward them but not the cops on them; it worked well for us. It was so new, and we were so effective. I actually heard a defense attorney once complain to the judge that the police are now using bicycles, and that was "…an unfair tactic." I had never seen a judge laugh out loud;

chuckles, yes, but not a belly laugh. Well, I thought the judge was going to fall out of his chair when he heard the attorney's argument.

When the judge regained his composure, he looked at the attorney with a concerned look and said, "Oh, you were serious?" When the attorney confirmed his statement, the judge just said, "Try again, counselor, because that's just not working for me." That was exactly the point in time we realized just how effective we were in our drug enforcement. My partner and I felt we had arrived given the defense attorney's lame argument – man, was he digging.

Drugs (mostly heroin) were very pervasive in Downtown Tacoma. We were bringing in six and sometimes twelve arrests almost any given day. We had patrol units staying close by so they could be a part of the fun when we went on sweeps. Our sweeps were quick, and when we called out, we were headed to do a sweep; other units knew we were going to snatch up some dealers and users. Once we had two or three in custody, we saw someone running, which let us to inform the patrol units, give a description, and notify which way the suspect was headed. This was what the patrol units lived for. They knew we would be doing all the paperwork, so all they had to do was catch our runner and bring them back to us to get the name and such. They booked the suspect, and we did all the work. A little bit of yippee-ki-yay right now, if you will.

What did all this mean? It meant we made over 5000 arrests for cocaine or heroin in the first two years of the bicycle patrol. Man, we were kicking it; busier than a one-legged man in a butt-kicking contest. Downtown Tacoma had just become a very difficult place for drug dealers to work their trade, and that was out intent.

My partner and I had a mission, and that was to make Downtown Tacoma a better place to come and enjoy. If you come Downtown right now, you will see a wonderful transition that we handed in, making it a place to enjoy. It wasn't just a two-cop show, but without getting rid of the dope, no one would have invested in the Downtown area like they are today. Investors were vacating Downtown in vast numbers prior to this drug enforcement program we embarked on, but now there is much to love in Downtown Tacoma. Many buildings were abandoned, only being used by addicts and crimes of all kinds. Now those same derelict properties are filled with trendy restaurants, condos, and nightclubs; the University of Washington also built a satellite campus in Downtown.

Drugs, assaults, and prostitution were out of control, so aside from the drug arrest, we were working with vice to rid the area of pimps and their crews. We all know both drugs and prostitution go hand and hand, so both had to be addressed at the same time.

Because there were so many arrests, faces began to blend together. It was easy to remember those who fought with us or repeat arrests, but the few that realized Tacoma was not the place to come to score or deal drugs, those folks were just another face. This all brings me to a family gathering during the Christmas season in 1991.

My wife and I got dressed up for a family gathering at my in-law's home. We always looked forward to going over there. My father-in-law was a dentist, and he had a beautiful home. Additionally, he never skimped on making those parties a fun time. Plus, my mother-in-law is a phenomenal cook, and she makes everything she touches a delicious meal. I definitely looked forward to her food during the holidays or whenever we had a chance to go over for a meal.

When we got to my in-law's home, there were many people already there, so we went through the normal hellos and the meeting of some new people as well. My in-laws always attracted many people to their gatherings. Many of the people there were co-workers of my father-in-law, and a few were patients, as well as other family members. Almost everyone there knew I was a cop, and as these things went when I was at gatherings, people wanted to talk about cops and loved to hear cop stories, much like the ones I have written about in this book.

As I was engaged in a funny story with some of the guests, my wife came up behind me and said she wanted me to meet someone. I turned around, and standing there was a tall man, thinning hair, medium build, and a bit rumpled in his attire. Standing next to him was a female, quite a bit shorter but equally as rumpled. Between them was a little girl about five or six years old who appeared to have a cold; she had a runny nose and looked a bit feverish (red face). I assumed the tyke was the couple's daughter. I also noticed the man's face was white, and he appeared to have a startled look on his face. At first, I thought nothing about it. I just figured he might have gotten his daughter's cold, and the look on his face was just a look of pain/discomfort. Nevertheless, I was introduced, and that was that. Note: I won't tell you what his name was or how he may be related to me because I don't want to embarrass his family.

Shortly after the introduction, I saw the man's mother, who was angry because he left without much warning, along with his wife. What the mother was angry about was he left the sniffling little one behind for his mother to take care of. Again I just figured this guy was getting sicker by the moment and nothing else. Poor guy had to go home and get some bed rest. At this point, I was just hoping I wasn't getting what these folks were passing around, especially when I shook his hand.

Sometime later, I found out that was not the reason he left.

Fast Forward Five Years

My wife and I were at a local Lowes when we ran into the man's mother. We hadn't seen her since the Christmas party, and so it was a nice semi reunion. We began to talk about all that had passed over the years just like anyone would do when you haven't seen someone for quite a while and eventually got around to the Christmas party at my in-laws five years earlier. What I found out was the look on the man's face when I first met him was not because he had contracted his daughter's illness but pure horror and fear. Why? Because he was one of the smart people whom I had arrested in those 5000. Apparently, I busted him for heroin possession and booked him into jail. He was smart because he never came back to Downtown Tacoma. I had no idea who he was when I was 'introduced' to him at the party. I mean, he was just another face, simple as that. I don't even know if his reason for not coming back to Downtown was because he knew who I was at the time of the arrest or just trying to stay away from our sweeps. We all honestly laughed about that, even his mom.

Let me digress…again. Just a thought and comment here: in my time working street-level drug enforcement, I have seen some real crap. I've seen how drugs consume people and how, at first, the users believe they can control the drug. It's a lie, everything about it. You don't control the drug; it's the other way around. You are the person following the commands of the narcotic. It's demanding and forceful.

There is a temptation to be a part of a crowd who are lying to you, just so you can join their misery. Before you even think about it, before you think, "Oh, this looks like fun," do your research. We google to find out about almost any topic we want to know about and see what information we can get. Most of those Google searches are just mundane things that nobody really cares about. So why not do the same about the effects of illegal drugs? Why not find out about something that you might just have to deal with for the rest of your life? What are the results, and how addictive can it be? Just make sense, doesn't it?

To bring that home and prove to you what I just said, I want to talk to you about what happened to a friend of mine. Basically, I am going to digress on the digress. When I was in the Navy, one of my shipmates brought aboard what was called peach powder heroin; it wasn't, obviously, from the peach. Its name came from its color. This was something you could buy off the streets in Southeast Asia, the Philippines, Taiwan, etc. My friend wanted me to snort it with him, but there was no way I was going anywhere near that crap. *My God, it's heroin, ya idiot!* I thought. "You can't be that stupid to try this shit, or are you?"

He decided it was a good idea to give it a try, saying, "I'm not worried about it. There's no way I can get addicted just trying it once." I couldn't believe how stupid he was being and that he was angry I wasn't joining him.

For the next three days, he was violently ill. He was experiencing intense stomach cramps and muscle spasms. The guy was in sheer agony. It was an ugly scene and the first time I had ever seen something like that. At the same time, my buddies and I did not want to see him get in trouble for one stupid act. I mean, he was already experiencing a living hell, so we hid him from our division chief. When asked, we just said he was working on a project somewhere he couldn't be seen. We hoped we wouldn't get caught, and, lucky for us, it worked. The chief just accepted our explanations and left it at that.

When he finally got past the sickness, he told me, "Man, I won't ever do that again." *Great,* I thought, but guess what? I was hoping he learned his lesson and that he was right, which was he wasn't going to get addicted to just one use of the heroin. Sadly he was wrong because he was back on it again – it took a week of battling with this demon before he scored the drug again and was back to it. Why? Because it only took just once, and he was hooked. This time he was on his own. No way was I or anyone else going to take the chance of getting in trouble for his stupidity. Needless to say, he was caught and subsequently court marshaled, sent to the brig, and eventually thrown out of the Navy on a bad conduct discharge. That just sucked.

I hope that made an impact.

Other Party Experiences

Another Christmas Party

This is a bit short but an experience most every cop has had to deal with sometime during their career. Unlike me, I am sure this type of experience probably did not happen at a Christmas party that was being held at their father-in-law's home. Yep, the same home I just discussed previously. Don't get the wrong idea; my father-in-law was a great guy and extremely supportive of the police and what I was doing.

Like any Christmas party, it started out with the usual hugs, Christmas greetings, and such. My wife and I were enjoying ourselves, and it seemed so was most everyone else. We were socializing, laughing, and enjoying conversations. I ended up in the living room talking to some of my wife's co-workers when I was semi-cornered by the husband of one of the dental assistants. At first, he was pleasant, but I soon realized that was a ruse to get me to talk to him.

First, let me tell you about three months prior; one of our officers and my friend was killed in the line of duty. This husband asked me why police had these massive possessions every time an officer was killed. "Don't you think that is rude to the rest of the public and very inconvenient?" he asked.

My answer was short and quick, "No." What more could I say – it was obvious this guy was anti-police and probably trying to get a reaction out of me. I wasn't going to go there, at least not yet.

He was about to make some other stupid remark when I said to him, "You know what's truly inconvenient? My friend dying to help protect the public." That statement didn't phase him a bit. He just went on to tell me that how these funerals are a huge amount of money paid by the taxpayer, but not everyone's funeral is paid for by the public. He also outlined how the officers get paid for being there, the cost for traffic control, the gas in the cars, and so on. Each and every time he said something, I'll have to admit I was getting a bit tenser with every word that came out of his stupid mouth. I wanted to punch him dead in the face.

One side of my brain was ignoring him while the other was about to rip his tongue out. Because I wasn't giving him the reaction, he tried to ratchet it up just a bit by telling me cab drivers deserve this type of procession. Still not going there, I said, "You bet, and they have the right to do so. Not my problem that they don't organize themselves to put something together like that. Plus," I told him, "they have a stressful job and get killed from time to time – probably as often as cops." There was that look; why hadn't he got to me yet? What was it going to take to really piss off this cop? I could see it written all over his face.

And then it came! "You know, even garbage truck drivers have a more stressful job than cops," he said.

That was it, and I let him know. "I have been here, trying to be a good guest in my father-in-law's home, listening to your fucking dribble, you anti-cop piece of shit—"

He interrupted, saying, "I'm not an anti-cop."

"Excuse me, but I am not finished, and you're a fucking liar," I responded as I got nose to nose to this 5 ft 4-inch little twerp, using everything possible to make him feel uncomfortable and as much intimidation as possible. When I saw the 'sweating bullets' look on his face, I let him know. "You are not about to compare what I do to a garbage truck driver's stress level." I further told him, "You can go fuck yourself, you little asshole. Do I make myself clear?"

"Ah, yeah," he said in a stammer. I am sure he was wondering if I was ready to rip his lips off, and that made me feel a bit better.

About then, my wife was walking by, and I said to her it was time to leave. I walked outside and waited for her in the driveway. That little incident caused the party to break up, and I felt bad about that, but I was greeted by those who witnessed the whole thing and couldn't believe I held my temper as long as I did. It was nice to hear so much support.

Then it was that guy's turn to leave. I could not believe he actually walked up to me and said, "Just wanted to wish you a Merry Christmas."

My answer was, "Fuck you." Just after that, my wife came out, and we left for home.

Oh, by the way, we did have a very Merry Christmas.

Know Your Audience

This is one that was kind of funny in a way. Shortly after I met my wife, she wanted to go to a party with her friends. She wanted me to meet them. "Okay," I told her, "but please don't tell them I'm a cop." My biggest reason for that is once people know that they want to tell you about the asshole cop they met. Cops will tell you that kind of thing happens more often than not. She said she would not but did say there were a few that already knew.

It was an outdoor party/barbeque. It was fun, and the usual was there: hot dogs, hamburgers, and a keg. Perfect. My wife got a glass of wine, and I went hunting for the keg. Found it!

It was in a garage, and there were a few guys standing around it, like guys do, talking. As I introduced myself to them, all but one, I recognized from the previous contact with my wife. He knew I was a cop and knew I really didn't want that divulged quite yet. Do you know what they were talking about? That asshole cop who gave one of the guys a ticket.

Oh yes, the cop was a jerk; why? Because this guy was on Interstate Five, on his motorcycle, traveling 100 MPH and popping wheelies. But the cop was mean and rude, maybe because you were driving recklessly with total disregard to public safety. Hmm, just maybe? Oh well, I bit my tongue again and then left, going back to sit with my honey. Oh well, I thought I'd just stick with her and leave when she was ready.

Just as I thought that the guy who was cited by the state trooper found me and let me know, "I didn't know you were a cop," and went on to say he likes cops and that he had some relative who was a cop and the routine apologetic phrases. Oh well, the guy was trying, so okay, I just let it go. I kind of thought it was a bit humorous to watch him grovel a bit. He even asked me if "everything was okay between him and me?" It was.

The Date From Hell

This is not a story that happened while I was not on duty but happened while I was a police officer. Also, while reading this, and if you are a movie buff, you will notice some parallels to the Bruce Willis/Kim Bassinger movie *Blind Date*. It wasn't until after the date did I make the connection to one of the scenes in the movie.

As a male police officer, you meet a ton of women. It's not bragging; it just happens and part of the territory of being a cop. Once they find out what you do for a living, cops get one of two reactions. Most are very willing to go out with you, and they feel quite safe. Others are more hostile, such as the girl I met via a friend who told me, "I smoke dope and don't date cops." Okay, that made it easy to decide what to do. I had a lot of fun as a single cop.

This date began one warm summer evening while I was riding my motorcycle. I came to a red traffic light and stopped. As I was waiting, a Buick Regal came up on my right and also stopped. The car was occupied by two women in their late 20s or early 30s. The driver rolled down her window and asked, "Hey, you wanna trade?"

I told her, "No, but I'll give you a ride."

To my surprise and, at the time, my delight, the driver got out of the car, saying, "okay," and straddled the rear seat. She was a tiny girl, standing all of about 5' 2" and hardly weighed in at 100 pounds. I remember she had dark hair and was wearing a loose-fitting dress. I was thinking, *okay, this should be fun*.

The passenger yelled at her friend. "Liz, what the fuck are you doing?" We both ignored her, and off we went. Liz wrapped her arms around my waist and held on. This girl was obviously quite bold, so I was going to give her the ride of her life. I mean, come on, what girl gets out of her car at an intersection and jumps on the back of some guy's motorcycle who she has no clue about. I could have been a deranged, homicidal maniac or some other crazed criminal. Of course, there was also the possibility she could have been some crazed criminal as well. At this point, I didn't care; she was a little hottie. So off we went.

We sped down the street toward the Narrows Bridge. We hit speeds of 80–90 as we crossed the Narrows and once on the other side made a U-turn to head back. As we crossed, we could see Liz's car going in the opposite direction, driven by her friend. We both waved at her as we flew by at Mach 5 or better. There was no doubt Liz was having a great time as she grabbed me even tighter and reached down for my crotch. This was becoming a good time, for sure.

We went back to where we met and got off the motorcycle to talk and wait for her friend to return. We engaged in a conversation for just a few minutes when Liz's friend showed up. The car came to a screeching halt, and her friend jumped out of the car. Her friend (who I found out later was Kathy) began screaming at Liz about how reckless she was; she didn't know me and had no clue what I was going to do to her. She was right, and I agreed with Kathy. I think Liz was a bit surprised at my reaction. I eventually did identify myself as a cop, and that seemed to relax Kathy a little, but she reiterated that Liz didn't know that when she flung her leg over my motorcycle seat.

The three of us just talked for a while and got to know each other. After a while, I asked if the two of them would like to join me at a comedy club in town. I told Kathy to bring a date, just so she understood the invitation was actually meant for Liz. They both agreed, and Kathy assured me she would bring her boyfriend. It was set for Tuesday night, and today was Sunday. I wasn't quite ready to have Liz know where I lived, so we agreed to meet at the comedy club.

I left the intersection feeling quite proud of myself. Here was this very petite and quite cute lady who I just met agreeing to meet me for dinner and a comedy show. *What could go wrong,* I thought. Given how spontaneous this chick was, I thought I would have to screw it up in a seriously bad way not to get lucky with this one.

Tuesday came, and I arrived at the bar for the comedy club about 20 minutes before Liz and Kathy were going to show up. I figured if I got stood up, I was sure I could find someone in the bar to join me at the club upstairs.

Though I was in the process of flirting with some girl when Liz, Kathy and, what appeared to be Kathy's boyfriend, showed up. I was happy to see them. We had a couple of drinks and some bar food to start before heading upstairs where the comedy club was. I was a bit surprised that Liz was able to down her two Scotch & waters like a sailor. I wrote it off as nervous given this quasi-blind date. So upstairs we went.

We did a bit more drinking, with some jokes but a bit loud laugh from Liz. Nevertheless, and I'll be honest with you all, at this point, I was hoping to get this little pistol in the sack, so putting up with her being a bit loud and slightly obnoxious was a price I was willing to pay. What I didn't know was what was on the horizon of this date.

By the time the first comedian came on stage, Liz was pretty well looped. The comedian hardy got the first line out when she screamed out, "That's not fucking funny, you suck!" I told her to chill out, but she just ignored me and kept up her onslaught on this poor guy. At first, he bantered back, coming at her with a few good insults; well deserved, I have to admit. At first, it seemed cute that this tiny girl was boisterous, but after a while, many people began to become annoyed.

Suddenly without warning, Liz stood up, screamed a loud "fuck you," and tried to throw her drink at the guy. However, I was able to pull her back down in her seat, so most of the drink landed on the table. At that point, I told her we were going out of there, and even the club manager came by and told us to leave. Liz wanted nothing to do with that and said she wasn't leaving. The entire crowd now was booing us, so I told her again we had to leave. She refused and took a swing at me. So I picked her up in her drunken state, threw her over my shoulder, and walked out to the applause of the crowd. Down the stairs we went, back to the bar/restaurant, all the while she was hitting me, screaming obscenities, and trying to wiggle free.

When we got to the bottom of the stairs, she tried to run past me to go back to the club. She was easy to handle, but she tried to hit me several times. Trying to reason with her was a waste of time as she was now acting like she was possessed, growling at me. I had to tell her if she continued this way, I was going to have to arrest her—the last thing I wanted to do. Well, that seemed to piss her off even more. "Oh, so now you're going to be a cop on me, are you?" she asked in a demeaning, sarcastic tone. I told her she would make the decision for me. She was too drunk to understand that and how it applied.

During this exchange with Liz, the bouncer was watching me the entire time, so I finally had to ID myself to him and told him to call 911 and to ask for only one car to respond. I was clear as to what I wanted, but that's not what he did. He called in with, "Off duty officer fighting with a customer in the front foyer area," and that ended up getting the response I did not want. I heard sirens coming from everywhere. *Son of a bitch*, I thought. Just what I needed. A bunch of my cop buddies showing up, laughing at me.

When the first car showed up, I was happy to see my friend Roger and put Liz in the back of his car, fighting the entire way. I immediately told Roger to cancel any other cars that were on the way. I surely did not need cops rushing to my aid for something that wasn't necessary, not to mention how embarrassing it was to have to possibly arrest my date. All I could think was how this had gotten out of control. I explained the entire incident to Roger, and at the end, he asked if I wanted him to arrest Liz. "No, that's not what I wanted. I just wanted her to go away."

Just as I was finishing the story to Roger, Kathy and her boyfriend showed up at the patrol car. "Where the hell have you two been?" I asked.

What I got from Kathy was, "Well, we thought you two wanted to be alone or something."

I thought, *are you kidding me?* "What part of being kicked out and carrying this bobcat over my shoulder made you think I wanted to be alone with her?" I told them. "Now, what I want is for you two to take this little runt home."

Kathy asked if she could talk to Liz, and I told her if that was what it would take to calm her down. After a few minutes, Liz asked to talk to me. She apologized and asked to be let out of the car. Upon my request, Roger let her out. Liz came up to me, getting very close. She began rubbing her crotch against me. She told me she wanted to make up for all this and would make the rest of the night 'worthwhile.' As much as I originally wanted to take this girl home and do very nasty things, and still wanted this girl in the worst way; at this point, I did not want to take her home because then she would know where I lived. Just what I didn't need; this had 'fatal attraction' written all over it. So despite all my male hormones, I said no. I had to say no several times because she would not take that for an answer. It wasn't until I told her I didn't want to take advantage of her due to her intoxicated state but assured her I would call her the next day so we could talk. That answer seemed to be acceptable, and she followed Kathy and her boyfriend to their car. I thanked God that she was leaving.

Liz walked about 20–25 feet and stopped. *Oh, no, don't you dare turn around*, I thought. *Oh, no! She turned around! Shit!* Not what I wanted to see. She stopped and said, "It seems my dates always end like this." If I had any inclination of calling her the next day (which I did not), those thoughts ran for cover when she said that.

I never saw her again, and if I ever do, it will be too soon.

But I Love You!

One of the many benefits of being a police officer is you meet many members of the opposite sex who are more than happy to date or even sleep with you. Of course, one needs to be very careful when pursuing those offers because you never know their intent is when you happen to meet them on a call or just in casual encounters. In those kinds of meetings, I always set up very casual meetings, like a coffee or just lunch. Once I felt comfortable, then I would ask them for a movie/dinner date. Of course, that doesn't always mean you get it right every time.

One of those encounters (which I had no idea would turn out the way it did) was Susie, my case in point. I met her at a deli my partner and I frequented when working swing shift. She was the clerk there, and she just struck me as adorable. We talked a great deal over about two months before I asked her out. Things went very well at the beginning of our relationship except for one thing – she drank too much. At first, I didn't look at it as a big deal, but as the relationship continued, I saw many faults in her alcohol use. When I would want to discuss it with her, she became agitated and a bit angry. You'd think that would send up a red flag for me, but to be quite honest with you, I was getting laid, and I had zero desire to get married, so I just ignored it.

After about three months, I began to question my decision of asking her out, not to mention sleeping with her. I did not want to just walk away from this relationship, given I did like her when she was sober. I decided I needed to see others, and I was not one of those guys to go behind the back of a woman I was dating and especially a sex partner. That had happened to me, and I knew that feeling when someone did that to another person. It's not pleasant. As difficult as it was going to be, I decided to let her know my feelings, but I had to catch her sober.

We had set a date to attend a party, so I thought I'd talk to her just before, so if she was upset, she could decide to go without me. We decided to meet at a local watering hole due to our schedules, and I didn't know where the party was taking place. When Susie arrived, I told her I needed to talk to her before we went to the party. I was about to drop a bombshell on her, so I wanted a neutral place where she would be less likely to go off on me. I told her my feelings and also told her if she was upset, I would understand. I also told her that I did not want to break up but would understand if she wanted to due to me asking to see others. Susie assured me she was okay with me seeing others and mentioned it allowed her to do the same. She was right, and I felt comfortable with that as well.

Despite my proclamation, Susie said she still wanted me to go to the party with her, and she would drive, leaving my car behind. *Okay*, I thought, given she knew where the party was at, but I later figured out she had an ulterior motive.

When we got to the party, everything seemed to go smoothly at first, but as she began to drink more and more, her alcohol bravery grew with every drink. She began telling everyone she could find that I was an 'asshole.' She started saying, pointing at me, "He wants to start fucking every bitches he can find." After being ridiculed and embarrassed way too many times,

I told Susie I was out of there and going to walk back to my car (about 15–20 blocks away).

She followed me out to the street and said she would take me back; we argued for a few moments, and it became apparent she was not going to take no for an answer. She was making a scene, and to keep the neighbors from calling the police, I agreed to go with her. Reluctantly, I got in the car as I was very concerned she might be too intoxicated to drive.

Susie drove an older VW Bug, stick shift. When she pulled away from the curb, she stalled the car. I figured she would just restart, and we'd get going. Nope, wrong once more. She turned to me and said, "I want a hug." I refused at first, telling her it would not mean anything, but once again, she would not accept "no" as an answer, so I hugged her. She restarted the car, and we got about a block down the street, stopping at a stop sign. She began to pull out when she killed the engine again. She immediately restarted the car but didn't move forward. Instead, she put the car in neutral, turned toward me, and said, "I want a kiss." Once again, I refused. I told her, once again, it would not mean anything. This turned into a true argument as I was going to stand my ground this time.

Eventually, I said, "Fuck it," and I tried to step out of the car. As I opened the door and I was about to step out, I felt the car surge forward with me hanging out the door. She then drove like some crazy person as we headed back to the bar we met at. No words were spoken on the way. When we pulled in behind my car, I got out as quickly as possible. As I walked up to my car, Susie got out and said she wanted to talk. As I got in my car, I just said to her, "Go home, Susie," and off I went.

When I arrived home, and as I got out of my car, Susie drove up and parked behind me. She begged me to talk to her, but again I refused. Susie was determined to get her way. Once inside, she began to scream as loud as he could. "But I love you!" I did not need to have my neighbors hear this nor need to field any complaints from them. I opened the door and told her to get inside.

Once inside, I told her we were over, but she began rubbing against me, telling me she wanted to make up for being so rude tonight. She said she wanted to go upstairs to my bedroom and make love. Then she unbuttoned her blouse so I could see her breast. Susie had one of the best sets of tits I've ever seen on a woman. So I caved, but before we went upstairs, I asked, "Are you sure you are okay with this?" She assured me she was and felt bad about her behavior earlier. "Okay," I said, and I started upstairs first.

My house was built in 1922, and the stairway was a narrow hall with a fairly steep staircase. When I got about halfway up the stairway, I felt something grabbed my belt and pulled me back down the stairs. I couldn't believe this woman just pulled me backward down my own set of stairs. I got up quickly, and my natural reaction was to grab her by the neck as I cocked my fist back to punch her in the face. I stopped short of that, thankfully, even though I would have been justified. I pushed her aside, went to the living room, picked up her shirt and bra, handed it to her, shoved her out the front door, and said, "Don't ever come near me again." She stood outside the door putting on her shirt, staring through the window on the door. I opened it again and told her if she did not leave, I would call the police and report a domestic violence assault. "You're going to jail if you don't leave." She left.

Since then, I have seen Susie around town, but that's it.

Roommates

At the end of my rookie year, I decided it was time to buy a house. So after a short search, I found a small bungalow house in the Northend District of Tacoma. The great little house had a full basement, four bedrooms, and a half-story upstairs. In the time I owned that house, I had a few roommates. I had interesting times there, but mostly fun times. Of my roommates, two were guys and three were girls (I always had two roommates at any given time). Both guys who lived there were co-workers, cops, but the girls were not. The girls were the most fun and employed outside of law enforcement. At the time of the purchase, I was only paying $600 a month (how I wish my mortgage payments were still at that level), so I split the rent three ways, a win-win for all of us. I got help with the mortgage, and they got an entire house and not an apartment with people above, beside, or below. Also, I split the utilities with each person.

Mark

Mark and I didn't know much about each other before he moved into my house. We had only two basic connections, and those were we were both cops at Tacoma and our barber, Carol. What actually brought Mark to me was that I heard he was looking to find a place to rent, so when I bought a house, I approached him and let him know I was looking for a roommate. Mark was divorced and had a son, Scott. Scott was a cool kid and by now must be well into his 30s. He played with my two kids, and at that time, all three were little, about 4–5 years old.

Mark had been going from place to place since the time of his divorce. I thought he might like a more permanent place to live. Note: This is quite typical in the law enforcement family where officers were getting tossed out by their spouses and looking for a place to hang their hats. Many times, these so-called temporary places to live become semi-permanent. That's exactly what this turned out when Mark moved in. Mark and I lived together in that house for just over a year, and in that year, we had a great time.

We got along very well, right from the beginning. We had the same sense of humor, which at times one might say was a bit morbid, and most women might think quite childish. I mean, we thought the *Three Stooges* were hilarious; women just don't get that. We'd laugh at things many people would find tragic or silly. One occasion that comes to mind was when we were sitting around talking about our day at work, and I told Mark about a deceased call I went on.

I will digress (as usual) a bit to outline what cops think is funny. Mark and I think this is funny; you may not.

Mark and I were trained by the same sergeant who made it a point to let us know we had to have the person or victim sign our reports. We were told, in no uncertain terms, if the report was not signed, then "you'd better damn well get your ass back out there and get it signed." This edict comes into play as I write about the call.

Back to the deceased call. When I got to the call, it was obviously a natural death, and there were no signs of foul play. The deceased was elderly, in the late 80s, and appeared to have died quickly while doing laundry. Throughout the house, there were no signs of struggle as everything was neat and orderly. The guy just keeled over and died. Nevertheless, these were the days no matter the means of death — natural or suspicious — we were still required to file a report that I was there and my findings. I obtained the victim's identification via his wallet in his back pocket, and that was consistent with mail and bottles of medication I found in the home.

I got the entire report completed but ran into a slight problem. How do I get this guy to sign the report? There was no one else, and the guy who called us had left for work, so who's going to sign it? I didn't want to bring my 'ass back out here' because this guy was unable to sign. I stood over his body and asked him but no response. I figured it would be okay if I just gave him some help. I mean, he was dead, so I was there to protect and serve, right? I felt it was my civic duty to give this guy a hand, literally. Doing my duty as an officer of the law and to appease my sergeant, I grabbed his hand and helped him sign the report. It was close to his actual signature (comparing it to his driver's license) — a little off, but not bad, and quite frankly, who the hell would know. I left after the medical examiner arrived, and I went to the station to submit the report.

Now I am sure most of you don't think that was extremely funny, but from a cop's point of view, it was hilarious. To top it off, I'd never heard anything about that report. When I turned in the report, the sergeant didn't look at the title; he only turned the report over to make sure it was signed. He didn't look to see who the signature was by, and that was all he cared about. **Prankster**

Mark was known for his pranks. Cops are, of course, known for doing pranks, but Mark was known for taking pranks to a professional and refined level. Here is the one he recently shared with me.

He went 'upstairs' to work on a nonpatrol job; you know, one of those foo-foo jobs where you have to act civil with lots of public contacts. Anyway, he was working with a very senior officer who was nicknamed 'Dandy Dave.' Dandy was a great guy and a great cop. I worked only a few times with him and always looked forward when I had those brief assignments with him. I would have never even thought of pranking him. Mark, on the other hand—no one was safe from his pranks.

One of Dandy's vices was he smoked…a lot. In the early to mid-80s, smoking inside a building was not illegal and, quite frankly, an accepted practice. Dandy smoked one of the nastiest and cancer-causing cigarettes; unfiltered Lucky Strike. I smoked in the past but had quit several years earlier. I would have never dreamed of smoking an unfiltered cigarette; that's a bit too hardcore for me.

Of course, Dandy used a lighter to light up his smokes, but in his desk drawer, he kept a number of matchbooks for backup if one of his disposals lighter failed. Those matchbooks were obtained from a local bail bondsman. Mark's prank was simple; Dandy would eventually have an empty lighter. It was just going to happen.

So here was the setup Mark concocted. One day when Dandy was out of the office, Mark took all of Dandy's matchbooks and put clear tape over the striking pad, trimming it perfectly to only cover the striking black strip. I asked Mark how long it took him to set up the prank. "About an hour," he said. Obviously, it was a slow day.

One never knows when the prank will finally have its day. Will it be today, tomorrow, or even take a year from now? You just have to be patient. In this case, it did not take too long to get the payoff. Dandy was at his desk working hard. Wait a minute! Nobody works hard at those foo-foo jobs! Sorry, but I had to clarify. The day finally came when Dandy was going to have a smoke, but his disposal lighter was out of fluid. He decided it was time to light up. He tried again and again, but the lighter was dry. So, after several attempts, he resorted to his backup stash of matchbooks (every cop always makes sure their backup is in place). After tossing the disposal lighter in the trash, he opened his desk drawer to deploy his backup. The first book, strike after strike, no dice. Second book, still nothing. Not one of the matches lit, and this went on and on throughout the entire stack of matchbooks. The guy needed his smoke.

One would think anyone going through these matchbooks would realize or eventually see there was something wrong other than the matchbook itself. Well, Dandy's near vision was not so good, and he was panicking due to his lack of nicotine. The combination and anyone who has ever smoked knows, at this moment, he was about to skyrocket through the roof. In no uncertain terms, Dandy told (or maybe it was a scream) everyone around to never get your matchbooks from this bail bondsman because they 'suck.'

After going through all the matchbooks and then seeing the smug look on Mark's face, he realized the prank that was set upon him. At that point, it did not take too long for Dandy to figure out he was getting pranked, given everyone around him was having a great belly laugh. I wasn't there, but something tells me, and my experience with Dandy, there were a lot of F-bombs flying around. I know I would have had a side ache, laughing at Dandy. I probably would have given it away long before he got through the first matchbook.

Tacoma Police Digest

In the mid-80s, we had a director of police services who came from Seattle PD. I can't remember his name, so I will just refer to him as Director. He was a total jackass; he would fly off screaming at you if you happen to slightly disagree or try to state your opinion in regards to his ideas or method of leadership, even if he was requesting one's input. He became so out of control he had to bring in a Seattle PD buddy to help him deal with these out-of-control Tacoma cops. Director became the joke of the department and obtained not only zero respect from the rank-and-file officers but the shortest tenure at TPD ever. Truly we were all very proud of driving him batty and having him removed.

Prior to Director's premature departure, the admin tried to help smooth over this tense relationship between rank & file and Director. In the infinite wisdom of our administration, which included Director, they thought the good idea was to publish a weekly newsletter. Oh, goody-goody! Won't that just make (inject heavy sarcasm here) have that tingly warm feeling all over. Riiiiggghhhhttt!

So within a week or so, the first of only a few newsletters hit out mail slots, the Tacoma Police Digest. I am sure the title of this periodical's initials (TPD) is not lost on you. It was okay, at best. It was very self-serving for the admin as it seemed to always have some story about how hard the administration was working for the officers on programs we never saw and how Chief, oops, sorry 'the Director' had your back and cared about the line officer. For most of us, that part was not only hard to swallow but impossible given this asshat was screaming at you for a nothing issue. Just a note: his relationship with the uniform officer became so bad he refused to exit his office to visit with us. I think he was scared to death.

The digest also talked about new officers, babies that were being born, items for officers for sale, which always seemed to be from someone in admin, etc. The digest was a joke and became fish wrap or garbage can liner for the most part.

The digest was out for about a month when suddenly a new newsletter appeared in our mail slots. The new periodical was titled Tacoma Police Indigestion. By its sheer name, one knew it was a complete spoof of the digest. Admin did not take kindly to this new and opposing 'newsletter.'

The TPI had exposed sexual affairs in admin, the wasteful spending going on, junket trips admin was doing (mostly so they could support the affairs without spouses knowing), etc. TPI looked a great deal like the digest, but there were added cartoon figures.

Director vowed to find out who was publishing this unauthorized TPI and when he found out who the culprit was, they would be disciplined. There were even interdepartmental memos that said that if any officer were caught with a copy of a TPI, that officer would get a minimum of "three days off without pay." This meant if you got one of those in your mail slot, you'd better turn it in to your sergeant. All that made the TPI even more valuable. I still have my copies in my stack of keepsakes from my days at Tacoma Police.

Guess what you never do, and you'd think this former cop, Director, would know better; don't threaten a cop. With that edict from his office, the TPI went underground, and officers began making copies to help distribute. Director directed his admin goons to collect TPIs no matter where they were, but there was no way they could keep up with us who were helping the distribution. There were so many areas the TPI was being dropped for collection. TPI showed up everywhere, stairwells, interview rooms, locker rooms (both men's and women's), restrooms, just to name a few. I think someone even went so far as to drop a stack in front of his office door while he was in there, just to piss him off. I truly wish I could have been a fly on the wall when he opened his office door. He would have gone on a spinner...zing!

For the most part, these things were being hoarded and cherished. But not by all. Some of the admin officers (captains, lieutenants, assistant chiefs, etc.) were a bit pissed off. Their secrets were out, and it didn't sit too well with them. Us, rank and file officers, absolutely loved it, though.

Everyone wanted to know who was writing TPI, but at the same time, everyone was glad they didn't know. Sometimes ignorance is a good thing, especially when Director tracked you down to 'interview' you as to your knowledge of who was behind this exposé.

I got featured once that some officers thought I'd be angry about. No way! As a matter of fact, I was quite honored by being featured. I laughed about what was said and still have the original copy stowed away protected in plastic. What was said?

First I have to tell you in my single days I enjoyed women. I still do, of course, but then I was a single cop, and let's say I had more fun than I should have. I loved everything about them, and I wasn't shy about approaching women and striking up a conversation. After Mark moved out, I lived with two girls, and because of that, my house got a nickname: 'Enzo's Stables.' I took it as the humor it was meant to be and nothing else. It was just funny. The author of TPI decided to exploit that in one of his entries. Printed on the last page of one of the issues, it said, "Officer Enzo is the proud father of triplets, and all three mothers are said to be doing fine." I laughed about that for some time and still see the humor in it.

For some time, I had no idea who the author was. It wasn't until this issue with me in it did I get a hint. Shortly after the issue featuring me, Mark came up to me and asked if the most recent issue bugged me. I thought he was asking because he was curious how I felt about it. It wasn't until I told him I thought it was just funny and I saw the relief on his face did I then know he was the author. I looked at him and said, "You dog! I am so proud of you." He denied anything to do with the periodical, but I didn't believe him.

Some 20+ years after that day, Mark and I met up, and he divulged he was the artist for the TPI but had nothing to do with the verbal comment; yeah, okay, Mark, we'll go with that.

Mark and I had some other fun stuff, but he eventually moved out. It came as a bit of a shock, not because he was moving out but where he went and why. I always expected him to buy a house, and that would be why he'd move out. Keep in mind, he was quite the lady's man, and he contributed to the nickname my house, so when he told me he was getting married, that came as a bit of a surprise. Mark getting married? That just did not compute with me. I thought, *okay, he decided on one of those many girls* — who were all very hot, I might add — *to settle down with*. It was not one of the many girls he was seeing but instead an old high school flame. Plus, he was moving to Provo, Utah.

What! Stop the presses — moving to Provo, the heart of the Mormon faith! Unbeknownst to me, Mark was…is a Mormon! When the hell did that happen? This was all a shock to me, to say the least. I can tell you Mark was not on a bicycle, going door to door telling anyone who would listen about the Book of Mormon.

I briefly met Mark's betrothed. She seemed very nice and understood my shock, to say the least. Oh well, this was his decision, and I wished them both well.

Jim

Jim lived in my house for less than a year before I had to ask him to leave. Two things come to mind, but I assure you there were many more.

Skis

The first one was when I came home one day. I remember it was a very warm July day, so I was a bit surprised to find Jim in the living room dressed in full snow ski gear, and I mean full ski gear. He was in full ski attire, looking like he was ready for the slopes. He was wearing a ski suit, boots, gloves, hat, wool cap, and goggles; he also had poles in hand, and his new Roosendaal skis attached to his boots, all on my solid wooden floors. "What are you doing, Jim?" I asked. He told me he was testing out the new equipment he just got a great deal on.

Me: "Jim, you realize this is July, and you're in the living room."

Jim: "Well yeah, but I needed to make sure it was all good."

Me: "Shouldn't that have been done before you purchased this stuff?"

Jim: "But it was such a good deal I couldn't pass it up."

Me: "Okay, but you could do this in the backyard instead of the living room."

Jim: "That would look silly."

Me: "Get out of the living room!"

I suppose I should have explained myself a bit better to him and make sure I outlined what I expected him to do at this moment. It seemed he needed a bit more detail. If you are in the living room of a house with skis attached to your feet and you need to move to another room, or in this case, out of the house, common sense would tell you to remove the skis first, right? Well, that's not how Jim processed my demand to go outside. As he picked up the first ski, he swung it around like a helicopter rotor, smashing into a lamp.

I couldn't help myself and told him, "Take those fucking things off!" He immediately removed the skis with a ton of "I'm sorry(s)."

Jim scurried into his room, and I noticed he was sweating profusely. Maybe, and I might be going out on a limb here, but I think wearing a full-fledged ski suit in July might just do that to a person...hmmm.

No Open Door Policy Here

Before I tell you this little story, one of the things you must know about my little bungalow. The front door has a window in it, not one you can open but just clear glass to see out or in. I had a set of blinds on the window for privacy and, at the same time to open them for additional light. When someone comes to the front door, and if all the interior doors were open, you would be able to see through the living room, through the hall, into the bathroom, and then into the backyard (if the bathroom window curtains were open). If I wanted privacy, all I had to do was just close the blinds on the front door. Simple, right? At all other times, one had the option to leave the blinds open.

This particular day was a day off, and I was headed home to whip up a lunch for a girl I was dating. I was so looking forward to having her over to treat her to my pasta salad. I wasn't expecting to come to the front door and see what I was about to witness. I came up to the door, and the blinds were open, the hall door was open, and so was the bathroom door. Remember what I said? If it was all open, one could see into the bathroom. Now that's not a big deal if all were unoccupied, but that day the bathroom was, indeed, occupied by Jim. There he was, sitting on the toilet, obviously going crap. Man, are you kidding me? Why wasn't the bathroom door closed? No, no, no; he can't be that stupid. And the view was only the beginning. When I opened the front door, the smell had engulfed every cubic foot of the house. The stench was overpowering, and I felt my eyebrows begin to sizzle. "Oh, my God!" I yelled. "What the fuck are you thinking?"

I walked to the bathroom, and as I started to close the bathroom, I could not believe what Jim was going to say, but he did. He said, "Hey, don't close the door; it'll stink in here!"

My response was, "That's where it's supposed to stink, dumb ass."

So I had to call my lunch date, and she was kind enough to meet me at a restaurant but fearing the house still lingering with the pungent odor, I had to turn her down for any other activities that would be indoors. She had quite a hearty laughed when I explained why.

You're Out

The previous incident I just wrote was pretty much the last straw for me, and when I told Mark, he felt the same way. Neither one of us had a clue how to tell Jim, but we got an unexpected incentive to tell him he was out.

Mark and I went to the same barber, Carol. Carol had her own business, and Mark and I always enjoyed getting our hair cut by her. She was good at what she did, and it made it even better that she was hot. Mark and I would rather go to a barber that was cute than some guy. Easy pick for both of us, so the combination was something that always kept us coming back.

Shortly after the incident, I just told you that Mark and I had back-to-back haircut appointments. While I was in the chair, Carol began talking about how she had to move because she did not like the neighborhood she was living in, and it was too far to commute. She also said she hadn't found a place yet. I don't know if she was baiting us, but if she was, I was cool with it.

I looked at Mark, and I could see he was thinking the same as I was. "So," I said, "I have a room opening up in my house, which is only a few blocks from here. Want to come to take a look at it?" Keep in mind, both Mark and I had been going to Carol for over a year, so it wasn't like we all didn't know each other. Asking her was a natural transition in this conversation. She agreed to come over to look at the room and seemed to be genuinely excited about the prospect of living with a couple of cops. She told me it would be two weeks before she could look at the house and another two weeks before she could move in because she was still tied to her lease. As far as I was concerned, that could not be more perfect.

As Mark and I left, we were high-fiving out the door. "So, what are you going to tell Jim?" Mark asked.

It was my house, so it was my duty to tell Jim. "I'll just have to figure it out."

When I got home, I figured I might as well get started on this so Jim could have time to move. Both

Mark and I confronted Jim, who was washing his face in the bathroom. When we began to speak to him, his face was turned away from us as he was looking in the mirror; I could only see the right side of his face. When he turned toward me, he had a massive shiner on his left eye. "What happened to you?" I asked. He told me he was out at a place called the Rain Tree, which is a known gang hangout, and someone recognized him as a cop. He was lucky to get out with just a shiner. "Man, that sucks, dude," I said. "Hate to make your day even worse, but both Mark and I are having a difficult time with you living here." He asked if I was kicking him out, and I said, "Yep." He took it better than I thought. No fuss, no bother, and he was out before two weeks had gone by. When Carol moved in, Mark and I had eye candy for the following year. I even pulled a stunt the first night Carol was there. After a long evening of conversation, Carol was seated on the couch. She stretched, which I have to say was one of the sexiest things I had ever seen a woman do and then said she was off to bed. Oh yes, this was going to be a wonderful relationship.

What happened to Jim? Jim had gone over to the traffic division and rode motorcycles. He seemed to enjoy that, and we continued to be friends, despite me kicking him out. Sadly, he had joined the ranks of officers killed in the line of duty on April 27, 2004. Jim was responding to help another officer when a motorist turned left in front of Jim's motorcycle despite the fact Jim had all emergency equipment activated.

Terri and Donelle

I want to combine these two together because they moved into my house about the same time. When Mark moved out to get married, Carol introduced me to Terri, and when Carol moved out, Terri introduced me to Donelle. This change transpired over a very short timetable, so it seemed like these two ladies moved in at the same time.

Both of them were, in my opinion, polar opposites but, for some reason, just seemed to work out without much difficulty. At the same time, both were exceptionally cute, and of all my roomies, I miss these two the most. Probably because they lived with me the longest, and we were like close friends, and I looked at them as my little sisters.

Terri was a petite blond that had this innocent look but was a very mischievous little one that always made me laugh. Donelle, on the other hand, was sexy in a hot biker chick sort of way. She was smart and could get her way not only through her sex appeal but through her intelligence.

When the girls moved in, we all agreed this was a platonic situation, and even though I found them both sexually alluring, I felt compelled to agree to this. It was not just because they were asking but because I liked them so much, and I wanted them to stick around. Both of these astounding women made me smile, and I looked forward to coming home to see what they were up to.

Most of my stories about these two focus on Terri as she and I had the most interaction. Donelle was not home as much as Terri and I were, but still, Donelle had her moments as well.

I'm Injured, Really

In police work, it is not uncommon to get injured; it kind of comes with the job. One time I hyperextended my right thumb, making me a liability. I could not hold a gun or write without much difficulty and discomfort, so I was ordered to go out on an OJI (On the Job Injury) leave until I was released by a doctor to come back to work. So off I went.

I made sure I told my partner to stop by for lunch or get something cold to drink, given it was mid to late summer and getting warmer every day. He said he would when time allowed, and because my house was in our district, that should be easy to do.

About five days into my convalescence, he called me and said he would stop by if I was home. "You bet," I said, "I'll be home all day."

The girls (as I always affectionately referred to Terri & Donelle) and I decided to go out to the front yard and catch some sun. Did I mention these two girls were quite cute? I know I did; I just thought I would brag a bit. Terri got into her French cut leopard pattern bikini, and Donelle put on a very revealing black satin bikini. They both went from cute to very hot. We grabbed our outdoor recliners and set them up in the front yard. Terri got on my right, and Donelle got on my left. I put together a cooler with beer and ice as well as some soft drinks for my partner when he showed up.

At this point, I had no clue what this would look like when my partner arrived. I was just out enjoying the sun with my roommates, nothing more. Once again, these girls were my buddies, no big deal. It wasn't until my partner showed up and seeing his reaction did I get what this all looked like.

As a patrol car came rolling down the street, I told the girls my partner was showing up. They had never met him, so they both got up as he pulled to the curb in front of my house. We all waved at him to come on up to the house. He stopped in front of the house and just sat in the driver's seat. We were all yelling at him to get out, and I waved a can of coke for him to enjoy. He didn't move. Terri asked in a puzzled manner, "Is he getting out?" I didn't know and could not understand why he was still in the car. After about two minutes, he looked directly at me and, with a scowl on his face giving me the hand gesture that he was none too happy with me; you know, 'the finger.' Then without a word, he drove away. *What the fuck!* I thought. The girls looked at me in utter confusion, and then suddenly, it dawned on me. He saw me on OJI leave, with two half-naked hot chicks, with beer, while he was in a patrol car driving around shagging calls. Also, I later found out the car he was driving had broken air conditioning. Oh man, that truly had to be a sight.

We talked later that day, and he said he wasn't actually angry at me it was just the scene he drove up on was just a 'are you kidding me?' moment. It was just too much to bear. The girls and I made it up to him when we all went to a great pub close by, Engine House #9.

Every Night

Because my house was in the district, I patrolled from time to time, and I would stop by to write reports or just get a quick lunch. I worked graveyard or swing shift, so it was a way to also make the girls feel more secure when I would stop by for lunch or a coffee. Sometimes they were there, and sometimes they weren't. In this tale, I was not with my usual partner as I was doing field training officer (FTO) duty. That meant I had a rookie with me. This particular rookie needed more assistance because he had two previous training officers that were lazy and gave him wrong information on how to respond to call, or how not to respond to calls, would be the correct to way to view his 'training.'

My rookie was assigned to me, and his field training was extended. The training lieutenant told me that he wanted me to make sure this rookie was fired by the end of the 30-day training period he was going to be with me. I couldn't believe this lieutenant had said that to me and couldn't help but believe this may have been more of a racial issue than inadequacy as the rookie was of Asian descent. I wasn't sure, but it just kind of gnawed at me. I was also ordered not to tell him he was supposed to be fired at the end of our training. What do you think I did when we first got into the car? Yep, I told him. With that in mind, it was time to get this rookie on track and make sure I did everything I could for him to successfully pass his probation.

In the time I was with this rookie, I saw a good officer who got bad training, and we had a good time together. On one of our graveyard shifts, we were about five reports down, so I put us out of service to write. We headed over to my house to brew up some coffee and maybe get a bite to eat.

As it is in law enforcement, rookies write all the reports, and this was no different. I set him up at the dining table as I put on the pot of coffee. I then sat on the couch, which had my back to the dining table but facing the fireplace. Above the fireplace was a large mirror that allowed me to see into the dining room.

After about a half-hour, Terri came in the front door, which was between the living room and dining room. It was about 2:00 a.m., and she took one look at the rookie and knew exactly what was going on (I had told my roomies about him). Without a word, Terri went into her room and, within a few minutes, came out with her tiniest teddy and crawled up next to me on the couch. She snuggled up very close to me, grabbing my right arm. She began to stroke my arm and nibble at my ear, and made sure my rookie could see. She then began to coyly say things such as, "I love living with a cop. It makes me feel so safe." I knew what she was trying to do, and by the looks of my rookie's face in the mirror, with his gaping mouth, it was working. The rookie couldn't believe what he was seeing. Terri continued her temptress onslaught by nibbling at my ear. Even though I was kind of enjoying this snuggling, I had to tell her to go to bed. Of course, Terri couldn't let it go, so she placed her right index finger to her mouth and, in her shyest of voices, asked, "Are you coming with me?" I told her no because I was working. With a pouty face, she said, "Well, okay."

She got up and walked past my now shocked rookie, and said good night to him, and blew me a kiss as she walked into her bedroom.

At this point, my rookie was about to explode and could not get his eyes off Terri until she closed her door. Immediately he asked, "How often does that happen?"

Keeping with the tone of things, I said, "Every night, man, every night."

I know what was going through his mind about that time. He wanted to know how does he get a part of this? I decided to leave it at that, but after a few days, I told him the truth and to forget about Terri.

Last Night Was Wonderful

As I stated, my relationship with my roommates was very platonic. If there was any hanky-panky going on, I would have bragged about it. That said, Brenda, my girlfriend at the time, thought quite differently.

I never understood her attitude about my roommates. She knew when she met me, I was living with two girls, and given my girlfriend was a stunning, tall German, I really had no desire to be with anyone else. This was truly a 'three's company' situation.

Not to mention, it seemed I was at her house a great deal more than I was home. Quite frankly, one time, when I came home and my roommates were both there. Terri asked (jokingly), "Hey, mister, do you live here?" Nevertheless, my girlfriend always accused me of sleeping with the girls, and that created a bit of a riff between my roomies and her.

Her attitude went on for the entire time I dated her, and it truly took its toll. I was getting to where I was fed up with Brenda, and though I liked her, I didn't like her enough to marry her. This became evident to me when she asked me if we could go look at rings together. I told her I wasn't ready for that type of commitment, and she assured me she was cool with how I felt. In looking back, I think this was a bit more of an attempt to get me in the store so I might change my mind, nevertheless off to Shane Company in Seattle we went.

When we got to the store, Brenda walked right in and headed to the counter, and immediately engaged a clerk to look at rings. She had no clue that I stopped at the entrance and could not cross the threshold. As a police officer, I never felt true fear until that very moment. I just knew if I walked into the store, I would be dead before I could exit.

Brenda was completely unaware I wasn't standing next to her as she was consumed with the clerk and pointing out rings she wanted to look at and was even speaking to me as if I was standing next to her. Suddenly she realized something was missing; me. When she finally came up for air, she looked up to see me still standing at the front door. "What are you doing?" she asked and motioned me to come to look. At this point, sweat was rolling down my face, and I stuttered, "I...I...can't do this!" The look on her face was not sadness but pure anger!

As soon as the clerk saw me, he very gently removed the rings Brenda selected and put them back in the case. Something told me the clerk had seen this play out before. She began marching directly at me and said, "I can't believe you embarrassed me like that." I reminded her I had already told her I was not ready for this, but that statement didn't settle too well with her. She answered in a sharp tone, "That's right, you did, didn't you?" Every guy who is reading this right now knows exactly what the voice inflections are with that statement. So with that, I figured I needed to catch a bus, but she assured me she would take me home. She did, but without a word, she drove back to Tacoma, and she took me directly home. As soon as I got out of the car and before I could fully close the door, she drove off.

I know I have digressed a great deal, but this incident was truly the beginning of the end of this relationship needed to set up the actual end. Unbeknownst to me, Terri had a prank up her sleeve, which caused the true end of this relationship.

On Dock Street in Tacoma, there is a place called Dock Street Landing. A great watering hole and a fun pub. My squad decided to have a squad party there in a couple of days, so I told my roommates to stop in because given there were going to be a number of single guys, and I was sure my buddies would all love to meet them as well. I also told Brenda and let her know I wanted to go, and she said she wanted to go as well. We agreed she would drive. She picked me up in her Mercedes 450SL, and being it was summer, it was fun to run around with the top down.

Brenda picked me up on the day of the party, and when she did, she asked if my roommates were coming, and honestly, I didn't know, so that's what I told her. When we got there, there were a number of guys, and we began engaging all of them in banter and fun conversation. After being there for about 30 minutes Terri and Donelle showed up. When they walked in, the place went silent, and all eyes were riveted on the girls.

There was no doubt they were dressed to meet guys, dressed similarly but opposite at the same time. Let me explain. Terri was wearing a white leather miniskirt with white fishnet stockings. She had on a white leather short jacket, and you could see a hint of a red lacy bra peeking out at the opening of the jacket. Donelle was wearing a black leather miniskirt, black fishnet stockings, and a black, short leather jacket with the hint of a blue lacy bra. They looked exceptionally hot! I introduced my roomies to the now drooling squad and barely got their names out when guys were grabbing chairs to have them sit next to them. Terri ignored the pleas to come sit next to one of my friends but elected to walk directly toward me. I noticed, even though she was walking in my direction, she was not actually looking at me as much as she was looking at Brenda, who was sitting on my right. At this point, if looks could kill, both of them would be dead. Terri walked up to my left side. As she turned around, she deliberately bent, so her butt was accentuated toward Brenda. This placed her head to my right and between Brenda and me. I kind of knew what she was attempting to do but had no clue what she was about to go as far as she did. She placed her left arm around my shoulders, grabbed my chin with her right hand.

I was thinking she was going to tell a secret, but that wasn't quite it. She stuck her tongue into my right ear and said in a sultry voice and just loud enough for Brenda to hear, "Last night was wonderful."

Keep in mind, Terri was creating a scene that these horny cops were all dying to experience, so they were quite focused on what Terri was doing. Plus, Donelle had this big grin on her face, so I do believe she knew exactly what Terri was up to.

When Brenda heard what Terri said, she jumped up and screamed at me. "I fucking knew it, you asshole!" The place went silent – oh crap! Enzo's in major trouble! When Brenda pushed her chair away from the table, it fell backward, and she stumbled over it as she stormed out of the bar screaming obscenities at Terri and me. Brenda got in the car and was burning rubber through the parking lot as she left. Obviously, that ended the relationship right then and there.

Terri, at this point, had this extremely satisfied look on her face and was quite pleased with what she had just accomplished. The looks on the faces of the cops were priceless, and I think Terri was pleased with that result as well. I told Terri she could not go home with any of the cops, given I needed a ride. She didn't care. She came to do what she did and succeeded.

Most of the guys there were disappointed as Terri was no longer available and couldn't understand why we were both laughing about what happened. Admittedly, I was disappointed. I wasn't going to get laid on a regular basis, but man, that relationship had become way too much work. It was getting to be over the top with unjustified jealousy on Brenda's part. It was time to put it all behind me. Not exactly how I had my day planned but, quite frankly, I didn't care.

Moving On

The girls eventually moved out. Terri bought her own place, and Donelle was working in Olympia, so she moved there to be closer to work. I truly do miss the girls. In our short time together, we had some fun, and I think of them often.

Bad Dog

Don't you love pets? Me too. I'm a big dog guy. One of my pleasures is coming home and being greeted by my dog. It just seemed like yesterday that my wonderful Rhodesian ridgeback had left this earth, and I truly miss her and miss that greeting I'd get when I walked through the door. I'm not so big on cats, but I do get the connection people may have toward them. With that in mind, I'm going to embark on a tale that has nothing to do with the love of one's pet, but it does have to do with a couple of dogs.

My partner and I were on routine patrol when we observed a guy we knew was wanted for dealing cocaine. I'll call our suspect 'Augie Doggie.' We knew of an outstanding felony warrant, but by the looks of where he was sitting, we had to believe Augie did not know. There he was, sitting on the front porch of 2331 South Sheridan without a care in the world. As we drove up closer, Al called out to Augie, saying, "How you doing, Augie?"

Augie made no attempt to leave or run away, but he did respond with the usual vernacular of every other jerk out there of "fuck you;" you know that limited vocabulary response when you can't think of anything witty or intelligent to say. My partner was driving the prowl car and said we needed to go get Augie. I never like jumping out of the car, so I wasn't keen on that at all. I told him we needed to wait for another unit to cover the back of the property. I don't think Al's hearing was as sharp as it should have been that day because he got out and began walking toward Augie. All I could think was, *aw man, are you kidding me?* I got out of the car as well. I mean, at this point, there was nothing else I could do. As soon as we exited the car, I advised dispatch where we were and who we were contacting.

The walkway to the front porch, where Augie was sitting, was about 20–25 feet long. That was just enough for Augie to figure out what was up. He knew being contacted by police was just not in his best interest. He immediately bolted to the right side of the house (as we were facing it). My partner began to chase, and I radioed in, saying we were in a foot pursuit.

As Augie ran to the right, he went through a chain-link fence gate leading to the backyard. My partner was on Augie's heels, and I was a few steps behind. As he ran through the gate, he went to the back of the house and ran along the backside of the structure. When Augie got to the middle of the back wall, there was a door that looked as if it was access to the crawl space or basement. Augie opened the door and yelled, "Sic 'em!"

Damn it, I thought. That was not what I wanted to hear. I knew a lot of the drug dealers in this area, known as The Hilltop, trained pit-bull dogs for illegal fighting.

Both my partner and Augie ran past the door, but my few steps behind put me in a tough situation. It was just enough to see not one but two pit-bull dogs coming out from under the home. This is what I expected, but I had hoped they maybe were training Pekinese. Nope.

One was a tan color, and the other was black and white. As they exited, the dogs were snarling, so I drew my weapon. I knew if I began to run, the dogs would immediately attack. By facing them and slowly walking backward, I could have my gun trained on them as they were assessing me, plus there was no way I'd be able to outrun these two animals. As I squared off on the dogs, I pointed my weapon at them and began saying things like, "Bad dog, sit, stay," and so on. I figured I had nothing to lose by using any 'doggie talk' I could think of. As I was doing that, I was slowly backing up toward a gate that was just around the corner of the left side of the house. I figured if I could just hold them off long enough, I might just be able to get through the gate before they decided to attack. I knew what was coming but wasn't sure exactly when they would decide I was a viable target and take the bite.

As for my partner, I had no idea what was going on with him, given I had my own problems right now. Sorry, but my partner was on his own there. That's what he got for not waiting for backup.

As I slowly backed up and got closer to the gate, the tan dog must have realized my great escape was close, so he decided to come after me. My gun was pointed directly at the dog, and the dog grabbed my grip on my weapon, chomping down on my right hand and part of my left.

My reason for waiting so long was because I really didn't want to shoot the dogs (they were only doing what the owner trained them to do), but now I had little choice, so I had to take action to get this mutt off my hands. Once he latched onto me, I lifted the dog off the ground using the leverage of my weapon (Glock Mod 21 -- .45 cal) and turned my gun into the belly of the dog. At that, I fired until the dog let go. It took six rounds going through the dog's abdomen before it dropped to the ground. This dog was not going to let go no matter how painful it was getting for him.

While dealing with the tan dog, I lost track of the black and white. When I turned around to go out the gate that was now near me, the other dog was standing between me and that gate as if to say, "You aren't leaving yet." The dog was snarling and looked like it was about to go for the bite. I saw this show before, so I was not about to wait this time.

I pointed my weapon at the dog, and I fired two shots into its butt as I said, "Fuck you!" I know the dog didn't understand me, but I just had to say that. Two rounds in the ass were just enough for him. Maybe because he saw what happened to his partner, and the two rounds in the ass were plenty for him.

While this was all going on, my sergeant had arrived and was on the opposite side of the house when I was firing at the dogs. During all this interaction with the dogs, I had no idea who was there or who was not.

When he heard me fire the six rounds, he thought I was getting shot and called out a "shots fired, possible officer down!" This kind of call gets everyone rolling at Mach speed to that location of the callout. I mean Pierce County deputies, City of Fircrest, City of Ruston, State Patrol, and of course, the entire Tacoma PD—all arrived. I heard sirens coming from everywhere. I wasn't listening to my radio, so I had no idea where the sirens were headed.

After the first six rounds, there was a delay, and then the sergeant heard the next two shots I fired, to which he assumed I was now returning fire. As far as he was concerned, this was getting uglier by the moment, and we had a gun battle going on.

Then I walked out to the front of the house with blood all over me, and that clinched what he had suspected. There was no doubt I had been shot, and only by the grace of God did I survive. I could see cops and cars everywhere, and once I found out what he was going through, I felt sorry for him. He must have been going through some serious stress during all that. I mean, I knew what was going on, but he did not. He assumed the worse, and I was glad he did.

When I got out to the front of the home, Augie's brother, a very large man, came at me saying, "You killed my dogs! You killed my dogs!" He was extremely angry, but I was in no mood to play footsie with this guy.

When he got too close, I brought my gun up to his head and said, "Take one more fucking step, and I'll kill you too!"

He must have seen the seriousness in my face because he immediately stopped, threw his hands in the air, and as he backed up, he said, "We cool, white boy, we cool." I don't know if I would have been justified, so I was glad he backed off. Would I have shot him? Probably.

As I looked around, I could see many of the officers who responded were a bit shocked that I was standing. I suppose they all expected me to have bullet holes in me and looking like Swiss cheese. I was happy to disappoint them. Nevertheless, I wondered if anyone had called for medical aid, given my right hand was a bit mangled and my left hand was also damaged. Nope, no one had, even after I came out and was standing there bleeding all over the ground. So I pulled out my radio and asked for medical aid to show up. Once I did that, my sergeant came over and said, "Man, I'm sorry. I should have done that." *Ah, ya think?*

I told him, "No worries."

I looked at the street, and given the number of police cars there, I figured I was going to have to walk down the street a block or so to meet the responding ambulance. So this was where the parking became a problem. But my good buddy, Mike, was driving medic unit, and a little thing like a bunch of cop cars was not going to stop him. Mike took the paramedic unit up onto the sidewalk and made quick order of getting to me instead of me getting to him. When Mike arrived, he said, "You need a ride, sailor?" Man, I just had to laugh at that. I jumped in the back of the unit, and away we went.

Just as I was leaving, a crowd began forming in the area, and as usual, in these things, misinformation was rampant. A rumor began that I had shot an unarmed man. I was also told later that when the paramedic unit left with me, some actually thought the so-called 'unarmed man' was in that unit. Thankfully that was all dispelled quickly, and once people realized it was a couple of dogs, no one seemed to care any longer.

While I was in the paramedic unit vehicle, I was surprised that my hand did not hurt. Though my hand, especially my right hand, was gouged heavily, there was no pain. How could that be? I was thankful for that but not sure of what that meant. Given I am right-handed, I was a little concerned, as well but expected to have a full recovery. That said, I had no feeling, so this could be something quite serious.

Once I got to the hospital, my partner showed up. I asked him to contact my fiancée, Tina. I found out after the fact, but she didn't believe him at first when he told her I had been injured and was in the hospital. The reason was, my partner is a jokester, and she just thought he was being his normal self. After some time, she realized he was not joking this time and made her way to St Joseph's Hospital.

Once she got there, she was escorted to my room and saw me joking with other officers and hospital staff, mostly the nurses. I still did not feel any pain, and even though one might think that's cool, it bothered me as I was hoping all my receptors and nerves weren't damaged beyond repair. No feeling in my right hand could be a serious danger, such as gun retention. Hard to be a cop without being able to hold on to a gun.

When Tina arrived, the doctor was there examining my right hand. Tina is not shy when it comes to blood, given she is a dental hygienist, so that sort of stuff was no big deal for her. She immediately asked the doctor if she could view what he was doing. I think the doctor, at first, was going to say no, but when he looked up at her, he was very agreeable. I don't know if I have said this yet, but Tina is quite adorable, so the doc was very willing to have her sit beside him. Hey doc, eat your heart out.

He showed her all the tendons and whatever else was in there as he lifted the skin. I had no clue what they were talking about, but they both were speaking the same language. By the way, I don't get jealous because I have never had a reason to be with her. These two were having a great conversation, and given the topic was scientific, and I didn't get it, there was no reason for me to interject anything and look stupid.

After a while, the doctor decided to send me off to surgery. Anyone who's been in a hospital when you have to go off to surgery and because it's not life-threatening, it might take a while. I fell into that category. So I had to wait; no worries, I was in no big rush.

While I was waiting, Tina decided this was a good time to go have a smoke. In those days, she smoked, so off she went outside. Thankfully, she gave up that habit.

Let me digress for a moment. Earlier, when I first arrived at the hospital, I was told that I should be prepared for a contract out on me. The dogs I shot were prizefighters, and Augies's bother was none too happy with me. Though he backed off to keep from getting killed, he wanted some revenge for losing his moneymakers. When I got that information, I was fairly aloof about it; basically, it was neither a big deal nor anything I couldn't handle. But at the same time, it was not something I wanted Tina to know about.

Okay, back to Tina going out for a smoke. When she exited the room, I yelled out to her to come right back. I still was not interested in telling her about the possible contract, but I surely did not want her to go out to the street alone. I told her she needed to be escorted by an officer for her safety. I told her there might be some gang activity because of what happened, but I think she kind of figured it out anyway. Nothing ever came of the contact, but as we all know in law enforcement, once you let your guard down is when bad stuff will come and bite you in the ass or hand, as it were.

Shortly after her return, I was contacted by a nurse and told I'd be headed into surgery. I told Tina I'd call her or have someone else call her when I was ready to be picked up. She left when I got wheeled off to a kind of staging area. I was hooked up to a number of monitors along with the one that went ding (Monty Python, *The Meaning of Life*).

Let's digress again for just a moment or two. In those days, I was doing a great deal of not just weight lifting but also a great deal of bicycling. With all this aerobic exercise, I learned how to manipulate my heart rate. I could adjust my heart rate low if I needed to sleep better. A lot of people who do a great deal of aerobic exercise can do the same.

After getting all hooked up to these machines, I was left alone in the room to wait. So I thought I'd just sit back and relax; no worries. I'll just wait for my turn and get out of here when they were done. After a few moments, one of the machines began to blast a high shrill sound, almost like a siren. As quickly as that happened, the nurse who dropped me off in the room came running in. When she saw me just sitting there, she looked at the machine, and it said 42. As I moved about, it went up to 48, and the sound stopped. "Are you okay?" she asked. I really didn't understand her concern because I was just fine, and I told her that. She left, and that was that.

At this point, I really didn't know what was up, but when the machine went off again at 42, I realized that it was the heart monitor, given the sound had her running once again. This time she didn't have the concern on her face as the first time. She had more of a 'what the hell?' look. She asked me if I did a lot of aerobic-type activity, and I told her about my cycling activities. Her facial expression then went to 'aw, that's it!' look. She left again after the machine stopped beeping.

Okay, so I'm a bit of a jerk from time to time, and this was one of those times. On the first two responses I got from her, when the alarm went off, I wasn't trying to get the machine to react. But all of a sudden, there was a third time! Yeah, it was all me this time. I just wanted to see how low I could get my heart rate down. Within seconds of my attempt, it dropped, not to 42 but to 36 very quickly. The machine seemed to scream even louder. The nurse walked in this time, gave me a scowl, walked over to the machine, and shut it off. As she was walking out of the room, she looked at me and said, "We're done with this, right?" in a very emphatic way.

She was a bit irked with me, so I really didn't want to piss off the woman who would be assisting my surgeon, so I, very meekly, said, "Okay."

The surgery went well. There was a positive side to this entire incident. Given my right hand was the most injured and I am right-handed, I could not hold a gun or even a pen to write reports, so I was forced to go on OJI time off until released by a doctor to return to work.

Tacoma PD used to have the 'Darigold Award.' If you don't know what Darigold is, it's a large dairy company located in Seattle. To get the award, one must milk the injury one gets on duty. I think I might be in the top ten.

So, how long did I 'milk' it? Rehab took a long time, about three months. That was just enough time for Tina and me to plan a trip to Disneyland. One side of me felt like I was cheating, but another side said, "I don't care." We had a great time. One of the things that happened at Disneyland was that I was denied to go on the rides due to this crazy apparatus built for my hand. The physical therapists, who I think are frustrated engineers, made this odd-looking thing that had a bridge on the top where rubber bands were attached, which led to my fingers for exercise therapy. So to get on the rides, I took this odd-looking thing off and put it in the rental car. My mistake was I put it on the dashboard. It was a bit warm outside and even hotter in the car. When we got back to the car, the plastic apparatus had melted all over the dash. Thankfully the melted finger bridge lifted off the dash in one entire piece.

FYI: feeling in my right hand returned shortly after my surgery. It was good to feel some pain as I knew that had to be the healing process.

As for Augie, he was released from jail not too long after he was booked on the drug warrant, which is typical in our ultra-liberal area of Western Washington.

Nevertheless, that did not turn out to be a benefit for him. It seemed Augie was bragging about how he sic the dogs on me and was trying to make himself out to be a big man on the drug scene. His attitude was not sitting well with the major players in the Tacoma drug world. Augie had to get himself an old discarded TPD bulletproof vest because he was being threatened by those in charge that if he didn't shut up, it might result in his demise. Augie's not the brightest bulb in the chandelier because he was acting out the part of being the big tough guy. That was why he acquired a bulletproof vest. One problem, the vest only protects the upper body, and if you are going to use it because you are scared for your life, maybe you shouldn't tell everyone you are wearing it.

So the real kingpins decided to show him who were the real bosses. One night Augie was lured to go to a certain phone booth to get a call about him moving up the line of drug dealers. It was a setup. They told him through a messenger they wanted to use the phone booth just in case his home phone (cell phones weren't the thing yet) was being tapped. He fell for it; what an idiot.

While in the booth, the big guys did a drive-by shooting. Knowing he had a bulletproof vest on, they shot up his legs and lower torso. Augie survived and, from what I understand, learned to keep his mouth shut from then on. Message sent, message received.

One last comment about Augie. Years later, Augie was charged with a rape case of a teenage girl. One of my co-workers, who was on the case, went to the trial. He told me he wished I could have been there because the judge actually mentioned what happened to me at the sentencing hearing. When Augie was before Judge Tanner, he told the judge he had found Jesus, and now Jesus was a part of his life and hoped the judge would take that into consideration. The judge looked at him and asked, "Did you find Jesus while you were raping this girl? Did you find Jesus when you sic those dogs on that police officer?" Tanner also mentioned other cases, but I was shocked that Judge Tanner knew anything about my case. That was so cool. It gave me a newfound respect for Judge Tanner. I had always thought Judge Tanner wasn't all that cop-friendly, but given this hearing, I will have to admit I was wrong.

Augie got 25 years in federal prison (it would seem the rape occurred on federal property). My understanding is federal prisons are not so inclined to give early outs like state prisons, especially Washington State Prisons. Washington State is notorious for letting people out early.

So to Augie I say, I hope you like your new boyfriend in Englewood.

I am such a sucker for happy endings.

Fire!

During one of my injuries, I was assigned to work at the dispatch center. I got this injury off duty and banged up my knee, so the department was trying to help me out and gave me a desk assignment. That way, I didn't have to burn sick leave. It was not the most common thing to do, but it was a win-win for both the dispatchers and me. Dispatchers are truly overworked, so I could do some good to relieve the burden on them, and I saved sick leave time as well as learned what they go through on a daily basis.

I was aware that dispatchers took tons of calls that the field officers never see or even hear about, so I developed a newfound respect for them. While I was there for the two months of my rehab, I discovered the number of reports they took over the phone. Literally, hundreds of reports the field officer never knew existed were handled by the dispatch center. These reports were mostly mundane and very routine, mostly being insurance claim reports. This allowed the officer to be free to handle emergencies. Nevertheless, these reports still needed to be written; thus, the dispatcher would write a quick line or two, and the reportee would be happy.

So what was I doing there? There were those calls that were routed to me which required an officer to write. It was very boring, to say the least. The reports were yawners, and I would ask the routine investigative questions and decide if an officer needed to be sent. If no officer needed, then I would bang out a couple of lines, and that was it. If I decided it needed more attention, basically eyes on the ground to see and give me a bit more detail, I would let the dispatcher know to send a car, but for the most part, I took the call and wrote the report. So what makes this experience worthy of adding it to my tales? There was one specific call that has stuck in my memory, and after you read it, I think it may be burned in yours as well. This is one of those which fit into the category of 'you just can't make this up.'

Early one morning, the dispatch center was a bit slow, so I was relaxing as I waited for my first call. It took about an hour, and I was getting quite bored. Then the call came in. The call I was sent started out differently because one of the dispatchers actually contacted me, saying I needed to take this call. It was odd to be personally contacted because they never alerted me of a call. Usually, they just highlighted the call on the computer, and I would get an alert tone. Plus, there were no details on the call. Usually, there was some short narrative, but not this time. It just said the female requested contact with a police officer. Okay, maybe she just didn't give the dispatcher much information. I should have had a hint because as I look back now, I remember the dispatcher had a bit of a twinkle in her eye and a big smile. Here I thought she was just flirting with me.

I made the phone call and asked for the caller, who I will call Hestia. If you don't know who Hestia is, check your Greek mythology, but something tells me you'll figure it out as you read this tale. She answered the phone and did identify herself as the one who made the original call. I asked her how I could be of assistance, to which she replied, "My pussy is burning." Of course, I was assuming I heard her wrong, so I asked her to repeat what she said. She stated, with serious conviction and very emphatic, "My pussy is on fire, my pussy is on fire!"

Okay, I thought. She couldn't mean what I was assuming right then, so I asked her, "Do you mean your cat?"

"No, damn it, my vagina is burning!" was her answer. I was somewhat surprised but also not if you know what I mean. Her response was so strange the only thing I could think of was to ask her how she could be talking to me if she had a part of her body in flames. She didn't know, but she said she could see the flames right now. So the obvious solution was to get the fire department on their way, but when I told her I'd be sending the firefighters, she said, "They won't come out anymore." Big surprise, right?

So about this time, I thought these dispatchers gave me this call just to mess with me, so why not have a bit of fun with it. It was painfully (pun intended) obvious this woman was not all there, lights were on, but they were very dim. I thought I'd strike up a conversation with her; here was our dialog.

Me: "How do you think the fire started?"

Hestia: "My ex-husband started it."

Me: "Well, how did he do that?"

Hestia: "I'm not sure because I was asleep when he started it."

Me: "How can we reach your ex-husband?"

Hestia: "You can't."

Me: "Why not?"

Hestia: "He's in prison."

Me: "So you are telling me he broke out of prison last night to light your pussy on fire and broke back into prison?"

Hestia: "Yes."

Me: "You are also telling me you don't know how this fire started because you were asleep, so how do you know your ex was the one who did it?"

Hestia: "Because I saw him."

Me: "You aren't making sense; you said you were asleep, so how could you have seen him?"

Hestia: "I just did."

Me: "Okay, let's forget about your husband right now. Where are you?"

Hestia: "At home."

Me: "I know that, but where in the house are you?"

Hestia: "I'm outside working in the yard."

Me: "So your pussy is on fire, but you are working outside. Isn't that painful?"

Hestia: "Yes, it is, but my yard work won't get done unless I do it."

Me: "I can appreciate that but for now, let's stop the yard work and concentrate on getting the fire out, shall we?"

Hestia: "Okay."

Me: "Go into the house for me, okay?"

Hestia: "Okay, but I don't know how that will help."

Me: "You'll see."

I could then hear a door open and the screen door slam.

Me: "Are you inside the house?"

Hestia: "Yes, I am."

Me: "Go to the nearest bathroom with a tub, please."

A few seconds went by.

Hestia: "Okay, I'm in the bathroom."

Me: "Hestia, would you please fill the tub up with cold water, please? No hot water."

Hestia: "Okay."

I could then hear the water running. After about a few minutes, the sound of the water stopped.

Me: "Is the tub full?"

Hestia: "Yes, it is."

Me: "Get in."

Hestia: "Should I get undressed?"

Me: "No, no, no! There is no time to waste; get in the tub right now!"

I could then hear splashing noises.

Hestia: "Oh my God, that feels so good. Oh, thank you, thank you. The fires out, and I feel wonderful."

Me: "You're welcome." And I hung up, feeling proud of soothing a hot pussy.

At that point, laughter erupted throughout the dispatch center. I stood and bowed and then gave all of them the 'finger.'

"Is This a Movie?"

Even though my partner got hurt in this incident, I actually felt sorry for the young lady who hit us. She felt her entire world just collapsed before her. I totally get it.

This all started with a call to Titlow Beach. For a detailed description of Titlow Beach Park, see the section titled 'Russians.' The call was a fight in the local bar located there, and it seemed it was getting out of hand. We were about 20–25 blocks away, so we flipped on the lights and siren and began our priority response. My partner was driving, and as we approached 6th Ave and Jackson, he slowed, which was something we always did to make sure everyone was stopped. Clearing the intersection and still with the emergency equipment activated, we entered the intersection. We had no idea what was about to happen.

We got about halfway through when in my left peripheral, I saw a yellow object coming at us at a fairly high rate of speed. It was a VW Bug. I don't know why the driver didn't hear us. Nevertheless, the driver of the Bug must have been distracted because it not only ignored the siren but all the stopped cars a well. As I saw the car come at us, I could only imagine the driver has to be deaf and maybe even blind. I mean, this Bug was scooting past all the obvious warnings as it headed into the intersection. I had only a moment to warn my partner we were about to get hit. I probably didn't need to tell him because if my memory is correct, I think I heard a 'mother fucker!' come out of his mouth.

Before I go into the details of what happened after being struck, you should know that we were driving a Ford LTD. Why is that important? Because it was truly the worse car ever purchased for police work. It was way too light and had pathetic back seat space for prisoner transport. Another issue was at every high-speed pursuit or response; the brakes would be smoking (literally) by the time we got to the call. Overall, it was a POS (Piece Of Shit).

Now with that all said, let's get to the meat of this incident.

Have you ever heard when something like this happens, it seems all time slows down? Guess what? It's true. Or at least it seems that way. It wasn't like it slowed, so my speech or thoughts were guttural slurs you hear in some movies. Not that at all. Maybe my mind was working faster, and that made all the action around me seem slower. I don't know.

I say all that because I had time to think about drunk drivers—how they come out of accidents unscathed. Why? Because they are completely relaxed. I know that has everything to do with their state of intoxication, but nevertheless, it works. So, thinking all that, I decided to relax as best I could. Then it happened – we got hit just behind the driver's door. With how light the car was and the force we were hit, the patrol car began to slide sideways across the intersection. As the car slid, I looked at my partner and said, "Hey, this is just like Disney Land!" I was just trying to do what I needed to do to relax, and for the most part, it worked. Looking at my partner, I noticed his face was white, and he had a death grip on the steering wheel.

I was about to tell him to relax when the car wheel hit the curb. It jolted the car, and suddenly the car began a roll up onto its right side. As I watched the pavement come toward my door, I looked at my partner, who was now in the air above me, and I said, "I don't think I like this part of the ride."

I honestly thought the car was about to roll completely over, but it did not—what a relief. I felt we dodged a 'bullet.' if you will. The car teetered at this point for a few seconds, with the driver's side up, and then fell back to the ground, jolting my partner very hard. When we landed, I looked at my partner and asked if he was okay. He did not answer right away, so I asked again. He slowly looked toward me and said, "Yeah, I think so." I told him I was going to check on the other driver, and he agreed that was a good idea.

Just as I was about to get out of the car, this citizen, who appeared from the several cars that had stopped for us, drove up alongside us and asked the stupidest question I've ever heard. "Is this for real, or are you guys making a movie?"

I tilted my head and asked, "Do you see any cameras?"

"Ah, no," he said.

Trying to stay as polite as the situation called for, I said, "Very good, now get the fuck out of the intersection!"

After making sure that my partner was okay, I went to check on the other driver. She could not have been a day over 18, and needless to say, she was sobbing a great deal. I asked if she needed medical aid, but all she did was cry. I told her she had to talk to me because I was worried about her. She turned her red and puffy face toward me and said, "I hit a police car!"

"Darling, it doesn't matter as long as you are okay," I told her. She nodded her head and said she was fine. I could see her car was not operational, the entire front end was smashed, and it appeared her front axle was broken.

Once I knew she was okay, I called out the incident to dispatch and advised a sergeant. When I began to walk back to the patrol car, I noticed the amount of damage to our car. The entire rear passenger door on the driver's side was destroyed. I thought, *man, did we get hit hard or what*. I had no clue a Bug could do this much damage, or maybe it was the construction of the LTD.

One of the other things I noticed was my partner. He was not looking so good. By the time I got to him, he was holding his head and looked like he just got hit by a car (pun intended). I didn't like what I saw, so I told dispatch that we needed medical aid for my partner. He took the brunt of the impact. We were hit on the driver's side, and when the car dropped, it hit the ground; he took that impact as well. It was no wonder he was not feeling so good. By the time medical aid showed up, which was fairly quick, he was lying on the sidewalk next to the car.

As soon as I called out that my partner needed help, it sparked a number of sirens from police cars who were in the area of the accident. Within 30 seconds, we had three other patrol cars on the scene. They took control of the traffic so I could stay with my partner. It seemed in very short order, and we also had an ambulance on the scene. The paramedics took one look at my partner and quickly scooped him up on the gurney, and off to Tacoma General Hospital they went.

Given I was involved in the accident, another unit had to write the accident report, so I gave my side (what I saw and experienced). I also collected information on witnesses and turned over the info to the investigating officers.

I was given a ride to the station by my sergeant. After finishing my report, I was ordered to take the rest of the day off. Hey, that worked for me.

I stopped by the hospital on my way home to see my partner. He seemed to be just fine. When I got to his room, I noticed two very cute nurses caring for him. He looked good and couldn't wipe that grin off his face either. He told me he still felt a bit woozy. I had the feeling he said that just loud enough for the nurses in the room and not so much for me to hear. No worries, man, you deserved a bit of coddling, so enjoy it while you can.

After my short visit, I left, and on the way home, I felt pretty good about myself. I know my partner took the biggest hit at that accident, but it's not like I wasn't jostled as well. I just kind of figured my workout was coming back to me in a way that helped me get through the impact. I'd like to think so.

Titlow Beach

Titlow Beach Park is a pleasant place to go for family picnics and such. For the size of the park, there is plenty of parking and a stellar view of Puget Sound, along with the Narrows Bridge. On a clear day, it is just a pleasant place to visit. Surrounding Titlow Beach is an affluent neighborhood, and the residents in that area are not at all pretentious. They are police friendly, and for the most part, the area is one of the quieter areas of Tacoma. There is, though, a Tavern near the water, which is more of a neighborhood gathering place and generates very limited trouble.

Calls to the park and surrounding area are far and few between, so getting this call was a bit of a surprise. The call came out at about 2:00 a.m. on a warm summer night in 2003. Dispatch broadcasted citizens were saying there was a large group of people fighting in the parking lot near the tavern. I get someone on one fights from time to time but rarely a 'large group;' basically, a rumble, if you will, and it just didn't seem quite right. Nevertheless, I headed in that direction.

Titlow Beach Park is at the bottom of a very long hill on 6th Avenue in Tacoma. When the call came out, I was at the top of the hill, so I told dispatch I would be headed to the area and would observe to see what was going on.

Near the parking lot where the fight was allegedly happening was a public swimming pool, which had a locker room building. The building was a cinderblock construction and quite large, so it made it easy to pull my car behind the building and observe the parking lot without being detected. Where I was observing from were very large trees, and I could easily conceal myself or use them for cover if need be.

I shut off my lights, moved in slowly, and parked behind the locker room building. As I moved into position, I rolled down my windows to hear what I could hear, but I heard nothing. Anyone who knows anything about a large fight, that large, one would be able to hear feet scoffing and people yelling. There was nothing.

When I got into position, I could clearly see the lot, and there was no one there except two cars and three guys who looked like they were talking. The cars were small, one white and one black. That explained why I didn't hear anything but didn't explain the reason for the call. Why would multiple citizens call in a 'rumble' type fight when it appeared nothing was going on? To get the answer, I decided to drive the rest of the way into the park and contact the men in the lot. As I approached, I let dispatch know there was no fight and I would be making contact with the three men in the parking lot for further investigation.

After pulling into the lot, I got out and walked up to the three men who were all standing next to the black car, an early 80s Mitsubishi Eclipse (the car description becomes important later in this tale). All three were white males, one who was about 6'5", at least. He looked taller and towered over my 5'10" height. He ended up becoming the spokesman for the three, who I will name Igor. I asked if I could speak to them, and Igor immediately said, "F**k you, pig," in a heavy Russian or Ukrainian accent. His remark was followed by chuckles from his two pals, who I named and called Heckle and Jeckle. When I called them that, all three had a quizzical look on their faces, so it gave me a slight chuckle inside. Just a quick note if you don't know who Heckle and Jeckle are, they are a post-World War II cartoon of two misfit magpies. Okay, I've digressed enough.

I looked at Igor and asked from where the comment, "F***k you, pig," came from. I had hardly said anything to him, and he decided to be a prick to me. I always loved when people decide how contact was going to go, friendly or like, in this case, not so friendly. Igor went on to tell me I had no right to talk to him and that "Amereeka sucks!" He went off on a tirade about me making an 'unlawful contact' and some other crap he may have seen on TV. I mostly ignored his ignorance and kept trying to investigate the alleged fight. The answers I received were a spew of profanity, so I decided to just give up on the investigation, satisfied that if anything that happened was most likely just a small skirmish.

Prior to leaving and during the investigation, I told the three men to give me their IDs or drivers' license. I was shocked when they handed them to me without any argument. Was this the result of their past Soviet indoctrination and just used to this sort of thing in Russia? Well, then good for the Soviet Union; at least one good thing came out of that mess. After getting their names, addresses, and dates of birth, I left but warned the three this contact would come back to haunt them, and I was sure if they were in Moscow right now, this contact would have gone a terribly different way. As I got in the car, I was barraged with their favorite four-letter F word, and the word wasn't 'free.'

As I drove out of the lot, a black male in his early 20s ran past my car toward my three Soviet rejects. I assumed he may be one of the vodka sippers' friends and was just waiting for me to leave, so I just continued on. You know the routine. Friends asking their buddies about the contact and how he heard them talk to the cop, remarking, "That was so cool, dude." I think you got the picture.

I drove off and was gone out of the lot for 15 minutes or so when I was advised by dispatch that there was another report of a large crowd fighting in the parking lot. *Really*? I thought. I told dispatch I would head down to the beach and check it out and advise.

This time I dispensed with the stealthy tactics and headed to the parking lot. I figured if something was actually happening, I always had the reverse to get out of there. As I got closer to the lot, I could see, once again, there was nothing, and even my jerk Iron Curtain friends had also departed. I told dispatch what I had found, or lack thereof, as it were, and any other units could cancel. At the same time, I surmised there must be something to these calls. I mean, really, why would someone call this in twice.

As I walked around the parking lot, looking for any evidence of a fight, a citizen contacted me. He walked up to me holding a camera; he asked me if I wanted to see the video he recorded. *Okay*, I thought, *I'll humor you if you want me to watch a video*. What he had was the entire contact I made with Igor and the magpies. As I watched the video of me making contact, the citizen stated he started filming because he was hoping for some "Rodney King stuff" and was disappointed he only got this. Really, dude? The video showed me coming in, making contact, and leaving. Boring, right? Then it also showed the young black male running past me – all stuff I was aware of. Ho-hum.

What I did not see was after the young black male, who I will name 'Rocky,' ran past me, and he wasn't contacting a friend but instead a nemesis, or at least it looked that way to me. Rocky ran right up to Igor and began to beat the living Russian crap out of him. Then, seemingly out of nowhere, the parking lot filled with people attacking the three Russians. This looked like it was a reenactment of the Russo-Japanese War. Just a reference note here, the Russo-Japanese war was the war the Russians got their butts kicked by the Japanese. See, not only is this a book about my tales but a history lesson as well. Advice to students; don't cite this on any term paper; it just won't go over very well with your professor/teacher.

Igor was getting beat so bad he fell to the pavement, but that didn't stop Rocky. Igor was just trying to get away and began belly-crawling on the pavement. Rocky finally got tired of beating on Igor, so he just turned around and walked away. When Igor realized Rocky was done with him, Igor got up and walked to the white car I told you about earlier. I could not see the entire white car but could see the left rear corner of it. Igor was at the trunk when it opened, and Igor reached into the trunk. Suddenly Igor showed back up into the video frame with a rifle.

He was holding the rifle at waist height, pointed at the crowd. Igor fired off two rounds, and people began to scatter in all directions. The reason Igor only fired two rounds was that his cheap knock-off AK47 jammed. He continued to walk through the parking lot to the far south edge, and I could see his arm movement trying to pull the slide back and forth to clear the jam this piece of crap rifle was experiencing. After about five pulls, Igor gave up, turned toward the camera, and then threw the rifle over his head into a hedge. That hedge was directly behind where I was standing while watching the video. I had the citizen pause the video and immediately turned around and then saw the brown wood stock of the weapon. I grabbed rubber gloves from my belt and put the rifle in the trunk of the prowl car.

There was more to the video, and I wanted to see if it looked like anyone got hit. At this point in the film, there wasn't anyone left in the lot, and everyone was running, but no one was holding a part of their body or any blood on the pavement. So much for Igor's aim. Igor dragged himself into the white car, and Heckle & Jeckle got into the black car. Then, both cars drove out of the lot.

I told the citizen we had to confiscate the video, and he was okay with that. I took his name down and address and told him it would be returned as soon as I could catch Igor and the magpies. I also called my sergeant to come down and look at the video.

The plot thickens. Earlier in the evening, I was aware of an armed robbery that occurred at a convenience store that was on 6th Avenue about 20–25 blocks from Titlow Beach. I thought it best to have the officers who took that call view the video as well. I wanted to see if these guys fit the description of their suspect(s).

After watching the video, the sergeant was a bit surprised by the fight he viewed, and the officers who took the robbery call said the Russians I contacted were a perfect match, along with the black car they were standing in front of when I contacted them. I gave the officers everything I found out about the trio, as well as what I got off of the state IDs, and the search was on. I so wanted so much to find these guys and hook them on the robbery charge.

Weeks had gone by, and I couldn't seem to find these guys anywhere. Even the addresses on their Washington State ID cards didn't pan out. It was like they just disappeared into the city, or maybe they just left, I didn't know.

During those weeks, my wife had ridden along with me, and when I told her about these jokers, she was excited to help track them down. My wife is a 'let's go get 'em' sort of person. I think she would have made a good cop. But as I stated, these guys were nowhere to be found. So my wife missed all the fun of taking these guys down. And given how Igor folded with Rocky's onslaught, I know my wife would have torn him apart.

All that said, we in law enforcement know that many times catching a bad guy is just dumb luck as well as many times stupidity of the crook. That's exactly where these guys, or at least where Igor fell into. Another one of those people where brilliance was not a part of his gene pool.

Approximately four weeks after the incident at Titlow Beach, I was dispatched to 6th & Pearl Streets for a traffic accident. When I got to the location, I recognized one of the cars — an early 80s black Mitsubishi Eclipse, the exact same car that the Three Stooges were at when I contacted them at the parking lot four weeks earlier. The car was unoccupied, and the driver was nowhere to be found. I also noticed the windshield on the passenger side was broken from the inside. It looked like what I had seen a hundred times before, head impact from not wearing a seatbelt. It looked like a major impact with the glass, so I just felt whoever hit it had not gone far before passing out or staggering somewhere.

Moments after I examined the car, the officers who took the robbery call four weeks ago arrived at the accident to help with traffic and crowd control. They recognized the description of the car, and I confirmed it was the car I told them about. I had a feeling one of those guys was here in the crowd, among the looky-loos or maybe nearby. I no sooner said that and then spotted Igor at the back of the crowd. I told one of the officers, and he asked if I was sure. There was no doubt, and as I started moving toward Igor, he must have seen the look in my eyes that I was going to take his dumb ass down. He tried to turn, but his noggin injury, which was an obvious sphere on his forehead, made him trip over his feet, and he landed hard on his head again. I actually broke out in loud laughter when he hit the sidewalk.

My pursuit was short, and handcuffing was relatively easy, all the while cursing at me. I told him he was under arrest and advised him of his rights.

That was followed by a profanity-laced "you have nothing on me" denial.

After putting Igor in the back of my car, I went back to the traffic accident. The other driver said Igor was not the driver, and the driver fled from the scene. Given Heckle and Jeckle were similar in the description, I couldn't quite figure out which one the witnesses were describing. I interviewed Igor, but he wasn't talking at all except for the F-bombs. I don't know where Igor learned English, but he should get his money back. Despite his poor grammar, he still had to go to the hospital. So that was where we went once I had the scene secured. The other officers waited for the tow truck and finished up the physical part of the call.

At the hospital, I cuffed Igor to the hospital bed, but when the doctor started studying the wound to get the glass chips out, Igor needed to be strapped down. Igor was screaming bloody murder and refused to keep his head still. This went on for some time, and I could see the doctor was getting very frustrated with Igor and was telling him to hold still, but Igor was having none of that. I ended up calling for the hospital security to bring wrist and ankle restraints. Once we got those on Igor, one of the security officers and I held him as best as we could as the medical staff continued to do what they needed to do. Because of Igor's childish acting out, the process was taking longer than originally expected. Watching Igor's responses to someone who was trying to help, I understood why Rocky was able to punish him as much as he did. Because Igor was a pussy!

The doctor let me know once the wound was finally prepped, he was going to put a couple of staples in to make sure it stayed closed. The doctor further told me it was going to be a bit painful for Igor, so we'd have to hold his head real tight. When the doctor put in the first staple, Igor went through the roof, then the second one went in, and Igor was screaming, "You f**king assholes!" That was the preverbal straw, and in a matter of five seconds or less, the staple gun went off 23 times. *Holy crap*, I thought. The security officer and I had such a tight grip on Igor he was going nowhere, but he screamed as I had never heard a person scream before. After creating a perfect Frankenstein scar, the doctor got up and asked his nurse to dress the wound, which she did. Inside I was having the best belly laugh of all time. The nurse had a look of horror and shock, and the security guard was equally shocked.

After all was done, I was walking Igor back to the car when the doctor contacted me and asked if he could talk to me. I told him I'd return after I put Igor in the car. Making sure Igor was secure, I went back to the ER. The doctor contacted me and apologized for his behavior. I told the doctor I had no idea what he was talking about and also said, "You know, I don't think I've ever had such a good time at a hospital like I did tonight." I left it at that and went out to transport Igor with the Frankenstein scar to jail.

What a lovely night it was.

Awards

In my time as a police officer, I was awarded the Lifeline Medal, the Service Medal, and the Medal of Valor. Interestingly enough, I was okay with getting the first two, but the Medal of Valor was a bit different.

A Medal of Valor is given to those who risk their lives, and traditionally, the officer is wounded in some way, usually by getting stabbed or shot. That is not why I got the Medal of Valor. Keep in mind a Medal of Valor is the most prestigious medal any officer can receive. It is not to be taken lightly or handed out without a careful inspection of the details leading to the award. I was honored that I was selected to receive the award, any officer would be, but I still had some reservations. I will explain in detail what lead to me being awarded this prestigious medal, but first, let's go through the details of the other two.

Lifeline Medal

This one is the easiest because of the story I told earlier in the chapter *Bad Dog*. Just to recap, when I was attacked by the two Pitbulls, there was much speculation that I would not be able to come back to work. My right hand was gnawed quite heavily, and given I was right-handed, the train of thought was I was done as a cop. I was even contacted by a couple of officers, asking me what I was planning on doing now that I was unable to return to the streets. The assumption was out there, and it seemed a foregone conclusion that my career was over. I half expected someone was going to ask me if I was headed back to forestry. Those questions truly upset me. I was not going anywhere.

Let me tell you something; those questions went in one ear and out the other. Rarely did I qualify them with an answer. There was no way I was planning on not being a cop. I loved forestry and still enjoyed being in the woods, but I liked being a cop a great deal more. Though I enjoyed my time off, it never entered my mind I wasn't going to be able to hold a gun or be behind the wheel of a patrol car.

All the expectations from others of a possible early retirement were what sparked being recommended and awarded the Lifeline Medal. It seemed the criterion for that award was when an officer might be forced to quit/retire due to the injuries sustained in the line of duty. Well, I fit that profile well, at least by those other than me.

I had no idea where the idea of me exiting law enforcement came from. I mean, nobody in the admin asked or even discussed how I felt about it or my expectations. I suppose someone might have talked to the doctor. Given this was an on-duty injury, the department might want to know some detail for manpower adjustments. I had no problem with that if that was what happened, but hey—you might want to talk to the guy with the mangled hands!

So under the guidelines of this medal, I fit the qualifications even though I was determined not to be a statistic and get back to work as soon as possible. When I was awarded the Lifeline Medal, I was happy to get it and proudly wore it as a triumphant display that I wasn't going to allow this injury to beat me, despite what others assumed.

To all departments out there, never underestimate your officers

Service Medal

My partner and I did a lot of things, but the one that had the biggest impact on us was Bicycle Patrol in Downtown Tacoma. Since the time we had been on bicycles, we had established a reputation of being good cops on bikes. We were exceptionally dedicated to the program. There were two other officers who were members of the Bike Patrol but didn't have the same commitment as my partner and me. They seemed to always find a reason to be in a car (heavy sarcasm here). "Oh my, I think I saw a drop of rain; we can't ride today!"

My original partner left the bike patrol shortly after it started. He wasn't really into it as much as me, and when he was offered a position in Vice, he jumped at the chance. That put me in a position to look for another partner. Because my new bike partner and I had worked together before, he was my first choice. Also, I knew my partner to be an avid rider as well, so with that in mind, I went to my lieutenant and told him who I wanted as my new partner on bicycles. At first, the lieutenant was not too keen on the idea. There seemed to be some sort of dislike for him by the lieutenant, but I insisted, and after threatening the LT that I would leave the bikes if I did not get him as my partner, the LT relented. Before you know it, we were both on the saddle chasing down crime.

Though my partner was not part of the first crop of bicycle officers, he truly wanted to do it much more than the other three I worked with prior to him.

Before my partner came to the bikes, no one seemed to want to take them to a higher level. It just struck me that the other two riders just looked at it as a ho-hum part of a job. The uniqueness of this type of policing wore off very soon with them. That was one of my biggest reasons for selecting the person I did as my partner.

He was dedicated to the program as much as I was, and that was what led to us getting recognized around the country. We were both on the same page and looked at how we could go national. What was going to make our program stand out above all others? Suddenly we got lucky, due solely to greed.

As things go in Washington State, Seattle Police Department Bicycle Patrol was contacted by the Washington State Criminal Justice Training Center (WSCJTC) to develop a bicycle officer training course.

Departments around the state were putting together bicycle patrols but wanted officers to go through some sort of formal training. Because Seattle was the first to develop a legitimate program, the WSCJTC contacted them to the training. The two most experienced said they could do it but wanted $5000 for a one-week program. Given that was a shock to the WSCJTC budget, they told them they would get back to them; you know, "don't call us, we'll call you" sort of thing. Tacoma was only about two weeks behind Seattle, so they called us. We jumped at it, and we were going to do it for free. Tacoma had a budget for academy training, and we could go on duty and not as a contractor. Win-win for all.

We developed training programs that were not only recognized by the department but also by the State of Washington and began teaching 40-hour courses within about two months of being contacted. The course included nutrition, officer safety, takedown procedures, gearing, bicycle maintenance, etc., as well as a competition on the last day for some bragging rights of the individual departments. One of the favorite things the officers loved was the soccer games we had from the seat of a bicycle – that actually turned into a blood bath, but it was still the biggest hit.

Only after about a year our training program became recognized by the largest police bicycle organization in the world, the International Police Mountain Bike Association (IPMBA). We were invited to join their ranks and asked to help write a large part of the first edition of the Complete Guide to Police Cycling. Our input was critical as we were the only ones in the country that had a formal training program – other areas were looking at our program to follow for their own states and police departments. No one had a 40-hour training session. Our week-long training was the most detailed and complete, thus eventually adopted by IPMBA as their training program.

Not only that, but we organized, advertised, generated sponsors, and planned the 8th Annual Police on Bikes Conference in Tacoma. It was a huge affair where hundreds of officers from around the country, as well as from Australia, the United Kingdom, Canada, Mexico, and Ireland showed up.

We begged for donations and freebies from anyone and any company that wanted to advertise. To help coerce those local companies, I even stirred the pot to get our way; it was not beneath me at all. As an example, I created a boycott against a local, national coffee chain. I told bicycle cops around the country to no longer go into that national chain and to tell them why they were staying out. What was the reason? They wouldn't give us their iconic paper bags to give to our attendees with some of their goodies — and you know what, it worked! It seemed all these stores around the country were calling corporate, asking permission to supply our conference with coffee and the bags. It didn't take long before I got a phone call from the corporate headquarters in Seattle letting us know they had a change of heart. Many officers were happy to hear the boycott was called off once we got what we were after.

My partner was able to score free shuttle vans from Tacoma Dodge to pick up attendees at Sea-Tac Airport and also shuttle the attendees about town. Tacoma cops volunteered to drive the vans and loved interacting with cops from around the country and the world. The vans had other uses as well, such as if an officer had too much to drink, they could call us, and we'd gladly pick them up. That way, there were no DUIs in our group.

There was a hospitality room with kegs of beer, and local wineries supplied bottle after bottle of wine. Deli's and pizzerias supplied a great deal of food for heavily slashed prices, just because it was cops. The community came out with donations in support of this law enforcement gathering. Even though I was one of the organizers, I was quite impressed with what was all going on.

Everything we did took hundreds of hours to put together, but it turned out to be top-notch. And this didn't even mention the competition that was never seen before, as well as the hot-rod show we organized during the registration. Our attendees were pampered and kept busy from the minute they arrived to the second they departed.

At the end of the conference, we were voted the 'Best Conference Ever' and held that distinction for the next three years. Plus, because it was so upscale and went so smoothly, I was elected Vice President of IPMBA, and my partner was appointed Education and Training Czar.

Because we brought such a positive light to the City of Tacoma and the Tacoma Police Department, the city decided to award us the Service Medal. We both thought that it was pretty cool that the city recognized us for the hard work and how we featured the City of Tacoma. I have to admit, when my partner first brought this up to me (he woke me out of a dead sleep), I was none too keen on it. But as I got into it, it truly became a labor of love. Seeing how it was all coming together made us both very proud. It is something we both can look back on fondly.

Medal of Valor

Earlier in this segment, I said I had some difficulty getting the highest award in law enforcement. It wasn't so much the medal; I mean, this is a prestigious award. I suppose I never felt I did something that achieved the level of Medal of Valor. As I stated earlier, this is reserved for those who were shot or stabbed in the line of duty. It was for those officers who nearly died, and that didn't happen to me. Nevertheless, I accepted it because it was offered, and I knew what an honor it was. I will outline the story that led me to get my award, and you can decide if I deserved it or not.

It was an early evening in the fall when I was on routine patrol in the Hilltop area of Tacoma. I turned a corner at South 19th, and Martin Luther King Way headed west on 19th. About three blocks in front of me, I saw a house that was totally engulfed in flames. As I approached the house, I called out to dispatch that

I was outside a house on fire. I parked my car across the street and ran up to the house. I could see the back door on the ground floor of this two-story house was wide open.

The smoke was coming out of the door, rolling rapidly against the upper portion of the door jamb, which allowed me to see under the smoke into the structure. Even though what I could see was hazy, I could tell someone was inside. I remembered my Boy Scout and Navy training and crawled under the smoke to gain access to the building. As I got in, the ceiling was higher than the door jamb, so I was able to stand up. Once inside and standing up, the smoke was somewhat intense but mostly above my head, and the fire inside lit up the interior in a soft yellow glow. What I could see was a blur of human forms.

The people were in was a larger room that included a living room area to the left and a small kitchen to the right. As I drew closer, I could tell there were three people in the room. A woman who was on the floor in the living room, just lying there. She was motionless, so I didn't know if she was alive or dead. On the couch on the far wall from me was a man who was lying there but looked to be moving about, kind of squirming around on the couch. The third person was another woman who was in the kitchen slapping at the main body of the fire with a kitchen towel. I scared her half to death when I grabbed the towel out of her hand. There was so much noise from the fire burning and her slapping at it, which was doing more harm than good; basically, she was stoking it up. I yelled at her to grab her friend on the floor as I grabbed the guy on the couch. I knew I had to get all three out of the house to fresh air.

I was able to get the man out fairly quickly and laid him on the grass. Because he was still fairly conscious once he was outside, he was able to breathe on his own. As soon as I knew he was okay, I went back in to help my dishtowel wheedling friend. She was having a great deal of difficulty moving the girl on the floor. I don't know why, given the girl was petite, but maybe the towel girl had sucked in too much smoke by now. I was able to pick up the limp girl and take her out and place her next to the man, who now seemed to be just fine. I turned around to see where Towel Girl was and realized she had gone back into the fire. *Are you kidding me?* I thought. I looked at the man and asked him, "Do you know CPR?" He said he did, so I told him to help the girl next to him.

I went back into the burning building, and there she was but this time looking around the room for something. I yelled, "Give it up!" I then grabbed her around the waist and pulled her out the back door. Once outside, she told me she had to go back in. At this point, I was a bit annoyed with her and asked, "Why in the world would you want to go back in there?"

She said, "I have no pants on." Through it all, I never noticed she only had a shirt on and her underwear. I gave her my jacket and wrapped it around her waist. I told her to help her male friend with CPR and get the limp girl away from the house. She promised she would not go back in and immediately went to help the male.

I heard some screaming in the front of the house, so I ran around the building to see what was happening. Another officer, Greg Hopkins, arrived, and people were yelling that there were babies upstairs. By now, the entire structure, which was a duplex, was engulfed in flames. Black smoke was pouring up the stairwell to the second story. All I could think was, *oh my God, if there are kids up there, they are probably dead.* Greg and I knew we had to try to get up there and find these kids, just in case. If there was any chance at all we could save them; we had to give it a try. We both began crawling on the stairway leading up. Though I couldn't see the steps because of the smoke, I could feel them, so I kept as close to the stair platforms as we could. If there was any air at all, that was where it would be. It didn't take long to realize there was no oxygen as the fire was consuming it all as well as displacing it with smoke. Nevertheless, Greg and I continued to try and advance up the stairwell. I couldn't see Greg, and I was sure he could not see me either. I could feel him next to me, and through the noise of the fire, I could barely hear his footsteps.

As we climbed the stairs, I was thinking of the kids but also thought, *what am I sucking into my lungs? How much poison is entering my body?* At about what I believed was halfway up the stairs, I could feel my lungs being filled with smoke. Then I began to think, *will I be able to see once I get up there; am I going to die on the stairs?*

Suddenly I felt a tug on my leg, pulling me back down the stairs. It was Greg. He was pulling me back to the bottom where there was some 'fresh' air, saying, "They're dead, they're dead!" I knew in my heart that he was right. There was just no way those kids could have survived that smoke, but I still was questioning myself: what if?

I looked at Greg and said, "We've got to try again." So we did, but by then, the smoke had gotten thicker. Compound that with our lungs, which were already full of smoke. With the even thicker smoke, we made it only a few steps before it was obvious that if we continued, we'd be dead as well. This time I called the retreat. I pulled on Greg, and we both retreated.

When we got back to the front porch, the fire was so intense that by then, the glass windows were breaking around us. Greg and I were greeted by the same crowd who began yelling at us, saying such things as "you just going to let them die?" and "you killed those kids!" As I tried to respond, with every word, black smoke came out of my mouth, but that didn't deter a woman from trying to incite others to assault Greg and me. I gave up; there was no way I could even talk, and I didn't need to be reminded what was going on in the back of my mind right then. I also saw shocked faces from the crowd as the black smoke poured out of my mouth.

The fire department showed up shortly thereafter and was able to put the fire out quickly. Once they had it under control and the smoke was at a minimum, I asked them to check upstairs. I told them what the crowd was saying, and the firefighters let me know there were no children upstairs. What? I ran up the stairs, and there was nothing, not even a child's bed.

When I went back downstairs, a few of the crowd was still there. There was still that one loudmouth woman who was slinging the insults the most. I wanted to go punch her in the face, but I resisted that impulse. Then I wanted to tell her to go fuck herself, but I resisted that impulse as well. I just walked up to her and said, "You will be happy to know the children are all safe and sound because they were never there." Then I just walked across the street, got in my car, and drove to the station to write my report.

My sergeant, Jerry Gross (RIP), contacted me at the station and had me give him a rundown of what happened. After outlining the entire event, he said to only give him the full report. He also emphasized writing it with as much detail and "don't leave anything out." Okay, I did. It took me about two hours to write the entire thing. Jerry had left by the time I finished the report, so I put it in his mail slot. I didn't know why he wanted me to submit the report to him, but he was the sergeant, and you do what the boss says.

What Jerry was doing was submitting Greg and me for the Lifesaving Medal. Jerry did not tell us he was doing that just in case the Awards Board decided against it. What Jerry did not know, and obviously Greg and I did not know either, was the Awards Board booted it up to Medal of Valor.

I know I said I wasn't sure if I deserved the highest award in law enforcement, but I will also tell you I have my medal prominently displayed in my den in a shadow box my wife made for me. It's not many cops who get this award, so for my sergeant who took the time to write up the incident is something I will always cherish.

God rest your soul, Jerry.

Pursuits

It's inevitable that a cop will get into a pursuit, whether on foot or a car chase. It just seems bad guys just don't want to get caught (heavy sarcasm here). When we get into those pursuits, especially car pursuits, it's an adrenalin boost. For the most part, they are fun, but in the back of your mind, you know they can be quite dangerous, which can lead to something very disastrous for the officer or maybe an innocent bystander. I don't give a rat's about the suspect who is running; they put themselves in that position to get hurt or killed.

In a car pursuit, you always think about the danger of crashing. Will I get hurt or killed? Do I really need to chase this guy? Does the crime really make it worth the risk? Those are just a few of the questions running through your mind as you head down the road at a breakneck speed or maybe around a blind corner in a foot pursuit.

On the other hand, you are also thinking about how you are just not going to let this jackass get away. How dare this bonehead run from me? It's easy to get caught up in the moment and lose track of the idea he/she could be caught another day where there might be less risk.

Most of us think it's the car pursuit that is the most hazardous, but foot pursuits are no less dangerous. The suspect could run around the corner of a building, and you forget your basic training when you round the corner, and you're staring down the barrel of a .45 or getting a 2x4 in the chops. If you are lucky, you may have time to look for cover and draw your weapon. Keep in mind this guy has zero reservation to blow your brains out or giving you a permanent concussion. He wants to get away, and you are now impeding on that mission. He is doing nothing but trying to eliminate that little obstacle in front of him; you. Ladies and gentlemen, he couldn't care less who you are or how nice a person you are.

The suspect is desperate, and if taking you out means he can get away, that's exactly what he will do.

Getting caught up in the moment is exactly what happened to my partner once when he was chasing a domestic violence suspect. It was in an area where there were several apartment buildings. These buildings were built on a steep hillside that we affectionately referred to as 'Sniper Heights.' On the backside of the complex was a retaining wall that was about 25 feet tall. We all knew about the wall, it was something which was built several years before I became a police officer, and Sniper Heights got its name from an incident when some guy, years before, had tried to snipe some folks at the businesses below. Nevertheless, on that day, the DV suspect tried to flee and ran around the back of the building where the wall was located. Our suspect must have only lived there a short time because off he went falling the full 25 feet. Okay, no big deal, right? He was the bad guy, and we didn't really give a damn if he got hurt. The problem was my partner followed, even though I was yelling at him to "Stop, damn it! Stop!" So suspect fell, then my partner landed on top of him, breaking both his ankles. Also, at the bottom of the wall were large massive Himalayan blackberry bushes. If you don't know much about blackberry bushes, the

Himalayan has the largest thrones and will tear you up in a heartbeat. Because the suspect landed first, he got the brunt of the blackberries, and when my partner landed on him, he was able to sit on the suspect. That including every time our bad boy moved, he got cut up even more. If it wasn't for my partner's now broken ankles, this would have been a true win-win situation. We had to call the fire department out to use those big ladders to get both of them back on top of the wall. A firefighter went down the ladder and helped cuff up the suspect. In the process, our suspect got a bit more cut up by the thorns. He had to be rolled over a few times to get the cuffs on correctly. I mean, they had to be just right, you know (wink wink). I took the position of supervising, which didn't sit well with my partner. Hey, I was not the one who went over the wall. By the way, the suspect was bleeding almost everywhere. And we didn't do it to him.

My partner was a bit more difficult to get out of. Once again, a firefighter had him get on his back and then walked up the ladder. Due to his ankles, he was unable to put pressure on his feet to climb on the rungs. I did make sure my partner got the first ambulance, and off to the hospital he went. The suspect was whining a great deal saying he needed medical attention. I let him know he was going as soon as an ambulance showed up. For some reason, there was a mix-up on the address where the ambulance was supposed to go, sorry dude (not really). There was about a 15-minute delay for some reason, but it finally showed up, and our suspect got that one.

I wasn't really going to write about this pursuit, but given it definitely pointed out the dangers officers encounter and, in this case, the suspect as well. Truly suspects should be aware it's just not worth the risk to flee.

As I was writing, I heard of an incident north of where I live (somewhere around Everett, WA) where a suspect who was being chased on a misdemeanor crime ran out onto Interstate 5 around 5 p.m. (rush hour) as officers were yelling at him to not go there. When he entered I-5, the cops broke off the pursuit; there was no way they were headed out into that heavy traffic. I'm sure you all can imagine what happened. The suspect was hit by several cars (per the news report) and subsequently died. Stupid, stupid, stupid.

I have digressed a lot here, but you get my point.

Water Fountain

Criminals are not always the brightest bulb in a chandelier. If they were, they'd put that brainpower to something honest. This guy was truly one of those who fit the above description.

I was dispatched to a possible drug deal in progress in Downtown Tacoma. The area I was sent to was well known as an area that had been previously known for drugs and prostitution activity, but now businesses in the area had been doing everything they could to change that image and make it a great place to visit. The area has the Pantages Theater, Rialto Theater, Bostwick Building, Farmer's Street Market, and so on. The area comprises several streets that have seen a resurgence and now becoming a trendy place to go and even hang out. It also hosts a great alcohol-free, family-friendly New Year's Eve gathering. This area had sprouted new businesses and was rapidly becoming a great place to take the family as well as a nightlife for a 'clubbing' area nearby. Having drug dealing to even barely sneak in was just unacceptable.

As I approached the area, I parked in an ally up the hill and behind a building. I was given a description of a white male in a brown older sedan who was dealing out of his car. I could see the car from my vantage point, which was between two larger buildings. I grabbed my binoculars and could easily see the man in the car passing small objects to individuals and getting some cash back. The individuals would then scurry away – all the indications were that this guy was selling something illicit. I returned to my car and headed toward the suspect to make contact with him. As soon as I turned onto Jefferson, he saw me and knew the gig was up. The suspect began to speed away south, and the pursuit was on.

Before we continue on with this pursuit, I have to explain a bit about this street. Jefferson runs south and turns into Broadway at the 9th Street crossing there. At that junction, there is a traffic light with a slight turn to the right, easy enough to follow. As Broadway continues south, it comes to 11th. Here is where it becomes a slight problem if you are not paying attention. My suspect was not paying attention, which is bad for him but good for me.

At 11th & Broadway, there is a quick jog to the right and back to the left to avoid a very large water fountain. The fountain is made of large blocks of concrete, which is about twice the width of most cars and about 15 feet tall. If you are going the speed limit (25 MPH), you still have to slow a bit to get around it. Pursuits never go the speed limit or anywhere near it. All one has to do is watch a few real-life cop programs to know that.

Back to the pursuit. Here we went, getting up to about 50 MPH. So what was he doing that caused him not to pay attention? Hiding his dope? Nope. Looking for a gun? Nope. Getting his dope ready to throw out the window, as most dope dealers do? Not that either. He was looking in the rearview mirror, giving me 'the finger.' Yep, that was what he was doing as we approached the fountain. I saw it coming and decided to slow as he approached at mock 5. I did see him turn his head away from the rearview mirror at the last moment, just enough time to say something like, "Ah, shit!" When he made an impact with the fountain, the fountain won. He hit the fountain so hard that the back end of his car left the ground about three feet or so. At first, I thought it might actually go completely over (or maybe I was hoping it would), but lucky for him, it didn't. I had already called out the pursuit, so other officers were on the way. I told them to slow down and alerted the suspect had crashed. As I exited my patrol car, I called for medical aid to come. Slowly I walked up to the car with the gun drawn; you never know what was going to happen, so precaution is the key to going home. I was pretty sure he was hurt and may even be dead, but as I approached, I was ordering him to put his hands out the window. Unknown to me at that time was he was not completely unconscious but so groggy that he couldn't understand anything I was saying. Once I got to the window, I could see he did not have any weapon in his hands, so I holstered. His head was bleeding, and his entire body was weaving about like some drunkard. He was saying things like "motherfucker, son of a bitch, etc." Before he could get his wits about him, I dragged him through the open driver's door window. I mean, I literally dragged him through the open window. It was easy because he wasn't wearing a seatbelt, so threading this needle wasn't a bit difficult. You know, now that I think of it, I don't think I've ever seen a crook wear a seatbelt. I put the cuffs on him and waited for medical aid.

I know what most of you are thinking: never move someone who has been injured in a traffic accident; it may injure them even more. He was a stinking, pathetic drug dealer; I didn't care! Plus, my safety was more important than his need to remain seated in the car. It would have been my luck if he came out of the stupor all the while seated in the car, and then the chase would have been on again. For any bleeding hearts out there, he survived intact.

An inventory of his clothes and car showed he had 14 bindles of black tar heroin and a little over $800, which I seized. A search warrant on the car retrieved 50 more bindles of white powder that tested positive for cocaine, two handguns (.38 S&W and a 9MM Beretta), and a little over $5000, which was seized as well. It was a good day.

Corvette Bank Robber

This is a pursuit that was never pursued by the rookie I had in my car or me. That said, this guy owned a beater Corvette, but a Corvette, nonetheless. Every time this guy would stick up a bank, he had the drop on us by the sure speed of his car, and I must admit his ability behind the wheel. His car outran us and could outmaneuver us, as well.

One late winter afternoon, when it was getting dark much earlier than the previous month, he struck again, just as the bank was closing. It appeared he had gotten a bit cocky on this one as he waited to see cops getting near, and like the fox he was, the hounds began the chase. My rookie was chomping at the bit to head into the area to help with the chase. I told him, "No." The surprise on his face was that of 'are you kidding me?' sort of look.

I told him, "Listen to the radio; those officers will tell you where this guy is going." If the pursuit is too far away, we would not only be risking our lives but that of citizens as well if we tried to catch up with the crowd. Also, given this guy always disappeared in the Northend of Tacoma, right where we were!

We listened, and guess what, the pursuit was headed right toward us. As the pursuit progressed, we could hear, over the radio, the direction and the streets the chase was on. I looked at my rookie and asked, "What are you hearing?"

He looked at me with a big smile and said, "They are headed right at us!"

"Indeed they are, and we are about to have some fun," I replied.

I had a hunch, and I acted on it. I turned onto a residential street (South 14th) toward Pine. As I turned, the Corvette came around the corner of Pine & 14th at a high rate of speed, and there we were facing grill to grill. Immediately, I called out we had the Corvette and where we were.

Then without hesitation, I hit the gas-bearing down on him and yelled at my rookie to "Hold on!"

In a very excited voice, my rookie said, "Let's get 'em!" The Corvette wasn't backing up, and he decided to head at us as well. As we approached each other, he tried, for the last time, to use his driving skills and go around us on my right side. Though he tried, the Corvette was no match for the curb.

As soon as he turned, the 'Vette struck the curb so hard the car rolled up on the driver's side by about 6–8 inches. At the same time, I turned sharply, nearly at a 90-degree angle, into the passenger door, which caused the 'Vette to roll onto the driver's side. Note: The look on the suspect's face was priceless – total shock.

Before we could get out of the patrol car, the 'Vette rolled over on its top. Concerned he might try to get away or shoot it out with us, we came around the diver's side with guns drawn. There he was, half in and half out, crawling out of the car. I ran up, put my foot on his neck, and could see he did not have his weapon (it seemed he lost it when the car hit the curb).

Shortly after we had this guy stuffed in the patrol car, other units showed up to take custody of him and book him.

My rookie was so excited to be a part of it, and we both got a bunch of kudos for it.

Real Estate

During my career, my wife and I invested in some rental property. At one point, we were at a high of owning 43 rental units comprising of a 21 unit apartment building, four houses, four four-plexes, and a duplex. Things were going well, but that was before 2007 when the real estate bubble burst. That is another story for another time or maybe another book.

One would think I may have had an advantage over tenants given my law enforcement employment. Actually, there are some advantages but also some serious disadvantages. When I interviewed prospective tenants, I would always work into the conversation that I was a police officer. I got one of two responses; either "That's cool" or "Hey, I have this other appointment, so let me get back to you." The latter perspective tenant couldn't get out of the rental property fast enough, sometimes tripping over themselves as they skedaddled on their way, getting as far as they could from that cop. The advantages would include a couple of tales related to our apartment building (Caribbean West Apartments) we owned in Lakewood, WA.

Hans

A tenant, Hans, was a nice German man who lived alone in a one-BR apartment in the 21 unit apartment building. His apartment was on the lower level (a two-story building). He pretty much kept to himself, and when my wife and I bought the building, we were told he entertained prostitutes from time to time. I engaged the old owner as to the description of the 'lady of the night.' The description was of someone who I recognized to be a known prostitute; I will call her M&M. That woman was just plain nasty, and I've had to fight with her in the past. She could hold her own, so I never underestimated her ability to throw a good punch. That said, I had given her a bloody nose on a previous arrest, so she knew not to mess with me either. Just because she's a woman, I'd be happy to knock her running lights out if that is what it would take to get her under control.

For those who may be offended that I gave a woman a busted nose, you have never met M&M. She was big and more than happy to use her size against any person, man or woman. She would have even given an MMA fighter a go, so I wasn't taking any chances with her.

At this point, I wasn't positive he had M&M as a 'guest,' but it would be easy to figure out, so I decided to engage him in a conversation about it. One of the things Hans liked to do was sit out in front of his apartment just talking to people walking by. Once I had ownership of the property, I'd show up most every other day and talk to the tenants as I strolled through doing various light chores. This day I specifically was going to talk to Hans.

When I came on the property, Hans greeted me in his usual way in his somewhat thick German accent. "Hello, Mr. Enzo." He had a big smile on his face and seemed to be in a very good mood.

I said, "Hi to you as well, Hans." Most of the time, that was the end of our encounter, and we both went on with our business. Today that was about to change. I said to Hans, "I think you and I have a friend in common."

A big grin came across his face, and he was excited to find out who the landlord and tenant each knew when he said, "Oh vonderful, who coos dat be?"

"Yes," I said, "M&M." His smile and enthusiasm left his face immediately. I knew at that moment that I was right; it was M&M.

He stammered as he said, "Oh. I don't nose her alls dat vell."

"Well, that's not what I hear, Hans." Before he could say anymore, I said, "If she puts one toe on this property from here on, I will make you homeless. I don't care if you fuck her, but you aren't doing it here. I will not have that skanky whore on this property. Do I make myself clear, Hans?"

"Yas, Misa Enzo."

"I'm so glad you understand. Hope you have a wonderful day," I said to him as I walked away, and we went on with our business.

This went well for some time, but one night M&M showed up on the property looking for Hans. It seemed she had lost one of her best customers, and she wanted him back. Hans immediately called the manager and let her know who was there. The manager called me and let me know she called the police but also wanted to let me know Hans was in a frenzy. Hans seemed to be exceptionally concerned he was going to be 'homeless' if M&M didn't leave, the manager told me. I had to chuckle at that, but I told my manager the threat I made to Hans so she would be on the same page.

I then called Hans, and when he realized I was the one calling him, there was absolute fear in his voice. I asked Hans if he called the police, and he told me the manager did. Okay, that worked. I asked if M&M was still there, and he told me she was. "Ya," he said. He went on to tell me he did not let her in the apartment and how he was trying to get rid of her etc., etc.

He was going on so long I finally had to interrupt him and told him, "Go ahead and hand her the phone. Tell her a friend wants to talk to her."

The next I heard was from M&M. "Who da fuck is dis?" she said so eloquently.

"This is Officer Bracken with Tacoma Police."

"Bullshit, motha fucka," again she stated in her best English grammar.

"Let me refresh your memory. If you don't get your fucking fat ass off my property, I am going to come down there. I'm going to bust that fat nose of yours again and then book you into jail, so move!" To that, I heard a noise, which was the phone dropping and then Hans telling me she was leaving. Oh good, she remembered. Sometimes it just took a subtle persuasion to get a little cooperation. From that day on, I never saw M&M again, not even in Tacoma. I am such a big sucker for happy endings.

Hans was so concerned that I was going to evict him; his voice over the phone began to crack as he spoke about all the effort he made to have M&M leave – to no avail. I relieved Hans's concern and let him know this incident did not qualify him to have to take residency at some tent city somewhere. Even though M&M may have been his sex buddy for hire, she could be quite intimidating. No doubt he was in a bind, me threatening his residency status and M&M threatening to kick his ass if he wasn't going to pay her anymore. Hans was really between a big fat rock and a hard place.

Sadly, Hans died about 18 months after this incident. I know he was an alcoholic and, to some, just some lowlife person, but he always treated me with respect. I liked him, and at times I thought he was quite funny, even when he wasn't trying to be. RIP Hans.

FBI

The FBI was looking for this major drug dealer who had skipped out on his probation and was working with the Pierce County Drug Enforcement Task Force. FBI got intel that the person they were looking for was living at my apartment building. Actually, he was a guest of one of the tenants. Pierce County let the FBI know a cop owned the building, and the owner would be more than happy to cooperate. I was contacted by FBI agents at the PD. They showed me a picture of who they were looking for, and I immediately recognized the photo to be the boyfriend of the tenant in apartment 18 and was in and out periodically. That was not meant to be a pun. The only difference was the name on the warrant was different than the one he had given me. I suppose if the FBI was looking for you and you are shacked up at an apartment building a cop owns, I would have used an alias as well.

I let the agents know that ironically I was searching for a new manager, and he had put in his name for the position. I had not committed to him, given his rental status. So to make this work, I told the FBI agents I'd make an appointment to do a walking interview for the following day. I'd just let him know he was on the list and at least wanted to give him a shot at the job. So when I talked to him on the phone, he stated he was trying to turn his life around given he had a rough background and this opportunity was a start. Did I feel bad about lying to him? Not for a minute!

I told the agents he was well aware of me being a cop and was used to me being in uniform, so that was not an issue. We decided to have the agents show up at the building about an hour before I was to meet the suspect. In the laundry room, there was a back room where I kept tools, cleaning supplies, extra light bulbs, etc.—you get it. That was where they would hide when I brought the suspect into the laundry room to detail responsibilities.

Though the suspect told me over and over, he was trying to turn his life into a good path, one never knew what he would do if cornered. All precautions were taken: I brought him into the laundry, making sure to close the door behind me, and then stood in front of the door so he had no way out. There was no back door. That was the plan, and it went down smoothly. Once we went in the laundry and the door closed, the FBI agent came out from the back room. The suspect did not fight and stated, "I'm so glad this is finally over." He knew exactly what was going on and had no issue with it at all. Good, the last thing I needed was to fight with this guy. He went into handcuffs without the slightest bit of problem, and the arrest was mostly uneventful.

I went up to apartment 18 after the agents left with the suspect to let the girlfriend know what happened and that her boyfriend was not coming back. I showed her my copy of his last booking form, and she seemed genuinely surprised. She stated she had no idea he was wanted by the FBI or anything about his background or his real name. The name he gave her was the same, he told me. I took the form back and told her if she needed information, she would have to contact the Tacoma office of the FBI. I was a bit surprised when she said she didn't need to contact anyone, and then she shut the door saying, "That son of a bitch." Well, okay then.

Duplex

The only duplex we owned was in south Tacoma, and there was a bus stop directly in front of the property. Pierce County Sheriff's Office (PCSO) was working to catch a molester/rapist that was attacking females on the buses when they got a hold of me. One side of the duplex was unoccupied, and they asked if they could use that location to watch the stop to see if the suspect would show up. No problem at all. I gave them keys so they could come and go as they pleased. Additionally, I filled the fridge with water, soft drinks, and sandwiches for the cops to have. I was told later it was the best stakeout spot ever.

The great thing was by using that spot, they were able to make an arrest and actually catch the molester red-handed — another great happy ending to a story.

Mason Loop

Mason Loop was a four-plex in a low-income area. We rented apartments in that building to mostly Section 8 tenants. One would think that a Section 8 tenant would do everything to maintain their assistance status. But there are some who have other ideas.

I had a tenant, whom I was at first reluctant to rent. However, given the apartment was vacant for nearly two months, I decided my gut feeling was just that, a feeling. This guy paid his deposit and first month's rent in cash. I let him know I'd take the cash this time, but in the future, it would have to be money orders or a cashier's check. For the next four months, the money came in like clockwork, and I was a happy camper.

Because I was working so much overtime at the PD, I wasn't able to do my routine checks of any of my rental units. Because of my lack of time, the old adage, "When the cat's away, the mice will play," falls into play in this tale. For the most part, this was okay, given my tenants were all fairly good. We had occasional things happen, but nothing as serious as this one, as you'll see.

What I didn't know was this tenant was building a meth lab, and it was operating. Now I knew how he always had the rent money. But we didn't know about this new business the tenant was involved in until we were contacted by tenants in another nearby four-plex.

I had gone into surgery and was quite out of it, and of course, that was when we got the call about drug dealing out of one of our apartments. Tina took the call from the other four-plex tenant/owner. She didn't know who to call, so she had to wake me up. Through the haze, I told her to call the front desk and ask for 'Scum,' the nickname of the drug task force officer, because my mind wasn't working properly to give her his actual name (for safety, I will not be revealing that here). I was out of it, and she was lucky to get that out of me.

Tina made the call and was able to get a car dispatched to the apartment building to investigate. Now you will see just how stupid this jackass was. The officer came to the door and asked the tenant to be able to come in and look around, you know, just to make sure everything was okay. The tenant denied entry without a warrant. Okay, so now the officer asked if he could look in the garage area. "Sure, that'll be ok," the tenant told him. The officer walked into the garage and saw all the makings for a meth lab, glass tubing, glass beakers, etc. As the officer left, he thanked the tenant for his cooperation and proceeded to the station to write up the search warrant. Bingo, done deal. This just reminded me of the scene in Grinch when Jim Carey has a verbal exchange with the cave echo where he lived. When he yelled, "I'm an idiot," the echo would essentially call himself an idiot. But the echo responded exactly like it should with: "You're an idiot." That was what this tenant was.

The officer returned with a search warrant and a hazmat team. This was an upstairs apartment so escape for the tenant was limited unless he wanted to jump off the balcony into the arms of waiting officers. The arrest was made, and the evidence was collected. That all done and using $20,000 later for cleanup decontamination, we were able to re-rent the apartment.

Additionally, for me, it was on the evening news, and I had to take grief for about two months after the drug bust.

I did get some payback when this went to trial because this POS got ten years in prison for drug manufacturing and distribution. A civil suit against this guy would have been a huge waste of money. He had no money, and when he did, it was going into his arm or nose. I never pursued that just because it would have only lined the pocket of some attorney.

So it seemed my gut was right after all. One must listen to your gut, not only when you are hungry.

No Good Deed Goes Unpunished

I had a tenant who was, to say the least, a major pain in the butt. We will refer to her as Bertha. First, she got behind in her rent and was subject to eviction. Nevertheless, I gave her opportunity after opportunity to pay what she owed by allowing her to pay every two weeks some extra over a six-month period. She agreed but never kept her end of the bargain. Tina was telling me to throw her out, but I was a sucker and tried to make it happen so she wouldn't be on the streets. As you can tell by the title of this tale, it did not go so well for me.

I had to remind her constantly what she owed, and it was never on time. I began to get quite frustrated with her. Also, she wanted to pay her rent via sexual favors, and I was having none of that. It seemed that pissed her off as well. "Hey, Bertha, I'm married, or have I not mentioned that to you a thousand times or more!"

The thing that drove me off the edge was when she gave me two bogus checks. I get to the bank and was suspicious asked the teller before making deposits if the checks would be honored. I was told no. I lost it and called her, and of course, she didn't answer. I let her know in no uncertain terms I was coming after what she owed, and she might as well start packing; she was out! Admittedly, I was none too kind and used some unsavory language as I spoke. I was pissed.

So now, what does this have to do with police work and the theme of this book? Quite frankly, it shouldn't have made the cut for *Tales of a Street Bull*, except for one thing. She filed a formal complaint against me, took it to a known anti-cop employee at the City of Tacoma who worked at the mayor's office. To top that all off, she lied several times, saying I blocked her car in with my patrol car and wouldn't move after asking me to move the car, and I banged on her door with my gun and made threats of bodily harm, along with some other lies. So, of course, the department ran with it with an IA investigation. I felt as if the department was not on my side at all, and this was a witch hunt. When I got to the IA interview, I was told about the lies, and then I began submitting evidence for my defense. They actually had a surprised look on their faces when I told them I wasn't even there in uniform when I tried to make contact at Bertha's door, nor was I armed in any way – plus my manager was there at the time as a witness. I drove my truck to the building and parked in my reserved slot on the opposite end of the building. Her story was full of holes, and it was an attempt to make me look like some out-of-control cop. This was an off-duty private business, and the department had no authority to intercede, and that was my position.

Even though I submitted a ton of refutable evidence, the department must have decided it could not lose face, so I was given 30 days off without pay. After an appeal, it was reduced to three days. I wasn't happy about that either, but I just wanted to put this all behind me; it wasn't worth the fight.

Truly this incident was one of two things that caused me to just say I was done with police work. I was burned out on trying to help people just to get a complaint filed against me. People ask me why cops hang out with other cops all the time, and it is just because of this and other stories like this. We know what we deal with; most of the public doesn't know or doesn't care.

SAM

Early in my career, I developed a near hatred for drunk drivers. There are so many things they do that negatively impact not only their victims but also a network of people around the victims and the drunk as well. In my career, I know of such stories as the woman who, on her birthday, was hit by a drunk driver as she was crossing the street that resulted in her losing both her legs.

And then there was the drunken woman who drove over three miles home after hitting a bicyclist. She didn't just hit him and then left the scene — oh no, the cyclist flew up onto her car, and his head was protruding through the windshield as she drove. According to the doctor's speculation, the man could have been saved if she would have just stopped and called for medical aid. But as it were, she was too drunk to even know he was on her hood. Then there was the guy who texted, "Too drunk to give a shit," just before he hit a car at a traffic light, killing all three occupants.

Let's not forget the taxi driver and his pregnant passenger who were killed on a local freeway when a wrong-way drunk driver slammed head-on with the taxi, even though the taxi driver tried to get out of the way. In that case, some may say two people died; I say three.

Or when my ex-daughter-in-law was traveling on another local highway when a drunk going in the opposite direction at a very high rate of speed hit the muddy center median, throwing mud so forcefully that it penetrated the windshield of her car and filled the entire interior of the car with mud. Only by the grace of God did she not get killed or have her son with her as he would have been covered with mud, most likely killing him.

These are just a few of the stories of the things drunk drivers do. So to say I had a severe disdain for those who get behind the wheel intoxicated would be an understatement. I could go on and on with stories such as these. Drunk driving is the leading cause of fatal traffic accidents in the United States, and I dare say that is probably the case throughout the world. I use to think my mom was a bit harsh when she told me anyone caught drunk behind the wheel should be tried for attempted murder. I know that will never happen, but I can no longer dispute that idea.

Though I can speak about these types of incidents on and on, there was one case that paved the path to how I dealt with DUIs. That's the case with SAM.

Very early in my career and when I was still on FTO (Field Training Officer), my training officer and I were dispatched at about midnight to a possible fatality accident at South 60th and Alaska. I remember it being a warm summer evening, and it was clear, with no rain or fog.

Before getting into the details of the accident, I need to explain the road conditions and the players of the accident.

First, the road. Alaska Blvd is a semi-main street, two lanes, blacktop road that helps you get through a good section of town when the main streets are fairly backed up. Also, as it travels south at 60^{th,} it bends to the left and begins a gradual downhill trek passing a fairly scenic area alongside Wapato Lake.

The player was the drunkard, a mid-thirty male driving a 1972 Chrysler Imperial 4. Some of you may know this car, but for those who don't, it is a massive car. Some would refer to it as a land yacht. The victim, in this case, was SAM, a 16-year-old high school female driving a 1974 Triumph Spitfire. This car is small and low to the ground.

This was a David and Goliath mismatch. But in this scenario, David did not win.

Lastly, one must keep in mind cars are not built today like the cars were built in the 70s or 80s. Thank God for that. Technology has advanced to make it very possible you will survive an automobile traffic accident, that wasn't the case for these two cars.

The drunk was traveling south on Alaska, and as he got to the bend and downhill grade, he crossed over the center line and now was in the oncoming lane. At the same time, SAM was driving her Spitfire north on Alaska, and given the warm evening, she had the top down. There was no way she could see the Imperial coming from the other direction and that it had crossed over into her lane. She probably saw the glow of the headlights, but, just like everyone else, she would reasonably assume the oncoming car was in its own lane. Most likely, when she realized this massive car was on her side of the road, it was too late to react.

The Imperial struck the Spitfire head-on. It hit the sports car with such force the Imperial went completely over the top of the low Spitfire, coming to rest about 20 feet behind the small car (Give that some thought – the Imperial drove completely over the top of the Spitfire). The Imperial driver was so intoxicated that witnesses said he seemed to have no clue he just hit the Spitfire. His car died, and he was trying to restart it, but even for the land yacht he was driving, the car was done for and refused to restart.

A citizen who was awakened by the wreck called the police and reported it. We and another unit got the call and were told the Imperial driver was uncooperative and attempting to get away. As we headed to the location, we heard the other unit arrive, and shortly thereafter, they requested we "step it up." So as we say at Tacoma Police, we went 4-Bells (lights and sirens). When we arrived, my FTO, who was driving, stopped directly behind the Imperial. He told me to check on the Spitfire, and he went to help the other officers. As I ran up to the Spitfire, I was sure the driver, SAM, was dead. To my surprise, when I got beside her car, she turned and looked at me. I immediately called dispatch and told them to have medical aid "step it up" as the driver was still alive.

Even though SAM looked at me, I had no idea if she actually knew I was there, nor did she say anything. I bent down alongside her crushed car. The car almost appeared to be crushed around her. I could see her legs looked to be pinned or may have been amputated by her crushed car. The dashboard was flattened against them, and it looked as if her legs ran into the speedometer.

While there, I touched her on her upper left arm. I told her to hang on, medical aid was on the way, and she needed to fight through this. Honestly, I felt she was about to die, and I was trying to get her to feel she was going to survive. I wanted her to know she was not alone. As I spoke to her, there was something else bugging me other than the obvious. I looked, and after some time, I realized there was no steering wheel, or at least it wasn't visible. Finally, I could see the steering wheel had collapsed, and the steering column was shoved through her. Oh my God, I nearly puked but knew I had to be strong for her and fought my nausea back. It wasn't long and as you can imagine she died as I spoke with her.

I wanted to cry; I have never felt that way over a stranger, but this young girl did not deserve to die this way. She was the daughter of someone who, most likely, loved her dearly. I didn't know anything about her but a young life being snuffed out at such an early age was beyond tragic. As I got through my grief, I became angry immensely.

The guy who did this had fought with officers to try to escape and denied any responsibility. He was now under control, but how dare he try to get away when he killed this young lady. Honestly, I wanted to pull out my .38 cal Smith & Wesson and put a bullet in this guy's head. Though I wanted to, I'm smarter than that.

As I walked over to where the officers had the drunk in cuffs, I told dispatch to cancel medical aid and requested the fatality investigation team. As a good officer, I advised him of his rights but added, "Take advantage of it and shut the fuck up." I swear if this guy had said anything, I would have punched him in the face. I would have cared less he was in handcuffs. To add to the frustrations of this call was after putting him in the back of the patrol car, he fell asleep. Not a care in the world, he had. Once again, I wanted to get in the back seat and beat the crap out of this guy, and once again, I sucked it up.

While we waited for the 'fat team,' I taped off the area with yellow crime scene tape to keep people out and keep the 'lookie Lou's' away. Also, I called for cones to close off the road to keep traffic out; there was hardly any but still needed to cover that base. When the 'fat team' did show up, they immediately covered SAM and her car with a tarp.

We transported this POS to the station for DUI processing, which included a breathalyzer. As per his previous attitude, he refused to cooperate, so to the hospital he went for a blood draw. He was no more cooperative there either, but now I got to use physical force. In Washington State, in a fatality accident, we can take blood without your permission. Yea! I get to play. I called for the hospital security to bring restraints. When they got there, I asked our suspect to cooperate, and he again refused. So I grabbed him by the neck and slammed him to the hospital bed; security placed the restraints on the subject's wrist, and we had the tech come in and draw the blood. All the time, he was yelling, "You're not getting shit from me." So much for that idea, sir.

I was also quite pleased that our drunk failed booking, which means he pissed off the corrections officers. When that happens, there is a brown wave of uniformed corrections officers that come out to the front from every possible direction. They dragged him to the holding cell as they stripped off his clothes, totally disregarding if his shirt or pants were ripped in the process. In those days, one did not have to be very kind to a guy who just killed someone, no PC attitudes in those days.

So even though I got little satisfaction of this guy getting a bit roughed up at the end of this call, it was not the slightest bit satisfying. I mean, he just took the life of SAM—Sweet Angelic Miss—and nothing for me would ever satisfy that. I could not imagine what the family was going through right now, as I assumed they had been notified by the police chaplain.

At the beginning of this story, I told you this incident changed how I treated DUI arrest. In the early days of my career, officers were encouraged to not book the DUI arrest in jail but to try and find a sober person to release them to. It could be a spouse or friend. Additionally, it was discouraged to impound the car the drunk was driving unless it was involved in an accident—that one I never understood.

Not only was it the death of SAM that changed my attitude and how I dealt with DUIs but also what had happened prior to the collision. About four hours prior to this incident, the DUI arrestee was stopped by a Pierce County officer for—yep—DUI. The deputy processed the drunk as normal by placing him under arrest but released him via criminal citation. The deputy, following standard procedure, located and released the DUI to his sober wife. It seemed from there the drunk made it back to his car. I don't know if his wife drove him to where his car was or just how he got back to it; he just did. Nevertheless, he got back into his car, and when he was arrested by us, there was an empty six-pack of Miller beer and six empty cans on the floor. I cannot say for sure he drank the beers after the first arrest or before. I can say, with some confidence, if the drunk was booked into jail, he would not have been on the road within four hours of the first arrest. The process of transport and booking, then paying bail, takes longer than that. Also, if his car would have been impounded, he would have to pay for the car to be released. Well, after paying the bail, his cash flow would have been most likely too low to get the car out of hock. Compound that with the time it took to get out of jail and get to the impound yard, this guy would have never been on the road when SAM was there. And just maybe, he might have had time to sober up a bit to think more clearly. So, my policy was to book them and impound them. I made it as difficult as possible for every DUI found.

Smoker Black Gloves

Law enforcement is under attack constantly because a small number of officers give a black eye to the rest of the good, honest, and hard-working officers. Smoker Black Gloves comes under the 'small number,' giving cops a bad name despite what you hear in the media or how Holly-weird portrays us.

My first encounter with Smoker was when I backed him up when he was making contact with a drunk in a city park. The rules are no alcohol in the park, and this guy had a beer. It is not a big deal and especially if the contact is cooperative. This was one of those guys.

I got to Smoker's location just as he was making contact. As he stood in front of the subject, I stood to the rear. It was a summer day around 70 degrees, so our contact was wearing a T-shirt and jeans, fairly low-key and casual, making it easy to view his waistband and if he had some sort of weapon hidden on his person. Smoker was in front and could easily observe the same things at his front. If we felt the slightest bit nervous, a pat-down could have been done at any time.

As Smoker was talking to the drunk, the drunk repeatedly apologized, which is typical when you are dealing with drunks caught red-handed, if you will. The routine was to get ID from our contact, run him for any warrants, and, if none, send him on his way with a liquor violation citation. He'd still be placed under arrest but released on his promise to appear in court: a very simple contact and win-win for all of us. Smoker could get an arrest if that's what he wanted, and the drunk could get to go on his merry way to buy another beer and take it home this time. Don't ask me why the drunk just didn't do that in the beginning, but so be it. I suppose alcohol can make one's thoughts a bit blurry.

This contact showed all signs of heading in the direction of cooperation. Smoker, being who he was, took it in a way off-direction from simplicity. I hate when cops do that! God, I love simplicity.

As Smoker interviewed the drunkard, the drunkard naturally placed his hands in the rear pockets of his jeans, which I had seen over and over. That's just something people do when talking to someone, but also something cops don't like you do when they are contacting you for a crime or suspicion of a crime. The cop doesn't know if you are carrying a weapon of sorts. Naturally, Smoker told the drunk to take his hands out of his pockets. The drunk apologized again and complied. *Okay*, I thought, *I would have probably told the drunk the same thing*. At the same time, I would have looked at the officer who was standing behind the subject, me in this case, and asked if we were cool – referencing the possibility of anything to be concerned about. Smoker didn't do that. I was about to tell Smoker our contact was not armed, but it was his contact, so another rule is the officer making contact is allowed to follow through unless he asks the second officer for input, assuming all is going smoothly, which in this case and at this time it was.

So on with the interview. And, of course, what did the drunkard do again – yep, put his hands back in his rear pants pockets. Just as I was about to tell our contact to take his hands out of his pockets, Smoker punched the guy with a closed fist across his face, knocking the guy to the ground.

Holy shit, I thought. "Have you lost your fucking mind?" I said to Smoker as I stepped over the drunkard to push Smoker away. "What the hell did you do that for?" I asked as well.

"I told him to keep his hands out of his pockets. How do I know he doesn't have a weapon?" Smoker replied.

My answer and the obvious one was, "Because I was standing behind him, you dick." I told Smoker to get away from this guy, and I would handle it from here. I think that he realized he messed up because Smoker walked over to his car without arguing with me and waited.

I helped the drunkard up and sat him at a nearby picnic table, and I could see others in the park staring at me to see what I was going to do. I asked our contact if he wanted to file a complaint against the officer. I could not believe this guy's answer. "No, I should not have put my hands in my pockets." He even refused transport to get medical aid. *OMG, are you kidding me?* After getting over the shock of this guy's lack of desire to follow up on what happened to him, I copied down all the information from his ID because I was still writing my own report. There was no way I wasn't going to write a report if, for no other reason, this guy might just change his mind. I let the man leave the park after tossing the beer in a trash can and then walked over to Smoker.

"Man, you ever do that again with me, I'll knock the shit out of you," I told him and walked back to my car. I deliberately did not tell him I was writing a report because I just wanted to see if he was going to put pen to paper. FYI, he did not.

That was my first call with Smoker. I had heard stories about him, but I'm not one to just go by stories from others. I have found in many cases stories are exactly that. They get exaggerated, and what was a monster was actually an angry kitty. In this case, from what I just saw, the stories were spot on; Smoker was an asshole.

Law enforcement attracts two basic types of people: the ones who want to help others and the ones who want to control others. After this call, Smoker fell into the latter group, ones who give law enforcement a black eye.

After that call, I avoided Smoker. I wanted nothing to do with him and never backed him up unless there was at least another officer present aside from me. There was no way I was going to be put in the middle of his indiscretions without another witness. So what came of my report? At first, I thought it was being swept under the carpet but what I found out later was a dossier being put together to present to the union to rid the PD of this guy. It wasn't until Smoker's last call did it finally come to a head. I had the unlucky displeasure of being a part of that last call.

Here's what happened. There was a strong-arm robbery at a convenience store parking lot. The suspect was described as a black male with a large stature driving a green panel van. The victim was a female and stated her purse was taken, which contained her ID and credit cards. This was in a winter month, and as we know, darkness comes early during that part of the year, and this happened at about 6 p.m. on this day.

After a few hours, about three, Smoker called out; he spotted the van at an apartment complex. All I could think was, *no, not him; anybody but him. Oh well, let's hope nothing goes stupid on this call.*

He also stated the van was occupied by a person fitting the description of the suspect. Further info was there was a female (not the victim, of course) in the passenger seat, and the van was stationary. He requested back up to make a felony stop. My partner and I were only three blocks away when Smoker called it out, so we radioed where we were and were headed his way. After a few seconds, Smoker reported the van was on the move and headed west. When he was radioing, we were coming around the corner, putting ourselves behind Smoker, and he was behind the suspect vehicle. I told him, via radio, that we were right behind him and to make his stop when he was ready.

Before I go any further for those of you that don't know how a felony stop is supposed to go down, the lead car (in this case, Smoker's) turns on the lights, including the spotlight, to get the vehicle to stop. If they do, great. The officer places his car behind the suspect vehicle, offset to the left for full protection the patrol car can provide. The second car (ours) sets the car to the right of the suspect vehicle to see the passenger side or directly behind the lead officer's car. The second car driver takes a position on the right side of the lead patrol car. The pretty simple thing everyone learns in the academy. But—and here we go—Smoker decided to make up his own felony stop procedure; of course, without telling anyone else.

Instead of staying behind the van after turning on the emergency lights, Smoker sped up past the van and then turned his vehicle diagonally in front of the van, placing the passenger side toward the front left corner of the van. Having no clue what Smoker was up to, my partner ran up to the rear driver's side of the van as I grabbed the shotgun out of our car and covered the passenger side of the van.

At this point, I figured Smoker was going to use the car as cover, but he didn't do that either. Nope! He ran around the patrol car, placing himself between his car and the van. I could hear him yelling at the driver, saying, "Open the door, show me your hands; open the door, show me your hands."

How it should have gone was, "Show me your hands, now reach outside the window and open the door from the outside." The critical portion he was missing was telling the driver to open the door from the outside and not from the inside. Basically, Smoker was confusing the crap out of the suspect.

Suddenly, I heard a gunshot go off. *Oh man*, I thought, *this is turning out to be a gun battle*. Prior to the actual stop, Smoker said there was a female in the front passenger seat. It was obviously not the victim but was this female the 'Bonnie' of some sort of a Bonnie & Clyde scenario? I just didn't know. I had to make a decision, and that was if that passenger door opened and I saw a glint of metal, this woman was going to eat my shotgun. Then just as I made that decision, the door opened, and as I was about to drop the hammer, I noticed she opened the door with both hands. That's what saved her life. Both hands on the door, and even in the darkness, I could tell she had nothing in her hands except the door handle. She turned toward me, and I yelled at her to "Get on the ground." She made the dive quick as I'd ever seen. I moved up on her, placed her in handcuffs then placed her between me and the open van door as we backed toward my car.

I asked her if there was anyone else in the car, and she said, "No." As I got close to my car, another officer came up behind me and took her to his car as I continued to cover the passenger side. I still didn't know what was happening on the other side of the van and so far only heard the single shot, nor did I know if any other person or persons may still be in the van despite what she said. After a few minutes, my partner came back and said the van was clear and to come upfront.

What I found out was during this 'keystone cop' exchange of "open the door, show me your hands," Smoker fired a shot at the suspect, striking him in the fatty tissue (he was quite obese) of the upper chest. The bullet traveled across the fat and lodged in the right side. I'm surprised it didn't go all the way through and hit the female I took into custody. These are the days of the Smith & Weston .38's so it didn't say much for our guns or ammo.

By the time I got to the driver's side of the van, the suspect was taken out and lying on a blanket on the ground, awaiting medical aid. The suspect had been dressed with a bandage on his entry wound, but it was obvious he needed medical aid from a professional. Within minutes Tacoma Fire Medic One unit arrived, and it appeared the suspect was in good hands.

As I walked around the van looking at the scene, just to examine how this entire thing got messed up, Smoker came up to me and asked if he could talk to me. I was still not too keen on him, and now that he totally screwed up what appeared to be a simple felony stop, I was especially not fond of him now. Nevertheless, I reluctantly agreed. What he said was something I would have never thought he'd tell me in a million years. He said, "I don't think this is the right guy." I could not believe he just told me that. Why would you tell someone—who you know doesn't like you—that you just shot someone whom you didn't think was the actual suspect? My thoughts, at first, were: *you should have kept that to yourself and see how the chips fell.*

I won't lie for anyone, not even myself, and I was surely not going to lie for a guy I had no respect for and believed that he shouldn't have a badge. There was no doubt I would have to repeat it at the shooting review board. But After giving it some thought, this might just be a good thing as I would have to tell the board everything I knew. And guess what, I was asked exactly that question: "Officer, did Officer Black Gloves (using his nickname only in this book) make any statements to you concerning the suspect?" There it was, time to make sure the entire truth came out, and I did just that.

Do cops make mistakes? You bet we do. Could this be just a mistake when Smoker shot this guy? Of course, it could have been. The problem was Smoker made several mistakes to the point of making him dangerous, and if I could have a hand in dumping this guy, I was happy to do my part.

So what happened to Smoker after this incident? Guess what, he wasn't fired! At least not for this. Smoker was able to convince the shooting review board that he was out sick when his academy class went over felony stop procedures. When I heard the outcome, I just couldn't believe he was going to get away with another stupid and dangerous mistake. This time a mistake that could have easily taken a life. I didn't feel sorry for the suspect getting shot, not at all; come on, he was a thief who used his size to intimidate his victims. That said, the problem was there was no way the suspect should have been shot because he was cooperating or at least trying to.

What happened to Smoker was nothing less than a slap in the face to those of us on that call and all other good cops around the nation. The administration decided because there might be a hint of what Smoker said about not being at the academy during the felony stop lectures and demonstrations, which I didn't believe, they decided to have Smoker go through remedial training for felony stops. I've got to tell you I thought that was a joke. How could that be the outcome of a guy who unjustly shot a guy? There ended up being a silver lining to what, at first, appeared to be a very dark cloud. Smoker decided this was beneath him, so he never showed up to his remedial training!

He was as stupid as I thought he was dangerous. The department gave him the break of a lifetime and even served it on a solid silver platter. Smoker decided to grab the platter and tossed it all in the trash. Also, when department supervisors went out to his house to check why Smoker did not show, Smoker stood at his front window, giving those who showed up the 'finger.' What a moron. That was the incident that got him fired. The proverbial 'shoot yourself in the foot' scenario. Idiot!

Throughout this entire story, I never told you how Smoker got his nickname of Smoker Black Gloves. It is simple. Every time you saw him, he was wearing black leather gloves and always smoking a cigarette. When he was in his patrol car, when he was in his private car, when he was at turnout (what TV calls roll call), walking down the hall, headed to court (at least the gloves) — no matter when you saw him he had those gloves on and a cigarette in his mouth. He was easy to tag.

The Tacoma Narrows Bridge

The Narrows Bridge has a great deal of history from the time it opened in 1940 to the present day. More so than most any other bridge, as it is one of the few structures that collapsed shortly after its original opening. Some of you might have heard of the term Galloping Gertie. That originated just after the original Narrows Bridge opened. The bridge deck was well known for its movement during any moderate wind and was closed during heavy winds. This finally took its toll on November 7, 1940, when the entire driving deck broke apart and fell into the Narrows waterway below.

Surprisingly enough, no one was killed during the collapse, but a dog who was abandoned in a car went down with the vehicle. Don't get too upset about the dog, as a gentleman risked his life to try and save the dog from doom. When the man got to the car, the dog was so scared that it bit the would-be rescuer. The man had to save his own life, so he abandoned the rescue attempt and headed to safety.

You can see the entire incident on YouTube by putting 'Galloping Gertie' in the search bar.

The collapse only ruined the driving deck, but the two spans remained intact. The deck was rebuilt, and the bridge reopened in 1950. It remained a single bridge connecting Tacoma and the Kitsap Peninsula until a second bridge was finished in 2007.

Both driving decks on the two bridges are about 180 feet from the water below. Just like other structures like the Narrows Bridge, the lure of those bent on suicide were attracted to the ease of access to its decks so they can follow through with taking their life. At the time of this writing, 17 people have committed suicide from the bridge since its reopening.

There are also daredevils who think they could survive such a fall are also lured to the decks of places like the Narrows Bridge. One such incident involved two army soldiers. Both men jumped without any fanfare, but only one survived. After the survivor's stint, which landed him in the hospital due to multiple injuries, he was court marshaled, spent time in the stockade, and discharged. I am sure alcohol played a big role in that adventure.

In my career, I had the displeasure of responding to two suicide attempts on the bridge, and thankfully, they both decided not to follow through. This story I'm going to tell you about was not a suicide attempt, nor was it a daredevil feat, but instead pure stupidity, alcohol, and machismo bull shit.

I was dispatched to the bridge at about 2:00 a.m. to a possible suicide attempt. I was given a description of a white male who was on the outside of the walking path along the driving deck. This was in the days of just the single bridge, and I was aware there was a large I-beam that ran the length of the bridge between each span. The beam was wide enough to stand on it without much fear of falling, but on that day, it had rained a fair amount, and it made the beam a bit slippery.

When I arrived, I could see the man standing just on the other side of the railing, as well as other units who were there trying to speak to the man. As I approached, I could hear the other officers talking to the man to ascertain if he was suicidal or just exactly what he was doing. His answers were mostly "fuck you" and such. He was also laughing at the officers as he tried to goad them to come out on the beam with him. Of course, he resorted to taunts of 'chicken shit,' etc. If that was being 'chicken shit,' then I was just fine with that title.

Suddenly the man began to run down the beam, which scared me a bit. I said to him, "Dude, do you know how wet that beam is?"

His response: "Fuck you, you pussy!" He then looked down at the beam, and I assumed he was reassessing his macho tactics and might realize he was a bit stupid. I was wrong. Not only did he run on this wet beam, but he started dancing on it as well.

None of us wanted to reach out to try and grab this guy; 1) because it was about a 3–4 foot reach and 2) if he had a death wish, none of us wanted to reach out for him to grab on to us so we could join him to the watery grave below. Talking to this guy, who was acting like a court jester, was our only alternative, for the most part.

Then it happened. He started skipping along with dancing on the beam, and in a flash, he was gone. I mean, this guy just disappeared from sight. We then realized he fell backward to the outside of the beam and disappeared into the darkness. I couldn't see him but could hear him scream all the way to the water. I know what I'm about to say may seem a bit uncaring, but he didn't sound so tough as he fell to his demise. Let's keep in mind that we tried our best to get him to come back to the driving deck and made sure he was well aware of the dangers he was facing—only to be shunned as if we were the stupid ones. That may seem a bit heartless, but you kind of get that way when you try hard to help someone only to be told to "fuck off."

Even before the guy hit the water, I radioed dispatch and let them know he fell off the bridge. The fireboat was sent out, and after a couple of hours, his body was discovered near Fox Island.

Suicides

In my separate Tacoma Narrows Bridge section, it talked about suicides from it, and there are other areas where suicides are done. These are incidents where I have been a team member to try and stop the action and have witnessed them firsthand. It's never fun to try and talk someone off the ledge and especially to witness someone who actually succeeds in taking their life. These next two stories have both a pleasant and a bad outcome.

I'll Be Right Down

This was an incident where my sergeant, JM, was the one who called it out. It seemed he just happened to come onto it.

I entered an alley (Court C), and standing in the alley was the Sergeant looking up at a five-story building. At the top of the building was a man lying on the edge wall of the roof. Sgt JM was talking to the man as I exited my patrol car. The man was saying, "Just get out of the way so I can get this done."

After only a few moments, Sgt Moore said, "Don't do anything before I get up there to talk to you."

As soon as the Sgt walked into the doorway for the building, the guy said, "I'll be down before you get up here."

At that point, he rolled off the edge wall face down. I yelled to my sergeant. "Here he comes!"

When the man hit the pavement, I was a bit surprised by the sound of his body striking the concrete surface. It sounded as if someone took a burlap sack full of chains and tossed the bag off the building. After we transported the man to the hospital—he survived the fall but passed away about an hour afterward—I asked the doctor about what I heard. The doctor surmised the sound was all of his joints popping at the same time. That was a bit of a 'wow' moment for me. I don't think I will ever forget that sound.

Later I gave great thought to this call. I wished we could have made contact with him and help him through what was concerning him. This was so different than the dancing idiot on the Narrows Bridge. This guy wasn't taunting anyone, nor did he want to hurt anyone else. I can only think he was dealing with demons, and this was the only thing to do to relieve his torment. I pray his soul was accepted in Heaven.

Ferry Boat Launch

Then there were the three guys who launched themselves off the Vashon Island ferry boat car ramp. It was about 3:00 a.m. that witnesses said a car, occupied by three people, was traveling about 70–80 MPH down the hill from Point Defiance Park entrance to the ferry dock. The hill is long and somewhat steep, allowing even a small engine car to get up to a fast speed. Additionally, the ramp was pulled up with a one-armed barrier made of wood. A car traveling at a high rate of speed could easily break the arm and get a great deal of air. According to the witnesses, that's exactly what happened. With that in mind, and given the description of the events that night, the impact when the car hit the water would be severe.

Divers were called out and were to locate the car. They wrapped a cable to the frame, and we called out a crane to lift the car out of the water. The three young men were not wearing seat belts and might have been knocked unconscious, given they were all in odd positions and there was no attempt to exit the car.

To this day, I don't know if they were committing suicide or this was a prank gone wrong.

The Poopy Pants Rapist

I know the title of this story may strike a funny bone, but I want everyone to understand while reading this what this guy did was no less than horrible. He was a monster of the worst kind. What I did to him, by my hand, was the least I could do for the victim. I enjoyed every moment of this and was glad we got this call.

The call was a rape suspect, who I will refer to in this story as Poopy; he was in a red older Ford Taurus. We were further told he was caught in the act of forcing his five-year-old niece to commit oral sex on him. This was sick at the highest level.

When I heard that, I felt sick to my stomach and extreme anger. I immediately thought about my daughter, who was seven at the time, and how I would have felt if that had happened to her. I also thought about if this guy forced his niece to do this, what other little kid had he abused and gotten away with the same disgusting crime. This guy was one of those who are lower than the bottom of a cesspool.

In this case, he was able to escape the scene and run to his friend's house. Unbeknownst to his friend of what he did, Poopy was able to convince him to give him a ride to a nearby town.

According to witnesses who gave the description of the car said it was headed south on Jackson Avenue from 6th Ave. Great! We were at 12th & Jacksons; all we had to do was wait for just a moment or two for the car to go by. This was my lucky day because our wait was short. We pulled out after the car got about a block down the street.

Our strategy was to see if we could find a traffic-related violation to pull the car over, and we got one. We ran the license plate and found out the registered owner of the Taurus had a suspended license. Perfect. That gave us the reason to stop the car as under a 'reasonable man standard.' We had every right to believe the registered owner was driving the car.

We put on the overhead lights, and just before 40th Street, where the road changed names to Bridgeport Way, began our 'traffic stop.' The car pulled into the Albertson's parking lot to the left, but the driver pulled the car all the way up close to the building. The Albertson's parking lot is very large, and where the car had stopped, it put us about 50 yards from the street. My partner was the driving officer this day, and he went up to the driver's side to contact the driver. Our suspect was in the front passenger seat.

I got out of the car, as per routine, and stood at the front of our car. As I stood there, the suspect got out of the Taurus. He was a white male, blond hair, slender build, and stood about 6'3". He was wearing a blue T-shirt and white shorts. However, I was quite disgusted with this piece of crap, yet I had to treat him with respect. I asked him to remain in the car for now until we got the traffic stop finished.

Instead of getting back in the car, he looked toward the street and then back at me. He did that several times, and I knew what he was doing; he was assessing his ability to get away. I was semi-sure he knew the real reason for the traffic stop and knew the gig was up. He had nothing to lose to try to get away, except, of course, my wrath. I once again asked him to remain in the car, but he wasn't having it. He took off like a rabbit toward the street. *Okay, here we go.* The chase was on.

As I ran after him, I yelled, "You better not let me catch you because I'm going to kick your ass!" I caught him in the middle of Bridgeport and had already extracted my nightstick, so I began using it. I hit him several times on his bare legs giving him welt after welt. I yelled at him to "get on the ground." Now that the statute of limitations had run out, I can tell you he was trying to get on the ground, but I was holding him up with my left arm while I swung freely with my right.

This was all happening in front of a restaurant by the name of Captain Nemo's (which has since been closed). I knew most of the waitresses there, and when they heard the commotion outside, they came out to see me smacking this guy. A couple of them yelled to me and said, "Hit him harder, Stu. Hit him harder." Well, I was hitting him as hard as I could. Even my partner told me later he could hear and feel the cracks all the back where he was at the traffic stop. Cool!

So as I was hitting this guy, I didn't realize he actually crapped his pants. Once I let him go to the ground for cuffing, I saw and smelled the brown liquid seeping down between his legs. *Are you kidding me? So he really is a piece of shit,* I thought. Nevertheless, I got him cuffed and stood him up. I told him he was under arrest and advised him of his rights. Then, of course, I had to point out the obvious. "I see you are quite the dude—diddling five-year-old and shitting your pants, all in one day. Yep, I'm sure your momma is quite proud of you. Wait until the guys at the big house find out what you're in for."

"They will never know," he said.

"Trust me, they will find out, and if they don't, I'll make sure everyone there knows." I not so gently informed him.

As we walked back to the patrol car, I saw that look on my partner's face. It was an 'oh my God, what the hell happened' look. He saw the brown streak and could smell it coming. That's when he told me he could hear and feel the hits and wasn't surprised our suspect shit his pants, not to mention the welts on both of his legs.

My partner had already placed the driver of the car in the back of our patrol car, and he was actually the registered owner – perfect again. The warrant was confirmed; additionally, my partner told me he was cooperative.

We devised a plan. We did not want Poopy in the back of our car. With that in mind, we decided to call out another patrol unit so we could 'separate' our two arrests. I didn't really need to do that, but hey, we did all the work so someone else can share in the arrest. I know, we're jerks.

A few minutes later, one of our friends, a female officer, showed up. My partner immediately got her out of her car as I stood downwind with Poopy. My partner walked her away from her patrol car as he explained the entire incident to her. When he got her far enough away, I scurried as I stuffed Poopy in the back of her car. As soon as I did that, my partner cut off the conversation and said, "Okay, see you at the station." We got in our car before she could, and off we went. As we drove out of the parking lot, I looked back and saw her get into the patrol car. She wasn't in there more than a second or two when she jumped out. She was not happy; she even appeared to be quite angry. And I believe she was using some very unladylike language.

As we left the parking lot, the driver of the car, who was now in our backseat, said, "That was not very nice of you guys." He then paused for a second and said, "It was funny though, but not nice." We had to agree.

At the station where we unloaded prisoners, there was a loading dock we would pull up to. To get to it, you turn off the street and drive down a long hill. We got there a few minutes before our female friend. We might have been exceeding the speed limit by just a few MPHs. As we exited our car, we saw her coming down the hill at a, let's say, rapid pace. She slammed on the brakes, slammed the car into park, jumped out, and said, "You sons a bitches!"

"What?" I said very inquisitively.

"You know exactly what I'm talking about! This guy shit his pants!" she said, quite angrily.

"Oh my goodness that must have happened after we put him in the car," I told her.

Her answer was, "You're full of shit, Enzo. Get this asshole out of my car." I did.

When we got to the booking desk with these two guys, it was busy with other arrests. I wanted to make sure the correction officers knew who they were dealing with, so in a loud voice, I asked for a booking form so I could fill it out while I waited because I wanted to "make sure we get this guy who raped his five-year-old niece booked quickly."

Silence draped the entire booking area. Suspects and corrections officers alike stared at Poopy. One of the larger suspects pointed at Poopy and said, "You are mine." When I looked at Poopy, I saw fear cover his entire face. Sometimes it's just fun being a cop. I don't know what happened to Poopy in prison, and I don't care.

Traffic Stops

"You don't know what you are talking about."

During my career at Tacoma PD, I never worked the traffic side of law enforcement; it just seemed boring. In patrol, the calls were always different; one moment, you could be on a robbery, next to a burglary, maybe a homicide or rape, or maybe even a traffic accident. It always jumped around, and that's what made it more interesting for me. In traffic, you wrote tickets, or you responded to a traffic accident; that was the main core of your existence. Some of my calls, as you've read in this book, were a combination of exciting, fun, and tragic or any other adjective you would like to describe them as. You just never knew what you'd get from call to call.

Aside from thinking traffic was just sheer boredom, my other reason for not working traffic was I hated giving tickets just for the sake of filling a quota. As a patrol officer and not a traffic officer, I could have gone my entire 22 years at TPD without ever giving out even one traffic notice of infraction, and it wouldn't have stirred the slightest concern. Patrol officers were there to be available for calls of service, which is what we did. Traffic officers, on the other hand, had to be available for traffic issues: violators and accidents.

Did TPD traffic officers have a quota? Yes, but not much of one as they had to produce at least one ticket for every unaccountable hour. Basically, if you were on a traffic accident or a patrol-type call (robbery, domestic violence, etc.), that was considered an accountable hour, so you didn't have to produce a ticket for that time. Pumping out a single ticket per hour was actually pretty easy to do, but still, something I just didn't think was much fun.

That does not mean I never gave out a ticket or made traffic stops. If I saw a violation, no matter how small, I would make the stop to talk to the driver. I always had the intention of giving them a verbal warning and sending them on their way. Of course, if, after making contact, I found out they had a revoked or suspended driver's license, they would get written up or even booked into jail. If they were revoked/suspended (a crime in Washington State), not only would I book them but write them for the original reason I stopped them as well, so as to justify the reason(s) leading to the arrest. Also, making traffic stops many times led to a warrant for the driver's arrest. A few of my traffic stops led to felony warrants, which made the traffic stop a bit more rewarding.

My reason for not enjoying the pleasures of giving traffic tickets was because I sympathized with people. Maybe they were running late for work or dropping off their kids to piano lessons, or how about sports events or truly a myriad of other things. Plus, it's not like I hadn't pushed the envelope from time to time because I was running behind schedule. The difference for me was most cops, not all, gave professional courtesy and let you walk on the minor violations. Was it 'right' to get those breaks? On the surface, almost everyone would say it wasn't, but let me ask this: what job doesn't have a perk or two? For me, the professional courtesy extended to firefighters, ER doctors, and nurses as well. My reason for them getting the breaks on minor violations was the last thing I needed. If I ever got shot,

I didn't need that trauma nurse, doctor, or medical aid firefighter to remember me as "the bastard that gave me a ticket" and then spit in my wound. Ooooooooo, no thank-you. I wanted them to remember me as the very nice police officer who was kind and gave them a break.

As for major violations, just like everyone else, we're screwed. For those who were reckless, that was different. As a cop, nurse, doctor, or firefighter, when you toy with other people's lives, you're going to be drawing the short straw with me and get a ticket or the arrest you deserved, not slack. This included a suspected DUI contact as that is not a traffic stop; it is clearly a crime of huge proportions. In my career, I've had a couple of firefighters, nurses, and a doctor on a DUI arrest.

Though I didn't like handing out tickets, there are those who find it necessary to talk themselves into a ticket. I never expected people to bow or even give me ultra respect just because I was a cop. I looked at stops as a sort of business contact. When I stop you for a traffic violation, you can disagree with me as much as you like; that is your right. But just don't argue with me on the street; that's what the courtroom was for. I used to love it when people would say, "I'll see you in court, officer." Good, that's your right to do so; let the judge decide who was correct. I had zero issues with going to court, plus I could always use the overtime pay.

I can't speak for all cops, but on routine traffic stops, my thoughts were always to walk up to the car and just give a warning. "Hey, your tabs need to be updated," or "slow down," or "you didn't stop at that stop sign back there" were my first thoughts. If all went as planned and you didn't have something other than a traffic violation, you were headed on your way in short order. If you were nice to me and you had a valid driver's license, this would be short and sweet. For the most part, my tactic went well. But as I just stated, for the most part, there's always got to be the exception to the rule.

This tale was one of the few times I was working the day shift. Side note: I didn't like the day shift at all because of the number of people that were out there. Plus, there were these people like the guy I'm going to tell you about. Those who tell you, "I know my rights" or "I pay your salary" or the ones I loved the best, "I'll have your badge for this;" you know that kind. I'm sure you may even have a friend or two that are like this guy.

These types of people were always fun to play with. I was bad about taunting them from time to time. First of all, the vast majority have no clue what the Bill of Rights states, and for their information, we all pay each other's salaries, whether by paying taxes or shopping at a retail store. As for the ones who wanted my badge would have no clue what to do with it once they got it.

On a side story, I was challenged by some guy in Downtown Tacoma who, out of the blue, just walked up to me and said, "If you weren't wearing that badge, I'd kick your ass!" My partner and I looked at each other with a 'what the hell' look.

But with the challenge, I took off my badge and handed it to my partner. I told the guy, "Let's rock."

Then he said, "Well if you didn't have that gun, I'd kick your ass!"

So I took off my gun belt and handed it to my partner, telling my loud-mouth friend, "Okay, pal, there's no anchor tied to your butt so let's get it on." Then he was about to give me another excuse or something else I was wearing he wanted me to remove, but I interrupted him, saying, "What? You need me to get naked before you get the balls to do something?" As soon as I finished my statement, I charged him, and he ran off like the scared little boy he really was.

I know I just digressed a bit here, but as I write this book of tales or memories—however, you see it—I just think of things that kind of relate to what I just mentioned, like the contact line from someone about "I'll have your badge." So now, let's get back to this traffic stop with my model citizen.

So as I was stating, I wasn't much of a fan of the day shift. On graveyard shift, it was basically crooks and victims out there, and not a great deal of traffic to get in your way. I really felt I was doing good police work there and not trying to be a public relations guy.

On this rare day shift, I found myself on one of Tacoma's busiest streets, South 38th. It was definitely a street that during the day I would have avoided. Traffic was always horrendous due to the number of businesses located along this thoroughfare. When I say I found myself there, it was just not my favorite place to be in Tacoma, and I only went there this day to get an Arby's sandwich and a large coke; Arby's in those days was not open on graveyard timings. The plan was to get my sandwich and get off that street. After getting my meal and as I was attempting to pull into traffic, I realized, once again, why I avoided this area of town. This street was the main access to the Tacoma Mall, every known fast food place on the planet, as well as other small shopping centers lined both sides of the street. 38th Street also is a major Interstate 5 junction that also leads to Highway 16 (The Narrows Bridge) and Downtown. During the day, there is a ton of stuff going on that street, making it virtually impossible to get around. Even if you have lights and sirens going, it is virtually impossible to get traffic out of your way; there just isn't any place for drivers to go to get out of the way of an emergency vehicle 'running code.' For all intents and purposes, it sucks to drive on 38th during the daylight hours.

But here I was trying to get back into traffic from the Arby's drive-through. It took me a while, but after some time, a good citizen finally took some pity on me, or maybe they just didn't like having a cop behind them, probably more likely the case and let me into traffic. Nevertheless, I was out and headed to my favorite hiding place to eat my lunch.

As I was headed to seclusion, I noticed an older car in front of me which had expired tabs. I called Records Division on the radio, and they confirmed that, indeed, the tabs were expired. They also informed me they were only two weeks overdue. *Okay*, I thought, *this will be an easy stop just to let the driver know about his expired tabs, and we'd both be on our way.* No problem, right?

I hit the overhead lights, but the driver did not pull over. It was a sunny day, so I figured he didn't see the lights, so I 'burped' the siren. That's when the driver pulled over to the side of the road, but where the driver stopped, we were blocking traffic, and that was not something you would want to do on this street if you could help it. Even for as short a time, this traffic stop would block traffic, making things worse than they already were. About a half a block down the street from where the driver stopped was an entrance to a large parking lot. That looked like a better choice to me, so I got on the external speaker for my patrol car and asked if the driver could 'please' pull into that lot. The driver complied. This was going well so far. This stop had all the makings of easy contact.

During all this, I could not see the driver, and actually, though I knew better, it looked as if no one was driving the car. I assumed at this point that the driver was small and probably a female. I know that may be sexist but don't get on some rant about me profiling as statistics back me up that; in general, females are smaller than men, so it was reasonable to assume it was a female.

The driver pulled into the parking lot but stopped in a place that was barely inside the lot, plus we were semi-blocking the entrance. I thought, *why is this person so stupid? Oh well, let's make this quick, and I'll just go up there, tell the driver about their expired tabs and get both of us on our way. Quick and easy, right? Yeah, okay.*

When I walked up to the driver's door, I was a bit surprised to see it was a man driving the car, and he appeared to be in his late 70s or early 80s. With him was an elderly woman, who I assumed was his wife. Before I could say one word, the driver said, "What the fuck do you want?" Was he kidding me? This was where we were starting this contact?

I asked, "You really don't want to begin this contact like that, do you?"

Again, he said, "What the fuck do you want, Officer?" (Now add a heavily sarcastic tone on the word 'officer' part.)

"Okay, if this is what you want to do, I want your fucking driver's license, the fucking registration, and proof of fucking insurance," I told him.

After getting the information, I still wanted this to be an easy contact and just be a warning, so I said, "Let's start over." I thought maybe we could calm this down a bit, get back on track, and I could get to my lunch, which in my mind was the most important thing right now (Side note here: my wife will tell you I get a bit grumpy when I'm hungry). Even though I was making the most valiant effort to get along with this guy, he still wanted to be a jerk to me. All he did was repeat what he said before with the same sarcastic inflection in his voice.

"Okay, if that's what you want, that is what I was going to deliver. Just trying to be the best public servant I could be."

I told the driver his tabs were expired, to which he stated, "You have no idea what the hell you're talking about." I then told him to exit his vehicle and come to the back of his car. He got out, and I could see he was all about 5'3" inches tall and was using a cane to dawdle to the rear of the car. When he got there, I showed him the tabs were expired, and he needed to renew them. There was no way he was going to admit fault, and he stated, "That's not my problem; it's the state's problem." I explained to him the tabs were his responsibility to get updated. Keep in mind that I was still just trying to make this a positive contact and end up as a warning – folks, this is how much I detested giving traffic tickets.

At the mention of his tabs being his responsibility, he became outrageously irate. His face turned so red I thought he was going to have a stroke right in front of me. Damn, then what — medical aid and no lunch; again, not to mention the reams of paperwork. What he did next changed the course of this entire stop. I knew he was angry, but not so much he would do the absolute idiotic thing he did. Suddenly he raised his cane over his head as if he were going to strike me with it. That was it! As he held the cane over his head in a striking pose, shaking it, I had every right to haul off and slug him, but I knew that would probably kill this little squatty body asshat. So instead of taking a slug at him, I reached up and grabbed the cane, holding it from coming down; I got close to his ear — basically nose to nose — and said, "If that cane comes any closer to me, I'm going to take it away from you and beat you to a bloody pulp and leave you here in this parking lot;

you hear me, old man!" (Add a heavily sarcastic tone to "you hear me, old man.")

I don't know if he saw the seriousness of the tone of my voice or he just got a word from God telling him not to do it, but as suddenly as he raised the cane, he lowered it to the ground when I let go, and with a grunt, he went dawdling back to the driver's door and got in the car. He sat there grunting and grumbling under his breath. I could not hear him, but I'm sure he was not reciting compliments about me. Have you heard of the movie *Grumpy Old Men*? I think the movie must have gotten their title from this guy.

Did I write the ticket? You bet I did. Why? Because he was a true definition of an asshole. I don't know what climbed up his butt, but he took a verbal warning and elevated it to a traffic ticket. Stupid, stupid, stupid! By the way, when I came up to the car to have him sign the ticket, he first refused. I thought, *okay, I really want to put you in jail right now; damn the sandwich,* but I was required to inform him his refusal to sign will result in his arrest and booking into jail. If he refused again, it was a crime, and I would have no issue in carting his butt to the Pierce County Jail. Inside I was hoping he would refuse again, but he didn't, as

I'm sure common sense took over. So he decided to sign the ticket with a grunt or two. Damn it; I wanted so much to cart this ass to jail. After giving him his copy, and as I turned to go back to my car, I heard his wife say, "When are you going to learn to just shut up?"

Back at my car, I had another one of those lunches cops all over the world can relate to—a cold sandwich and all the ice melted in my coke. Crap!

My Uncle's a Judge

As I have said, I never liked giving out traffic tickets, but sometimes being nice does not pay off.

I was on routine patrol driving north on Broadway Street in Downtown Tacoma when suddenly a yellow VW Bug pulled in front of me, causing me to brake very abruptly to avoid hitting the VW. I was thinking, *how could this driver miss seeing a police car? Oh well, no accident, no damage to either car, so I'll just pull over the car and chat with the driver — no need for a ticket, just a chat.*

On came the overhead lights, and the driver stopped, not on the right side of the road, but right there in the middle of the lane. I got on the loudspeaker and asked the driver to pull the car to the right. No movement at all, so I asked again—still nothing. This was not starting out very well.

I got out of my car and walked up to the driver's door, and told him to roll down his window. Instead, he opened the door. I asked the driver, a 20 something male, to roll down the window and close the door. The driver said the window did not roll down. That happens, so I let it be.

I asked him if he saw me when he pulled out from his parking spot. He said he did. Next question: "So why did you pull out in front of me?"

"You weren't that close," he said. His answer was more defensive and argumentative than explanation, so I began to feel this contact was not going to be an easy one. I asked for his driver's license and registration. He fumbled through his wallet and handed me his Washington State Driver's License but said he did not know where the registration was.

I looked at the driver's license and felt I recognized the name but couldn't place it. Oh well, no biggie, I'd just take the license and run it for warrants and driver's status. I had the license in my left hand, so as I turned to walk back to my car, the driver snatched the license out of my hand, saying, "You can't have this." Oh man, we were really headed down that path. I told him to surrender his license and advised him if he did not, I was going to be forced to arrest him. So then, this verbal warning was headed to an arrest. Why do people do this shit?

His answer was that there was no way he would give up that license. With that, I placed him under arrest. That didn't matter because he was not getting out of the car. I expected him to try and start the car, but he didn't do that either. What he did do was get a death grip on the steering wheel. I grabbed his left wrist and his hair and tried as I might, but he was not letting go. Time and time again, I pulled and ordered him out of the car, but nothing was working.

Suddenly a citizen (male) came up to the passenger side of the Bug and asked, "Do you need help, Officer?"

"Sure, if you'd be willing to assist," I replied. What happened next was nothing near what I expected in the way of help.

The citizen came around the car, ducked under my right arm, faced the driver, and delivered 6–7 punches to the left side of the face of the diver. That's what it took for the suspect to let go of the steering wheel. I had so much pulling force on the driver that when he let go of the steering wheel, all three of us fell backward onto the pavement. The driver was quite stunned from the citizen's blows and the falling out of the car, so I was able to right myself quickly and get him into handcuffs before he even came close to regaining full consciousness. Once I had him upright, he became aware of what was happening and began telling me about his uncle, the superior court judge. That was it—the reason why the name on his license was so familiar to me.

Oh dandy, I thought! Not only did this traffic stop went from a warning to an arrest, but it also went from municipal court to superior court—perfect.

After putting my driver in the back seat of the patrol car, I thanked my citizen and made sure to get all his information. If for no other reason but to send him a thankyou.

When I got back to the patrol car, I could see my suspect's left side of the face swelling up, so I would have to take him to the hospital before taking him to jail. At the hospital, it was all going quite well until his uncle, the superior court judge, showed up. I had no idea how he found out about the arrest other than someone recognized this guy and called his uncle. His uncle showed his disdain for me, saying, "This isn't over yet, Officer." He also told me to release his nephew to his custody.

"Is that a court order, your honor?" I asked.

"Yes, it is," was his reply. *Good, you can have the little bastard*, I thought.

Just before I was about to leave, the good judge said (very sarcastically), "My nephew is mentally deficient, or couldn't you tell that?"

I responded with, "To answer your question, no, because I'm a cop and not a psychiatrist, and if that's the case, how did he get a driver's license?" No answer; he just walked away.

As you can imagine, the internal affairs investigation started within days of this incident at the behest of the 'good' judge. I had no worries; I had a witness, the union, and the law behind me, so I thought, *bring it on, folks*.

US Marshal's Office

I only worked for the US Marshal's office in Seattle from November 2004 to December 2006 as a court security officer. I actually hate every bit of my two years working there. When I tell people I was a Special Deputy US Marshal, it seems quite glamorous to them or maybe impressive, not sure why. Quite frankly, it was one of the most boring jobs I've ever done. Not only that, but the Marshal Service actually looked down their nose at us retired cops. An example of the attitude toward us street cops was when I met the Marshal himself. When I was first hired, I was excited to begin another adventure. They acted friendly, and our meeting began well as he shook my hand and greeted me with all the routine pleasantries one would expect. Also, he outlined my duties, but just as the short meeting was about to end, he said, "Just one last thing."

"Sure, Marshal, what is it?" I asked.

"When you come to work here, park your fucking brain at the door because we really don't need you to think," he said. What? At first, I thought he was just joking, but the seriousness on his face was clear; this was no joke. After that meeting, I found out he had no use for us but had no control as to whether or not we were hired.

As I stayed for those two years, that attitude was pervasive throughout the Marshal Service, not only by the Marshal but by some of the deputies as well. Not all of them, obviously, but a good number of them. The deputies' attitude probably was nurtured because they might have been indoctrinated by him, and I think if they didn't follow in lockstep, their career there would be a bit difficult. After two years, with my wife and I working hard on our real estate business, I decided to just bag this little hell hole.

There are three short tales I can share which have a humorous outcome.

Before we get into this little story, you need to know a few things. First, the Marshals are based at the US Federal Court House in Seattle. The building is staffed 24/7 by us, the lowlife court security officers. I suppose doing what we did was just beneath them. We were staffed with a skeletal crew of two special deputies on the graveyard shift (11 p.m. to 7 a.m.).

Second, around the building are several cameras that are monitored from a control/command center. Each camera can be moved, and every one of them has a speaker where the person in the control center can speak to the person on the street. The cameras are mostly for watching people if they appear suspicious – they may be carrying a weapon or possibly even planting a bomb – that sort of stuff. The cameras are there to pick up any activity around the building, and on graveyard shift is where activity is the most interesting.

Third, each of the cameras has a speaker mounted near the top of the pole so the command center officer can communicate with the party near that particular camera.

Poor Little Puppy

Dates are a bit blurry, but the incidents are quite clear; I do remember this incident was a summer evening. I was in the control room one graveyard shift when a man and his dog came into the front courtyard area. This was common, even on the graveyard shift. The courtyard area is large, nicely landscaped with several park benches for people to enjoy.

The man walked into the area and sat on a bench directly under one of the cameras. I happen to noticed he had a newspaper in his hand. The dog he had with him was a border collie, black and white, and laid down under the bench. Okay, typical sort of scene, I didn't think much of it, so I went back to doing other things, but I turned on the speaker by the camera to hear anything going on, mainly because I was bored.

Suddenly I saw, in my peripheral vision, a fast movement across the screen and heard a sharp thump. Did I just see this guy smack the dog with the rolled newspaper? I could also see the dog trying to move away from the man, but the man was pulling the dog by its leash to be in front of him. I continued to watch, and I'd be damned if he didn't do it again. That just pissed me off. I get people's need to discipline their pets, but only if they did something wrong. Speakers on, and I didn't hear this guy admonishing the dog for something or the dog barking incessantly. No, the dog was quiet and doing much of nothing other than lying there. As I was about to get on the speaker and put the fear of God in this guy, he hit the dog a third time. He was not hitting the dog across the dog's rump; oh no, he was smacking the dog across the snout. This dog was cowering and trying to hide from this ass-hat, all the while Mr. Tough-guy pulling the dog toward him to take another smack at the animal.

Just as he was about to take another swing, I got on my microphone and said, "You hit that dog one more time, and I'm going to come out there, take that newspaper from you, and slap the dog-shit out of you." The look on this guy's face was priceless as his head swung about, looking for where that voice was coming from. His head looked as if it was on a swivel. I thought for sure he was about to do a Linda Blair exorcist head spin trying to see who was there.

"Yep, this is the voice of God," I said to him. At that point, he scooped up his dog and started hustling out of the courtyard in an attempt to obviously get away from that voice. The problem for him was that he walked alongside the building under several camera posts and then along the backside of the building, where there were even more posts. I just thought *this is going to be fun*. What do you think I did? If you guessed harassed him at each camera that he passed by, you got it. I was merciless as he reached every station, telling him I was on my way down to take that newspaper and beat him over the head with it, which of course, I wasn't, but he didn't need to know that.

As he passed a camera and I was telling him I was still watching, he would pick up his pace. By the time he reached the back of the building, this guy was a dead sprint. Fear was setting in a massive way. I was beginning to feel quite proud of myself. I kind of knew what he was thinking, "when will this guy leave me alone?"

Did I help the dog? I don't know for sure, but will this guy think twice before he smacks his dog for no good reason? I think so. So maybe I did help, at least for that night.

Come Back Here and Clean That Up

Once again, this was a summer night, and I was working the graveyard shift again (I enjoyed that shift because it was just my co-worker and me in the entire building). I saw a woman walking alongside the building, and my attention was drawn to her because of her suspicious activity. She would stop on the sidewalk and look up and down the street as if she was looking for someone or seeing if anyone was watching or maybe following her. She did that routine several times as she walked along the rear of the building.

I moved the closest camera near her to see what she was looking at or searching for but couldn't see anything up or down the street. She continued to walk slowly, and when she got in front of the loading dock area, which is an alcove, she walked directly to the large roll-up door. Now I thought that she was truly up to no good. I mean, what was she going to do at the roll-up doors? I alerted my partner, Paul, telling him we had something suspicious going on at the loading dock door. I gave him the description of the female and to use extreme caution.

Just after giving Paul the information on this suspicious person, I watched as she walked backward toward the roll-up door. This was getting stranger by the minute. *What is she doing?* I wondered. I could not see any place where she might be hiding any explosives.

Then suddenly, she dropped out of sight. She bent down, kneeled down, and something. Oh man, I didn't want to be on a shift where we had some bomber in a skirt. I immediately moved the camera down, and that's when I figured out exactly what she was up to. She was looking for a place to urinate. Down went her pants, and so did her underwear. I let Paul know this was not what I expected and to go ahead and cancel, and I would explain later.

I could not just let this go. No way. This was just too rich, and I had to come after her using the tools I had at my disposal. I got on the speaker, and in a loud, sharp voice, I said, "What the hell are you doing?" I don't know if I got her in midstream, but those pants went up in a flash, and she began to walk, semi trot, down the street. Was I done with her? Not on your life! I had to get one more dig in. I yelled, "Hey, come back and clean that up." She didn't miss a step or acknowledge my remarks, but I knew she heard me because she gave me, or at least the camera, the 'finger.' She was so special.

Love Is In the Air

This time I wasn't in the control room, and I remember it to be a cold winter's evening, which makes this tale a bit strange.

Paul was in the control room this time when he called me on the radio. He wanted me to head to the front entrance to make contact with two people there. I asked what was going on, and all he would tell me was I'd figure it out when I got there. Okay, so off I went. I figured it must be something unique given what he said. I was on the 7th floor at the time, so I jumped on the elevator, and as I approached the 3rd floor, I could hear a pounding noise coming from the front entrance door. The entrance doors were glass, and they led to a vast area that, when someone was knocking, echoed quite loudly. The noise that was being created sounded as if someone was banging on the doors.

When the elevator doors opened, the noise was very loud, and given the doors were made of glass, I was concerned that whoever was banging on the door might just break the glass. After passing the scanning machines, I could see exactly why Paul didn't tell me what was going on.

There they were. A couple in their 30s, having their way with each other. They were standing with the female against the door and the male driving it home. Before I actually reached the doors, I could tell these people had no clue I was there; they fell to the cold concrete. Her blouse was wide open, and her skirt was hiked up around her waist. As for the guy, his pants were past his buttocks, and he was going to town. There was no doubt these two had to be feeling the 28-degree temperature outside; how could they not? Now it was my job to ruin this romantic moment.

I bent down, getting as close to their ears as the glass door would allow, and said, "Don't you think you might find a better place to do this?" You know what; they didn't hear me. Damn it! So this time, I pounded on the door as loud as I could, and that got their attention. They both turned and saw me kneeling there. I just smiled and waved at them.

She was the first to react; I think he still wanted to keep going. She pushed her male friend off of her and franticly began putting herself back together. The guy, on the other hand, appeared angry but put himself back together as well, and without even a pleasant goodbye, off they scurried into the night. I waved, but they didn't wave back. Hmm, how rude.

Tina

One of the wonderful things that ever happened to me during my time as a police officer wasn't actually in the line of duty but after hours, so to speak. That was meeting, for the third time, my wife Tina. Wait a minute—the third time? Yep, you read that right. My wife and I met three times over a few years before we actually got together. Each time we 'met,' the previous encounters were not remembered, and no connection was made; until we actually truly met, the one that led us down the aisle. I know that may be a bit confusing, but as you read this tale, you'll see what I mean.

The first time we ever met was a quick greeting. Nothing to write home about, I assure you, especially for me. In the mid-80s, there was a nightclub in the upstairs part of a restaurant called C. I. Shenanigans. It was a truly fun place to go and located on Tacoma's waterfront. Everything about this nightspot was one of the more perfect settings for romantic encounters. This first encounter with Tina was extremely brief and not the slightest bit romantic. I simply walked up to her and asked her to dance, to which I was promptly turned down. I walked away with a heavily bruised ego, but I was never a guy who just gave up. Of course, it wasn't going to be her again, at least not that night. After being turned down, I just walked over to another girl and asked her, and she said yes. So there, take that my unknown future wife! I will explain a bit later how we figured out our ever so brief meeting.

The second time we met was a bit more extensive; it was on a call. My partner and I were dispatched for a possible burglary. We arrived at a large brick home, and we could hear an alarm going off from the upstairs portion of the house. I knocked on the front door, and we were greeted by Tina (I didn't know that at the time, nor I remembered the previous brief encounter). What I remember was a very cute blonde who greeted me. She said she tried to cancel the call, but the dispatcher would not allow her to do that. She also told my partner and me that the upstairs was occupied by another tenant, and there was probably no one up there at this time. It seemed the alarm had recently been installed due to a previous break-in.

Tina said she had called the neighbor at the rear of the house to see what that neighbor could see. The neighbor told her it looked as if the door was just slightly open. The upstairs apartment had its own entry at the rear of the house. My partner decided to go to the rear and went around the building to make entry. That left me to make an entry via the stairway inside the house that also led to the upstairs. That meant I was now alone with this little hottie, Tina. She showed me where the stairway was, and as I started up the stairs, Tina was following right behind me. Prior to going upstairs, I told her I needed to have her stay downstairs until we cleared the upstairs apartment; she was having none of that. It was obvious to me there was no way she was going to miss the action. I wasn't going to convince her to stay on the main level, so it was useless to argue with her.

As a pure procedure, I drew my weapon and told her to at least stay behind me, just in case. As I went up the stairs, she was directly behind me; she told me months later she thought that was cool when I drew my weapon. When we got to the top, my partner was already there fumbling with the alarm, trying desperately to get it to shut off, but to no avail. Tina made quick work of turning it off for him—I suppose knowing the alarm code helps. After talking to her and seeing there was no sign of forced entry, my partner and I decided it was just a door that was not latched correctly, and given there was a breeze earlier in the evening, that was probably what popped it open. We cleared the call and headed to the car.

When my partner and I got to the patrol car, I told him we needed to return for 'follow up,' given there are a couple of cuties that live there. Tina had a roommate, which I saw a picture of on an end table. My partner did not really respond in a way that I suspected he would, just kind of a casual, "Yeah, sure," sort of answer.

My partner was scheduled to take the next few days off, so I would be working alone. I thought that was perfect given his attitude and allowed me to make my own follow-up contacts. Armed with some pamphlets for how to keep a secure house and so on, I made my pilgrimage to that brick house to see if I could make contact and maybe just chat with this little blonde I met a few days earlier. I drove up to the house in my freshly washed patrol car, got out in my straight from the dry cleaners uniform, and rang the doorbell. No answer. Okay, let's try and knock on the door; still no answer. Crap! I wasn't ready to give up quite yet, so I went back three days in a row, but each time, it turned into a dead end. *Well, that sucks*, I thought, but I had a rule with myself when it came to women. If I tried three times and failed, then I used the basic baseball rule: three strikes, and I'm out. After giving it my best shot, I gave up. Have to admit I felt it was quite the bummer. She was adorable, and just the fact she was not a bit scared to walk up those stairs with me made her quite intriguing.

The third and final time we met has to do with Australia. My partner and I went to Australia for a six-week vacation; yep, six weeks down under, mate. As the Aussies say in Australia, "It was bloody well, rippa!" My partner and I had a great time in a great country with great people. When we got back, we decided to have an 'Australia party.' We bought a bunch of stuff in Australia, so it was a good excuse to have our friends over to my partner's house (his home was bigger than mine), show off our souvenirs, and drink as much Fosters Lager we wanted. We set up the party and got the invites out to all who wanted to come. In the process of getting that done, my partner told me his neighbor, Judy, wanted to meet me. It sounded good to me. Unbeknownst to me, my partner's girlfriend decided to invite Tina to the party. She had broken up with her boyfriend and just wanted to take her mind off of him and maybe meet some cops in the process. At this point, I still had no idea who she was, so even if someone told me Tina was coming, I would have just said, "Okay, the more girls, the better."

So as stated, I was supposed to be with Judy, and prior to Tina arriving, that was where I was headed. She was nice and not bad on the eyes and plus we were having a good time together. But then it happened, Tina arrived.

Here's how my attention was diverted. At some time during the party, my partner and I walked out onto the front porch, and at about that time, Tina arrived. I can't tell what time or how long we had been at this party, but I know it was still daylight, so early into the evening, I'd say. It was warm outside and just a great day. Here is what I saw, an adorable little blonde driving a 1989 black Mustang GT convertible.

Hold the phone here, boys! A chick who digs cars, this was so cool! I mean, this girl was driving the current mussel car from Ford, and it was even a convertible! I loved convertibles! My first car was a convertible (1963 Buick Skylark Convertible), and I had loved them ever since.

I wasn't much of a Ford fan, but hey, it had all the blocks checked: 1) hot car, 2) convertible, and 3) the best part – hot chick! Keep in mind that I was very attracted to her the second time I met her on that call. That had not changed just because a couple of years had gone by. Plus, she was driving a very fun car. This time the attraction was multiplied exponentially.

I looked at my partner and said, "I have to meet this girl." As my luck would have it with her from the previous contacts (still not remembered at this point), she didn't take a shine to me right off. When she came up to the house, her gaze was set on my friend Dave. Dave is a tall, dark and handsome sort of guy, and it seemed he was interested in Tina as well. They began chatting it up, so I just left that alone. I mean, come on, I was having a good time with Judy; I was already set for the evening.

What changed my luck with Tina that night was when Dave's girlfriend showed up. Oops, bad move, Dave. Good for me; awfully bad for Dave. His girlfriend was none too happy with him. Not because he was talking to Tina but because Dave snuck out without telling her about the party; thus, his girlfriend was not invited, and he could not be trusted. I am sure seeing him making goo-goo eyes at the blonde he was talking to didn't help his position at all. That sneaky action turned Tina off; she didn't want to get involved with someone who hid what they were up to.

I loved this, lucky me. Sorry, Dave! Yeah, sure, that's what I thought. As I watched Dave follow his girlfriend out of the party like a puppy dog, doing everything to ensure he didn't destroy his relationship with her, I had to chuckle. I decided to wait for a few minutes before I began to strike up a conversation with Tina.

She was disappointed, but nevertheless, we engaged in small talk. Even then, now that we were in close quarters and talking, neither of us still had made the connection of the two previous encounters.

As we spoke, there was more than that car that attracted me to her. I couldn't put my finger on it, but I just decided to stick with my plan, to at least get her number. As the night went on, I was more and more intrigued.

While talking to Tina, I had all but forgotten about Judy. On the other hand, Judy had not given up, and the green monster must have grabbed her. Judy walked up to us. Tina and I were talking when she stood on steps between the two of us, facing me, and said, "I am going home. I live next door; I sleep in the nude, and the door will be unlocked."

Okay, well, that was a bit awkward! Judy then walked out and went to her house. Almost every red-blooded American boy would have a seriously hard time saying no to that. Especially when Tina looked at me and said, "Go if you want to." I was getting the green light from her, but honestly, I was happy to give that offer up so I could spend more time with Tina and just get to know her better.

So I told her, "No, I want to talk to you."

Guys, I'm not making that up. I was more than happy to give up getting laid to spend time with a woman who was quite awesome and the most intriguing woman I met since my divorce. So the night went on; we talked and laughed. I don't know what time we went to our respective homes, but I remember the sun was coming up. We agreed to get together, but both of us reinforced this was all for fun and games and nothing to write home to mom about. As we left, neither of us still had a clue we had met before.

A couple of days went by before I called Tina. Again we talked for just a short time before I asked her to dinner. The answer was not what I expected, given how friendly we were at the party. She told me she could not because her dad was going into the hospital for some sort of heart procedure.

In my time being single, I've heard some whoppers when I'm being brushed off, but man, this is one of the best. I thought: *she's a pro at this*. I was about to say, "OK, it was at least nice meeting you," but before I could actually say something, she added, "…but please call me back." If a girl is trying to get rid of you, they would never ask for a callback. They would be happy you took the hint and just went away. If they don't want you to call back, they would never invite you to do exactly what they don't want you to do—her asking me to call again sparked me to call back in a few days. Additionally, at this point in my mind, I was only on strike one, so it was worth another try.

On my second call, we were able to connect for a dinner date. You know what; we had a great time and thoroughly enjoyed each other's company. For the next few days, we spent almost every possible minute with each other. Even so, I had to give her up for a week as she had a previous trip planned to go to New York City for a wedding of some friends of hers. Here's the kicker, the day before, we spent the night together — let's just say it was quite romantic.

Given she was leaving the next morning, I knew we had to get up early but didn't know her now ex-boyfriend was coming over to pick her up. It seemed he was the one paying the freight for the trip, so he was going as well.

I told her to have fun but have to admit I was a bit concerned given she was going with her ex-boyfriend. That's right, the one she broke up with shortly before the Aussie party. One side of me was troubled by that, but the other side said, don't worry about it, so I didn't. After she left, I actually felt calm and didn't feel a bit of concern. Maybe because of what happened as I was leaving and her ex was arriving.

The morning she was leaving arrived. This also has some comedic flair to it. I was roused out of bed from a dead sleep and hustled out the back door as her ex was headed to the front door. In my underwear, I scooped up all my clothes and headed to the alley behind her home. My past was quite sketchy as I had been with a number of women, but I had never felt like such a whore in my life as I ran through her backyard with my clothes bundled up under my arms. I had to hide between her fence and garage to get dressed. Getting dressed went smoothly, but now I had to get to my truck which was parked in front of her house.

I dressed as quickly as I could. Then, I had to walk down the alley and around the block to get to my truck. My truck at that time was very obvious – a red GMC 4x4. It wasn't like this guy could miss this thing, and maybe he wondered who it belonged to. So what did I do? I've got to get the truck, so off I went as bold as I could be. By the time I got to my truck, Tina's ex had been in the house and was then coming out to his car with a suitcase. There we were, face to face, and he had zero clue who I was. I greeted him with a hello, and he smiled and said hello back with a smile as well. I thought: *would you still have smiled at me if you knew what I had just done last night with your ex-girlfriend?* My guess was probably not. With smug pride, I drove home.

When she returned, I was ready to begin where we left off, and so was she. At this point, we had only been together for just a couple of days in the past week.

I decided to take this woman to Rosario Resort on Orcas Island in the San Juan Islands of Washington State. Rosario Resort is an amazing place, with stellar views, lots of activities, and if you want to have a romantic weekend, this is the place to go. We had nothing less than a great time. It was fun and extremely romantic. We toured the island, had wonderful waterside dinners, and did a bit of hiking, like to the top of Turtleback Mountain—all when we weren't in bed. Our relationship was now about two weeks old, and I must tell you we were having a great time, and there was never a moment I didn't want to be with her.

I am going to digress for just a second, so you understand what was happening, which no one, even me, expected to happen. First, let me say I know there is that new honeymoon effect that couples experience, and then as time passes, the newness wears off. I get that, but some inter-voice was screaming at me that was not what was going on. The voice was yelling, "Man, you have struck gold with this girl." Keep in mind that I was playing the field in a very heavy way. One thing cops don't have to concern themselves with, who want to be single, is difficulty finding a date or a bed partner. That is readily available if you want to take advantage of it, and yes, it's also available to married cops. I, for one, took complete advantage of that opportunity. I had nothing to hide.

Back to Rosario Resort. It was a beautiful day, and the forecast was for a beautiful weekend, so we took her convertible. The ferry ride there and back was perfect, adding to the romantic ambiance theme we both were experiencing. The water was like glass, making the ferry ride even better. The sun was shining, and the temps were neither cold nor hot. Everything about that weekend was beyond perfect. My thoughts were all over the place. I thought: *this is a woman I don't want to get away from.* In the past, if I met someone I liked, and she decided to go her own way, my thoughts were, *so be it.* I didn't really give a damn, but then that was entirely different.

After spending a wonderful weekend and on the ferry ride back home, I was looking at Tina and saying to myself, "Where am I going with this newfound relationship?" As thoughts raced through my head, even marriage slipped in there. *Whoa, whoa, whoa; back this truck up, boy — are you kidding me?* What was I thinking? How could I even consider the word I always cringed at — marriage — with a woman I had only known for two weeks? There were still so many women out there I had not met, and yet that didn't seem to matter right now.

Was it just this wonderful weekend we were having? Was it the ferry ride that added to the romance of this trip? I was asking myself: *do you really want to give up this free lifestyle you've enjoyed so much for the past eight years?* Honestly, I had no idea, but the voice was nagging me to ask, and then another voice also saying, "Runaway, ya big dummy!"

We were leaning on the rail when I looked at her and blurted out without a second thought, "What would you say if I asked you to marry me?"

She looked at me, a little bit of a quizzical look, and said, "Well, you'd have to ask me first." Oh my gosh, she didn't run away! She didn't hold up a crucifix toward me and say, "Die demon." With that, I had thoughts racing; the pain was entering my body from every direction, stabbing at me to ask and also not ask.

I was living the life of the ultimate bachelorhood. Girls were coming in and out of my house. I had experienced a large number of women in the eight years I had been divorced from my first wife. Many guys in the department were living vicariously through me, even my partner. So why was I thinking of asking this girl to marry me; I hardly knew her. I didn't know, and I couldn't believe what was about to come out of my mouth.

After a minute or so, I turned to her and said, "Will you marry me?" Once I said it out loud, it felt very right. The look on her face was not horror, maybe a bit surprised.

I was relieved when she smiled at me and asked, "You're serious, aren't you?"

I nodded my head in disbelief and thought for a moment. I was never more serious about anything in my life and told her, "Yes, I am."

She turned away for a moment and then looked at me and said, "Sure, I'd like that." She said yes! That was sooooooo cool! We embraced and kissed like we never had before. For the rest of the ferry ride and drive home, I was on cloud nine. I couldn't keep her too close to me for the rest of the trip. When did we meet? Saturday, May 14, 1989. It was then Sunday, May 28th, 1989. I have never regretted asking that question and look forward to waking up to her every day. Truly I am the lucky one in this relationship.

I told you I'd tell you how we figured out the previous contacts we had. Here's how it happened:

Being the bliss of our engagement, we decided we had to calm everything down a bit, so a few days later, we both decided on a bicycle ride. Cycling is one of my favorite pastimes, and it appeared Tina had a love for it as well.

It was just a routine ride from her house to the nearby University of Puget Sound Campus. It's a very beautiful campus that is somewhat serene in its Ivy League appearance, making any walk or bicycle ride very pleasant. As we rode around the campus, Tina said she wanted to go down a street that was nearby. As we turned onto the street, she pointed at a brick house and said she used to live there. At exactly the same time, she pointed out the house I was saying I had responded to an alarm call there. We looked at each other and said, virtually at the same time, "You were the cop who came inside" and "You were the one who followed me up the stairs."

She then had another light which came on when she said, "You asked me to dance at Shenanigans, didn't you?" Was she kidding me? No way was that possible. I know Tacoma is not the biggest city around, but still, the chances of running into each other three times were crazy.

I couldn't believe this was all coming together. I had never encountered anything like this. Despite her reluctance in our first encounter and me unable to catch her home on the second attempted encounter, we were destined to be together, but we couldn't see all the signs leading us there until that party. It would seem God had a plan, but I had to go all the way to a different hemisphere to find the woman I was going to fall in love with in my own hometown. That was just nuts.

Ride-a-longs

Tina went on a number of ride-a-longs with me. She was fun to have there, and when my good friend Zach was on a call with us, he would tell the reportees, victims, or suspects who asked who she was that she was our lieutenant, sergeant, captain, or assistant chief; whatever came to mind. She was observing her crew of officers to make sure we were doing the right thing, or at least that was what he told the citizens. It always seemed to work. She got to see how I worked and had some fun in the process.

One of the wild ones we got into once was when a police officer, Officer KP, was screaming for backup. Before I get into the actual part where Tina was involved, I have to say this incident should never have happened. It seemed in the north part of Tacoma, a complaint came in about a loud party. These were very routine and were normally handled by advising the party to keep it down, or we'd have to come back to break up the party. One of the things you never do is wade into the party until you have sufficient backup present. It could get quite dangerous, so having several officers was in the best interest of everyone, not just the cops. These were drunk people, and many times the alcohol did all the talking and made the drunkards feel tougher than they really were. One on one it's not usually a difficult thing, but in a party setting, it could easily be up to 100 or so; that's when it becomes a nightmare.

Officer KP got himself in a pickle because he didn't follow the basic rule. Not only did he wade into the party, but he also started checking IDs. In his misguided investigation, he discovered a person who was under 21 by a day but had an alcoholic beverage in his hand. The additional problem KP had was the person who was under 21 was the guest of honor. It would seem our underage friend was set to leave for the Marine Corp on the upcoming Monday (this was Sunday morning). We all took our job seriously, but discretion and common sense needed to come into play as well. In a case like this, one must not just look at the technicality of underage drinking, especially given the future jarhead was only one day away from age 21, but just get cooperation to stop the party and see how that goes before wading in. But that didn't happen, and KP placed the aspiring Marine under arrest. People don't take too kindly to police arresting the guest of honor at their party, so the hostilities began – thus the need for backup.

Though KP did the stupid instead of thinking it out, he still needed help. Once a cop is yelling for backup, the circumstances of how they got in that predicament didn't matter. All that matters was a brother/sister in blue needed help, so off we went. We started at South 12th & Union and had to get to North 48th & Ferdinand. A bit of a way to go, about four miles, but given the time of day (around 3:30 a.m.), there was little to no traffic to get in the way, so speed control was not really necessary. Not to mention I then had a great co-pilot to clear my right as I ran lights and flew past intersections.

We got in the patrol car and headed north on Union. We reached speeds of about 100 MPH, and Tina was making sure my right was clear. With lights flashing and the siren screaming, we would get air at the undulations at each intersection created by the very old maple trees that lined the center of Union Avenue. Our speed was the basic factor, as well as the trees that allowed us our short, low-level flying. Trees made the street quite beautiful, but the roots from those lovely trees also made the road surface quite uneven.

Note: Tina can be quite assertive when she wants to. Here's what I mean; not only was she clearing my right, and even though we were at about 100 MPH, she reminded me of my high school football coach. My coach would yell at us players when doing wind sprints, saying, "Get moving, faster, quit lollygagging!"

Tina was yelling, "Go faster!" during the entire time we were headed to the backup. Hey sweetie, thanks for the flashbacks.

We came from the longest distance of any of the officers responding, so when we arrived, there were a number of patrol cars already there. For the most part, we were doing the clean-up, stuffing people in the backseat of our car as well as other officers' cars.

The scene was very chaotic, and Tina decided she would wait in the car. But after I got a couple of the people under arrest in the back seat, she decided it best to be on the outside. I don't remember exactly how many arrests were made that night, but I found out I had stuffed the guest of honor in my car, along with another guy.

When I patted the guest of honor down, he had a sweatshirt on. I grabbed his front pocket and felt a small, thin object. I never just dig my hand into a pocket without at least asking first what I felt, so that was what I did. If the object felt what he said it was, then good. He said it was his cigarette lighter. Okay, it felt like it might be exactly that, and given I was sure it wasn't a gun, I left it there. That came into play a bit later.

I no sooner got him in the car when he began to cry like a baby. He was saying his life was in ruin because of the arrest, and the Marines would never take him now that he's going to jail. Though I had some sympathy, he was right about the Marines not taking him. I wondered if we were doing the Marines a favor. Really, if he was going to sob like a two-year-old over this, then what would he do in combat? Call out for mommy? Even the other guy in the car told him to "Get a set of balls, dude."

After securing my two guests, I went to help other officers. I could see another officer was looking for something. I asked him what he was looking for, and he told me his magazine to his weapon. He had looked everywhere, but it had come up missing. At this point, I didn't put two and two together, but the shape of his weapon's magazine (Sig Sauer) is a long narrow magazine, unlike what my weapon (Glock) has; a wider, stockier magazine. As you remember, I felt something very similar in the front pouch of the guest of honor's sweatshirt, but it was a cigarette lighter, right?

Not realizing what I had, I left shortly after trying to help this officer find his magazine. When we got to the jail, we drove into the Sally Port (a large bay where we were received by the jail). Tina wasn't going to, at first, join me in the elevator to the booking desk, but I told her she needed to have the entire police experience. At the booking desk, he was patted down again, and all private items are taken away from him. That so-called cigarette lighter was discovered by the corrections officer, who found the officer's missing magazine in the sweatshirt pouch. The corrections officer was none too happy with me but calmed down once I told her the magazine belonged to another officer and there was no gun connected to the clip that may have entered the jail.

Of course, my wayward Marine claimed he had nothing to do with the magazine, and it "was planted" on him. Oh well, not only was he being charged with a felony for assaulting a police officer but also possession of police equipment, yet another felony. If he had any chance of joining the Marines, he could kiss that goodbye. The Marine Corps can say thank you now.

As for the other guy who I transported with the sobbing Marine, he failed booking and was dragged off to a cell where Tina got her first look at the 'adjusted' booking process to help arrestees understand the need to have a more positive attitude.

We left the jail and called the office and let him know we had his magazine. We met later in the shift to get it back to him. He was happy, and so was I.

Naked Dad

Another call I had with Tina was a parent who called about having trouble with his son. What kind of trouble? I wasn't sure at this point other than being told the son was throwing his life away. When we arrived, we were greeted by the mother, who explained the son had a baseball scholarship to the University of Washington. The problem was the son would lose his scholarship if he broke the rules, one being, of course, no drug use. Well, it seemed the good son decided it was a good idea to celebrate the scholarship by smoking some marijuana. Well, in the days of that call, marijuana was not legal in Washington State, so that act of celebratory rebellion placed his scholarship in peril.

Mom was trying to mediate the dispute between Dad and Son, and Dad wanted the son out of the house. That's all well and good, but in Washington State, once a person has established residency, they have a legal right to the abode they have occupied. Believe it or not, in this case, Dad couldn't just throw his son out without an eviction notice and going through the eviction process. Even though Dad wanted Son out, there was no way I was going to tell the son he had to leave; basically, I couldn't. There was no way I had any legal right to toss the son out if he didn't want to leave.

As I was talking to Mom and getting ready to speak to the son, Dad came out of the bedroom and stood behind his wife. I couldn't see him all that well, and I was concentrated on making contact with the son. I didn't really notice him all that much, but Tina told me later he actually came out of the bedroom completely naked.

As he stood there, it was obvious he was quite intoxicated. He swayed back and forth. Tina let me know a few moments after I went to speak to the son; Dad must have realized there was some other female in the front foyer. He slowly reached down and covered his private parts with his hands, then retreated into what appeared to be the master bedroom. After five to ten minutes, he reappeared doused in baby powder and wearing a bathrobe. Don't ask me why he doused himself in baby powder; drunkards do some very strange stuff.

The son was toking on some illegal weed; it would appear he might have learned that behavior from his dad. I mean, why would one get drunk while trying to tell your kid not to get high? Some mixed messages there, it seemed.

After talking to the son, who was an ungrateful shit, given what he had, I returned to the front foyer area. That's when I really noticed Dad. He was as white as a sheet of paper. I thought, *what did this guy do; roll in baby powder?* I just ignored him because it appeared he was a part of the problem as much as the son. I told the parents their son could do whatever he wanted with the scholarship. That all said, the son had agreed to go to a friend's home, and because he was over 18, he didn't have to answer to them. Harsh as it might have been, that was the law, and that was all I could do about it. As I spoke to the parents, the son had exited through the rear door and left in his car. I could have chased after him and arrested him for DUI, but when I talked to him, he didn't seem quite that intoxicated. It appeared the marijuana had worn off.

After we left the house, Tina told me what happened when we first entered — the dad being naked — which I missed totally. I said, "How did I miss all that?"

She just looked at me, didn't say a word but just had that quizzical look of, 'yeah, how did you miss that?'

My Last Night as a Commissioned Police Office

Almost all police officers, when they are ready to retire, want to take it a bit easy for the last days of their career, maybe even the last few months. The reason being, they don't want to get killed on their last day of work. Many departments are more than happy to accommodate those offers with such jobs as the desk officer at the patrol desk or a sundry of other jobs that don't put the officer on the front line with all its dangers.

Then there were cops like me. I know, why not take the cushy job for one night, right? That was just not a part of my psyche; thus, not what I wanted to do. I stayed in the patrol car right up to the last minute until I was employed by Tacoma Police Department and my last graveyard shift. This last shift did not disappoint me.

It started out like any other shift, a bit quiet in the early hours, but around midnight, it began to pick up. My first encounter was when I backed up a female officer who was contacting two males in front of a convenience store. When I showed up, the males were yelling at the officer as they stood in front of the store. She was standing up to these two morons, but there was no doubt that she was ready to get some relief from them. Being my normal self, I got out and stepped in between the officer and the punks and said, "I think you need to have a seat on the curb." There was no doubt these mental midgets thought they could intimidate a female but knew a male would take their heads off, given a chance.

At first, they both just stood there and were doing the stare-down baloney that some guys do to try to intimidate. Given they weren't moving as quickly as I liked, I added, "If you'd like, I can help you with being seated." It seemed they understood my sarcasm and what I was saying—basically, I was ready to knock their dumb asses to the pavement if need be, and, quite frankly, I would have been happy to do so. In the back of my mind, I was saying, *oh, please open your mouth just one more time*. I was very disappointed when they sat down on their own.

I'm going to digress (once again) for a moment. This was my last day, so I was fairly immune to any repercussions from the vast majority of what I did on that night, you know — as long as I didn't do something criminal or quite stupid. A lieutenant put it very well but to his own chagrin. About a week earlier, when I was at the station and while two sergeants were standing within earshot, he said to me, "You know, you could do just about anything, and we wouldn't even have time to investigate it before you're out of here." I want to point out that this lieutenant was the one who called me out at a riot team meeting in front of the entire team. His rude comment was due to my concern about our chief who killed his wife and himself in front of their children. My comment, which was before the chief's homicide/suicide, was my concern about his ability to lead. That comment did not sit well with this lieutenant, and he let me know loudly and rudely.

So when he told me I could get away with just about anything, I decided to take my shot. With all the respect he deserved, I very 'nicely' said, "You know I am sure you are right, so fuck you," and then gave him the finger. Man, did that feel good to do!

The look on the sergeants' faces was priceless. They couldn't believe I did that. What did the lieutenant do? He just turned around and walked into his office, and I never saw him for the rest of that shift or for the rest of my career. He opened a door he should have never even looked at, and I was happy to not just open the door wide but shove him through it.

Alright, that's it, so back to the contact with the two pukes at the store. What I found out from the first officer was one of the males was 28, and the other was 15. It seems the 28-year-old was caught buying the 15-year-old a beer. One of the things that were bugging me about these guys was the 28 years old had a smug look on his face for most of this contact. The sarcastic look was annoying, at best. I felt it was necessary to make sure he understood the gravity of this crime.

I got close to his face, whom I will name Mr. Smuggy, and said, "A lieutenant let me know recently that I could do just about anything and the department would have no way of investigating it before I left, because this, sir, is the last day I'm a cop. I am retiring at the end of this shift. This is good for me but not so good for you because I'm about to wipe that fucking smug look off your face; you got me, pal?" He looked at me, and suddenly the smug look changed to fear. I'm sure that me smiling through the entire comment had nothing to do with the change of expression on his face; oh no, of course not. Nor do I think the wild look in my eyes had an influence on him either – I'm sure that had nothing to do with his decision to take this contact a bit more serious.

I don't know what he was thinking, but many people have this stereotype image of cops; when they are at the end of their career, they go off the deep end. This was the only time I would thank Holly-weird for propagating that image – it worked well for me that night.

After the first officer completed her investigation, Mr. Smuggy was arrested for contributing to a minor and taken to jail. Okay, that worked for me, and he seemed very happy that I wasn't the one taking him to the Gray Bar Hotel. Maybe he had heard about my elevator ride; I don't know. Oh well, I waved and smiled at him as the other officer carted him away.

I took the kid home, and his parents, who were none too happy their son was being brought home by the cops. They were even more upset when I told them who he was with. Sonny boy had asked me not to mention his partner in crime, to which I agreed, but I lied. So sue me; oh, that's right, he couldn't - it was my last day. I never told the truth to criminals. Why? Because they're criminals—even at 15. I got a thank you from the dad and went on to the next call.

Around 0230 hours, I was having a conversation with an officer in a parking lot that was just down the hill from a cemetery. For some reason, it's always quiet there (I know that was a stupid pun—oh, get over it). But tonight was going to be different. Suddenly the silence was broken by two gunshots that sounded like they came from the cemetery. I called it out to dispatch, and the two of us headed to the cemetery for an area check. Other units also came into the area, and we were able to fairly lock down the entire cemetery, hopefully to coral the shooter and possibly find a victim.

We didn't know if the shooter was shooting someone or just firing off a couple of rounds. Who knows what was up? A drunkard, someone high, a dispute, etc.—could have been anything. What we did know it wasn't a suicide as that would have been just one shot, unless, of course, the shooter was a bad shot and had to take aim again. Naw, I'm just joking.

The search continued, and at first, we found nothing. K-9 came out, and that's when we found the guy who was shot, hiding against a tombstone. He was pretty close to death when we found him, but due to the wonders of modern medical science, he survived the ordeal.

Note: This is going to sound terrible, and I will probably get grief for this, but when he was found, we all thought he was going to die. I mean, we all thought he had zero chance of survival. I actually thought, *how convenient this is? He doesn't even need to leave this place and just see what sites are open.* I know that's pretty rude, callas, juvenile, sick, etc., etc., and maybe you are right, but this is just more perverted cop humor.

I learned at the end of my shift that once paramedics stabilized our 'victim,' he was able to give a statement. It seemed he owed his drug supplier money for the drugs he was selling. Once again, I have to admit something here. While I was being told that by a very young officer, who was very thorough, I acted as if I was interested but truly wanted him to shut up because I really didn't give a shit about some dope dealer on the last day!

We never found the actual supplier on that night, but the detectives were able to track him down a couple of weeks later—after I retired. That worked for me.

The final call of the night was the dinger of them all. Let's start this story before I actually got the call. That began in Tacoma at a place called the West End Pub. The West End Pub is a neighborhood pub that has a good reputation. It is located on 6th Avenue, which is a busy street, even at 0200 hrs, and a few blocks from Union Ave, which is even a busier street than 6th Ave. This is all very significant as it leads to how this call ended up. Additionally, the players in this call include a 1967 Ford Mustang GT and three males in their mid-20s who were the driver and passengers in the Mustang.

This started out with the three males who were at the West End Pub and, of course, had been drinking quite heavily. I mean, it's a pub; of course, people will be drinking and drinking way too much. In the course of putting down a number of beers, the three became belligerent to other patrons. We all know when some people drink too much, they turn into flaming jerks, as an old adage goes, 'instant asshole, just add alcohol.' These guys were no different.

I'm not sure what they did to piss off customers at the pub, but in my experience at the West End Pub, regulars and others were always friendly and welcoming. Nevertheless, these three jokers were chased out of the pub by the patrons. They truly had to hit the epitome of being an asshole to be run out of this place.

These three stooges ran out of the pub and jumped into their car (Mustang), thinking they were being chased, and took off eastbound on 6th Ave toward Union and then turned south onto Union Ave. What we found out later was they were never being chased. Alcohol has the ability to make one even more stupid than one normally is. For these guys, the beer put them off the stupidity charts at record levels.

The driver/owner of the Mustang, who I will refer to as Mr. Happy, got up to — what we figured out in the investigation — around 110–120 MPH on Union Ave. One of the things we could be thankful for was there was little to no traffic at this time of the early morning, around 0200 hours.

In the car, aside from Mr. Happy, one of the three was in the front passenger seat and the third guy in the back seat.

Alcohol was also the fuel for stupid ideas and acts. The obvious was the speed of travel, but also maybe wearing a seat belt would have been a good idea. I know seatbelts might not have been a great deal of help given the speed they were traveling, but the sheer high risk of an accident was extreme, and a seatbelt might just have saved a life or at least reduce injury. The problem was alcohol ruled the common sense or lack thereof in this case, so none were wearing this potentially life-saving device.

As these mental midgets headed down Union Ave, they failed to take into consideration a hill. When Union reaches Hwy 16, you go under the Hwy 16 overpass. As you proceed and just after the overpass, there is a hill leading down to Center Street. The hill, under normal circumstances, is no big deal, but when traveling over 100+ MPH, it becomes a major issue. When our drunken fools got to the edge of the hill, the car went airborne.

If you've ever been on a rollercoaster or similar ride and go screaming down the hill, you know that moment of weightlessness. For our poor simpleton in the backseat, this became a serious issue. Gravity took its toll on our backseat rider when the car came down and struck the pavement with a force of 100+ MPH. The schmuck's head in the backseat hit the ceiling of the Mustang with the same force. Both of the front seat riders had something to hold on to but not the guy in the back. When his head hit the ceiling, it broke his neck in several locations, and he instantly became a quadriplegic. At that point, he went into a conscious shock, if you will—basically, freaking out and using not-so-medical terms. He repeated over and over. "I can't move; I can't move!" His buddies in the front seat had no clue and most likely didn't care, as they whooped it up when flying through the air and even at the impact during the landing. They probably didn't even know the damage they did to the car either.

When the Mustang hit the pavement, it blew out three of the tires, and the driver lost control as the car slid into the next intersection of Center Street. At the same time, a black Dodge pickup was traveling west on Center. The car struck the rear bumper of the Dodge, breaking the glass on the passenger door and striking the front passenger in the head with the corner of the truck's bumper. The front seat passenger was now out cold. As the car continued to slide across the intersection, the front passenger's head was hanging out the window.

Diagonally across the intersection at Center & Union is (still there) a car battery store with large rollup doors. On the edge of the doors are 4x4 steel beams. As the car slid, it careened through one of the rollup doors and into a bay but not before the front passenger, whose head was on the outside edge of the window sill, struck the 4x4 beam. The impact with the beam was so fast and dramatic that it took off the top of the passenger's head with a clean-cut as if cut with a very sharp chainsaw. When I arrived, I observed his brain and the top half of his skull were lying on the outside of the bay.

I got to the location just after the end of this mess, and firefighters were there as well. They were having some difficulty with the driver, Mr. Happy. He was quite upset that the firefighters were cutting off the top of the car to access getting him and his two buddies out. He was yelling the typical line of "I'm going to sue" and such. One of the things he said when the top was coming off was, "This is a fucking classic, you assholes!"

To which I had to respond; I mean, I could not let this opportunity go by. So my response was, in my best Inspector Clouseau French accent (*Pink Panther Strikes Again*), "Not anymore."

His response, I am sure you know what's coming, "Fuck you!" Can't someone come up with something different?

This guy couldn't care less about his dead partner in front or his friend in the backseat who was in total shock. Nice friend, right? He was just screaming about his car that was mostly damaged beyond repair due solely to his own drunken stupidity.

When the top came off, the firefighters were able to extract the driver, despite his whining. He sustained a broken left knee, so he had to go to the hospital before I could take him to jail for DUI, vehicular assault (friend in the backseat), and vehicular homicide (friend in the front seat). The guy in the backseat was also extracted, and due care was taken so as not to do more damage to him. He went to a different hospital than the driver, Mr. Happy. I have no idea how the backseat guy faired or what his condition is today.

Mr. Happy was transported to the Tacoma General Hospital, and prior to moving the ambulance, I decided to handcuff him to the gurney. Good thing I did because on the way to the hospital, he thrashed about, saying he'd jump out if it wasn't for the "fucking handcuffs."

Once at the ER, we brought our drunk driver inside and checked him in. We were able to get to a room in short order. There, I advised him of his rights, to which I got the usual two-word answer; it started with an F and ended with a U, more of the same from earlier. I also told Mr. Happy that we would be drawing blood for blood alcohol content. In his most uncooperative manner, he let me know he wasn't giving up blood unless I had a warrant. Just a note here: In the case of vehicular homicide, vehicular assault, or if the driver of the car is unconscious, an officer can have blood drawn without permission or a warrant. I had two of the three, and I was about to make the third reason a reality, so we were good to get this jerk's blood.

I might not need a warrant, and I was within my duty to get his blood; that did not mean he was going to give it up without a fight. That's exactly what he said as well—no way was he going to surrender his blood without a struggle. Not a huge problem; we just needed to get the right tools. A quick call to hospital security, and we'd get the first tools into place.

Hospital security brought down their very fashionable restraints that are made of thick, somewhat unforgiving leather. With a couple of us holding Mr. Happy, the security team went to work and secured both legs and wrists to the hospital bed. After that, he was secure and unable to move as freely as when he only had handcuffs attached to one wrist and to the bed. Nevertheless, he was still able to sit upright when we let him go. Also, once the tech came in, Mr. Happy would deliberately try to move his arm to make the tech's job virtually impossible, not to mention he was trying to bite us and spit on us. This guy was the height of jerkiness (believe it or not, that is really a word). To keep the spitting and biting down to a minimum, we had the lovely pull-over netting mask. What it didn't do was stop the thrashing about.

On the surface, this might seem like a major issue, but really it was not. I grabbed the back of his head by his hair and turned his face away from me. Then I walked to the head of the bed, all the while him trying to see where I went and yelling, "What the fuck are you doing?" At this point, I had a hold of his head with my left hand and quickly reached around his neck, planting the web of my thumb and forefinger just above his Adam's apple. Once there, I squeezed with my thumb and forefinger very tightly, cutting off blood flow or at least seriously reducing the blood to the brain. It didn't take long before he passed out. Goodnight, honey!

We rushed the tech in, and she was able to draw his blood with time to spare and without this jerk being a jerk. After about 30 mins or so, he woke up exactly where he left off, screaming we weren't taking his blood. As he yelled his verbal onslaught, I pointed at his right arm where the bandage was at. To that, he screamed, "You mother fuckers, I'm going to kick your ass…" and so on.

After he was released from the hospital, I transported Mr. Happy to jail. On our way there, he continued his verbal onslaught, and I attempted to warn him he might want to cut back on that sort of speech. "Up yours," was his answer.

"Just trying to give you a warning before you get to the jail. You don't want to fail booking," was my advice.

His answer: "I don't give a shit." *Okay, fair enough*, I thought as I was looking forward to the next scene.

At the booking desk, Mr. Happy did not disappoint. After about three or four F-bombs, I saw my final failed booking. This night was getting better and better. Brownshirts (corrections officers) came from everywhere; over the booking desk, around the booking desk, and you know what? It looked like they came out of the floor as they grabbed Mr. Happy and dragged him to the nearest holding cell. I didn't go in the holding cell to help, mostly because there was no more room, plus these guys were the professionals in this area; they didn't need my help. I'm not sure exactly how many corrections officers were in the holding cell with Mr. Happy, but I can tell you it was a bunch.

As the corrections officers worked their magic in the cell, I saw a shoe fly out into the hall, and then another. And suddenly, his pants came flying out, followed by Mr. Happy's shirt. At that, the troop of officers exited, and they closed the cell door with authority. Those doors are made of steel and are heavy. When they slammed shut, like this one was, it sounded like a bomb going off.

With all that, one would think Mr. Happy would just shut up; nope! He continued to vomit his verbal assault as I was leaving.

This was my last act as a Tacoma cop, and I enjoyed every moment. Nope, I didn't have to write the report. All my buddies on this last call said they would do the writing, and that was okay by me. Once I left the jail, I headed to my patrol car to head home, and I would be dropping off everything in a couple of days.

Was I sad about leaving police work? To some extent, but at the same time, I looked forward to something new.

What do I miss? Probably the same as many other professions—seeing the people you worked with on a daily basis. For the vast majority of officers whom I met in my career, I have a great deal of respect for all law enforcement professionals, which includes police officers, deputies, state troopers, federal marshals, corrections officers, constables, etc. If I left out a title or two, then please accept my sincerest apologies.

Many people do not understand law enforcement folks. They think we are hard to communicate with, and that is true to an extent. Most people have no clue what police officers do or see but then have the audacity to think they understand police work because of what they see on TV or in a movie. My wife hates watching police drama on TV with me because I rip it apart all the time.

Because of all that, cops will seek out other cops as friends because we understand each other. This is true in most professions. The biggest difference between law enforcement and other professions is that cops make life and death decisions almost every day. Keep that in mind.

About the Author

Enzo's career in law enforcement started back in 1983, and now for almost 38 years, he has been involved in this profession, in some fashion or another.

Tales of a Street Bull started out to be just a compilation of memorable calls to give to his children and grandchildren. After compiling, writing, and rewriting 'tales,' they took on a body of their own to a very full 4"3'-ring binder. At that point, his wife suggested publishing it so others could enjoy the stories and get a cop's point of view.

Made in the USA
Monee, IL
06 September 2021

77538394R00243